THE UNIVERSITY O[

WITHDRAWN FROM
THE LIBRARY

UNIVERSITY OF
WINCHESTER

D0549958

stage lighting
THE TECHNICIANS' GUIDE

an on-the-job reference tool
plus DVD video resources

SKIP MORT

UNIVERSITY OF WINCHESTER
LIBRARY

UNIVERSITY OF WINCHESTER

Methuen Drama

1 3 5 7 9 10 8 6 4 2

First published in 2011

Methuen Drama
Bloomsbury Publishing Plc
49–51 Bedford Square
London WC1B 3DP
www.methuendrama.com

Copyright © Skip Mort 2011

Skip Mort has asserted his rights under the Copyright, Designs and Patents Act,
1988, to be identified as the author of this work

A CIP catalogue record for this book is available from the British Library

PB ISBN: 978 1 408 12357 7
E PUB ISBN: 978 1 408 15386 4

Available in the USA from
Bloomsbury Academic & Professional,
175 Fifth Avenue/3rd Floor, New York, NY 10010
www.BloomsburyAcademicUSA.com

Typeset by Margaret Brain
Printed and bound by GraphyCems

This book is sold subject to the condition that it shall not, by way of trade or
otherwise, be lent, resold, hired out, or otherwise circulated in any form of binding
or cover other than that in which it is published and without a similar condition,
including this condition, being imposed on the
subsequent purchaser.

stage lighting
THE TECHNICIANS' GUIDE

an on-the-job reference tool
plus DVD video resources

SKIP MORT

methuen | drama

Stage Lighting – the technicians' guide

for Maurice

CONTENTS

FOREWORD

Stage Lighting – The Technicians' Guide is a very practical and useful book for beginners setting up a lighting system for a performance, and, for those already working in lighting, it is a very handy reference. The helpful layout allows you to quickly find the specific information you need, and then provides the necessary background knowledge along with suggestions for further reading. It always relates method to results, and not only explains the 'how', but also gives insight into the 'why'. It also contains useful explanations of terminology (as well as international variants for specialist terms).

The job of the technician and lighting designer is to utilise the vast amount of technology, both new and old, to produce what can often be perceived as 'invisible' stage lighting (and, in some cases, it is deliberately very overt). *The Technicians' Guide* demonstrates how to successfully achieve this objective alongside a safe working practice. It also helps people with a technical background to create their first designs.

The Technicians' Guide points the reader to current websites updated by manufacturers and trade bodies, so they can be sure that they are able to access information about the latest equipment and practices.

Lighting is a delicate combination of technical craft and artistic skill. A lighting designer or technician needs to understand how different effects and moods are created by subtle differences in the way light relates to performers and stage environments and how this is perceived in the eyes and minds of the audience. *The Technicians' Guide* will certainly help those working in this wonderfully emotive medium to achieve skilful and artistic results.

Rick Fisher

The Technicians' Guide is the conclusion of a six-year project which began with the development of 'Give me some Light!', three interactive lighting workshops on DVD designed for use in schools. My colleagues Maurice Marshal and David Whitehead gave me the opportunity to develop my initial ideas, together with Andy Webb and Mike Hill whose artistic direction, assistance and support has proved invaluable in producing the original project.

I am again indebted to David Whitehead who has acted as my technical editor, for meticulously reading the script, keeping me on track and his excellent contribution of 'Electricity – how does it work?' and 'An introduction to DMX'. Also Andy Webb has made a most valued contribution; he has helped and inspired me to develop the concept and content of *The Technicians' Guide* and contributed to the sections on lighting controls, DMX and digital projection. Finally, I would like to thank my wife Anne who has tirelessly supported the project and given me the space and time to write, and for reading and advising over the final script.

I would like to thank all those who have read and made contributions to the text; Chris van Goethen for advice in the early stages, Charlie Horne, Ziggy Jacobs for adding an American perspective, David Adams for advice on health and safety, Keith Rogers, Neil Vann for technical information and Rick Fisher for his interest and for contributing the descriptions of his lighting designs for *Swan Lake* and *Billy Elliot*.

Thanks are also due to Jenny Ridout, my publisher at Methuen Drama, for her encouragement and support and to the many throughout the stage lighting industry who have contributed so much material, especially Marie Southwood at Selecon for the endless supply of images.

The Technicians' Guide might never have been written without my friend and valued colleague Maurice who fostered my life-long interest in the theatre and who has encouraged and supported me at all the stages of the project. Maurice Marshal MBE was the Chief Electrician at the Northcott Theatre for 36 years and has devoted his life to the encouragement and training of so many young apprentices for the theatre profession. Therefore, it seems fitting to dedicate *The Technicians' Guide* to him.

Skip Mort trained at the Bristol Old Vic Theatre School. He is an educational consultant, writer, lighting designer, a former teacher and college lecturer.

Stage Lighting – the technicians' guide

– An on-the-job reference tool

This is not just another book to be read cover-to-cover, although you may wish to do so. The Technicians' Guide is an on-the-job resource that you can dip into on a need-to-know basis to find out how to do things and get started, to gather information and to extend your technical knowledge of stage lighting. It will provide you with a practical understanding and information on the safe use of lighting equipment, how to apply this knowledge to the creative and practical aspects of lighting design. The original concept of The Technicians' Guide was to provide a starter-level practical book on stage lighting. However, it has grown and developed to provide a foundation resource and reference tool for both students who are just starting out and technicians looking to go on to further professional training.

The guide is divided into three parts:

Part 1   Lighting Technician
Lanterns, Dimmers & Control – understanding and using the lighting system
Colour, Gobos & Effects – introducing the use of colour filters, gobos, motion and other effects

Part 2   Lighting Designer
Lighting the Performance Space – looking at the effects of the sources of light, the position and angle of illumination, using lanterns to light a performance space for drama, dance and musical theatre
Lighting the Show – applying the knowledge and experience of using the lighting equipment to the process of lighting design

Part 3   Resources
Technical info. – Reference data on equipment and manufacturers' products
Websites – contact details on manufacturers and suppliers of equipment
Key notes! – a section where you can keep a record of practical experience, additional training and production work that may eventually be used to produce a personal CV

➤ Each chapter is focused on a specific subject that is divided into three sections:
'**A quick start**' providing basic information, enough to get you started,
'**More info**' adding more detailed knowledge on the subject and
'**Extras!**' with extended technical information.

The three sections are colour coded throughout each chapter, allowing you to track your own way through the guide to mix and match or fast track though depending upon your personal level of interest.

➤ Tracking your way through the guide:

Chapter	1. From lantern to control	2. Lanterns – performance luminaires	3. Working with lanterns
A quick start	The lighting system		Rigging lanterns
DVD video clips	Understanding the lighting system	Five types of lanterns	Adjusting lanterns
More info		Adjusting lanterns	Lantern maintenance
Extras!		How do they work?	Electrical safety

➤ **Throughout each section** there are panels of additional information, '**Did you know that**'. '**Global jargon**' provides a wider international focus making the guide suitable for use by students in other English-speaking countries. '**Fast forward** on the DVD' provides a reference to the accompanying resource of video clips demonstrating the practical use of the equipment, examples of lighting techniques and effects providing a quick introduction to some of the content of the guide.

➤ **At the end of each section** there are '**Tips**' and '**Resources**'. There are also '**Points for action**' to follow up, to gather further information or to try things out for yourself. They are divided up according to the anticipated time that they will take under the headings '**Quickies!**', '**Takes longer**' and '**A proper job!**'

'I hope that you find The Technicians' Guide *a useful on-the-job practical reference resource when lighting your own productions. I pass on to you all the hints, tips and information that I have gathered by rubbing shoulders with others along the way as a lighting technician.*

Enjoy your lighting!'

Skip Mort 2011

Lanterns, Dimmers & Control

Getting down to basics – *looking at the individual parts of the lighting system and understanding how the equipment works, practical introduction to using the equipment, good working practice, health and safety.*

1 From lantern to control

A quick start – The lighting system

Understanding and using the lighting system

A quick start – The lighting system

Using the lighting system may at first seem rather complicated and confusing. How do you get the lantern hanging on the overhead bar to work from the control desk – where do you start?

Lanterns/Luminaires – Spotlights – Fixtures – Instruments – Units

These are the names that are used worldwide to describe the housing that contains the light source called the lamp, a reflector and for some a lens system to project the beam of light. The lighting units can be either static or automated and can have a range of different types of lamp sources.

Three parts of the lighting system

1 **Lanterns/performance luminaires**
   Lanterns produce light and they are hung on overhead lighting bars, attached to vertical booms or mounted on lighting stands. The lanterns are powered via flexible cables or fixed circuits terminated in outlet sockets that are hardwired via patch panels to dimmer units or to an independent switched circuit for DMX controlled fixtures.

   Acclaim Fresnel – Philips Selecon

3

2 Dimmers

Generic lanterns[1] are controlled by a dimmer unit. These are electronic devices that control the level or intensity of light produced by the lantern. The individual dimmer units are mounted in modular racks or portable packs.

Beta Pack – Zero88

3 Control

The dimmer units are controlled by miniature sliding faders on the lighting control desk. The desk may be positioned away from the dimmers as a remote control so that the operator can see clearly the action of the drama. Memory desks can be programmed to control DMX fixtures moving lights and LED fixtures.

Smartfade lighting desk – ETC

» **Fast Forward** on the DVD to **1.1 Understanding the lighting system**

Two types of dimmer systems

Dimmer racks

➤ **Hardwired systems use dimmer racks**

On permanent hardwired installations, the electrical wiring from the circuit outlet sockets is contained in metal trunking or conduit and connected direct to the dimmer units. The sockets are distributed throughout the stage and auditorium.

■ **Studio or small stage installations** – the circuits are usually terminated in sockets on or above fixed lighting bars or terminated at stage/floor level for side lighting

■ **Internally Wired Bars (IWBs)** are used on installations in the UK. The circuit outlet sockets are mounted directly on the bar with the cables running internally

■ **Circuit outlet sockets** may be paired together and wired direct to the same dimmer control channel

■ **Larger stages and installations** the dimmer circuits may be terminated in outlet patch panels mounted

Chilli Dimmer Rack – Zero88

[1] See 'Lighting jargon – Lanterns'

Sidebar: **A quick start**   **1 FROM LANTERN TO CONTROL**

adjacent to the lighting bars that are suspended from the flying grid. The outlet sockets on the bars are connected by a multicore cable ending with a 'spider'[2] of flexible cables terminated in plug tops which are hard patched into the dimmer outlet patch panel

■ **Fixed wired outlet sockets** on lighting bars or dimmer outlet patch panels are usually numbered by the dimmer circuit/channel fader number that is controlling them

➤ Using a hardwired system

A lantern connected to circuit outlet socket No.1 on the bar or dimmer outlet patch panel will be controlled by dimmer No.1 and channel fader No.1 on the lighting desk programmed with a 1:1 soft patch (see 'Lighting jargon – Lighting control desks').

Dimmer packs

➤ Hard patch systems use dimmer packs

Dimmer packs consist of six dimmer units mounted in a portable rack. Each dimmer unit has a single or pair of outlet sockets mounted either on the front or back providing the flexibility to hard patch any lantern to any dimmer. They are used for small stages and studio installations and for temporary rigs in the UK, Europe and the Southern Hemisphere.

Dimmer pack & cable patch – GMSL

■ The circuit outlet sockets on the bars are hardwired back to a cable patch being terminated in flexible cables with numbered plug tops

■ The cable patch is mounted below the dimmer packs allowing the individual circuit outlet sockets on the bars to be hard patched to any of the dimmer units

■ Hard patching makes it possible to have a larger number of circuit outlet sockets than the number of dimmer units so that they can be widely distributed over the lighting bars and at floor level. This provides a greater flexibility to position the lanterns anywhere in the rig without the need for additional cabling

■ Lanterns can be paired together but care must be taken to prevent overloading the individual dimmer units

■ Hard patching is used on temporary lighting rigs for shows where flexible cables are used to connect the lanterns to the dimmer units. In North America, this is called 'hooking up'

[2] See 'Lighting jargon – Lanterns'

1 FROM LANTERN TO CONTROL   A quick start

➤ **Using a hard patching system**

A lantern hanging on a lighting bar is plugged into a circuit outlet socket No.12 which is terminated with a matching numbered plug top at the cable patch. If plug top No.12 is connected or patched to dimmer unit No.1, the lantern will then be controlled by channel fader No.1 on the lighting control desk.[3] The lantern and the area of lighting will now be called by the same channel fader number, No.1.

Did you know that –

■ Lantern or 'Lanthorn' is an early English name for a source of light enclosed in a housing as used by William Shakespeare in his plays[4]

■ 'Magic lantern' was the term used for the early glass slide projectors as used in Victorian and Edwardian times in the UK

■ Bunches of cables taped together from a lighting bar are traditionally called 'tripe' in the UK and the 'Snake' in North America as they describe what they look like

■ 'Socapex' and 'Lectriflex' are names frequently used for multicores named after the make and type of the multipin plugs or sockets used to terminate the multicore

■ 'Soco' is a term used in North America for a multicore cable

GLOBAL JARGON

■ **Lanterns** (United Kingdom/UK) – Fixtures, Instruments, Units, (North America/NA)

■ **Fittings & Fixtures** – also used in UK, Fixtures relating to moving lights

■ **Luminaires** (Northern Europe/NE) – International term, also used in North America(NA) & Southern Hemisphere (NZ & Aus)

■ **Spotlights** (NE) – Fresnels and PCs

■ **Patching** (UK) – Hooking up (NA)

■ **Lamps** – Light source not a stage light or lantern

---

[3] That is, providing the lighting control desk is on a 1:1 default patch. See soft patching, Chapter 5 'Lighting control – Extras!'

[4] *The Art of Stage Lighting*, Frederick Bentham

QUICK TIPS

- The lanterns are always called by the channel fader number that they are controlled by
- When planning the areas of lighting, it is easier to remember and recall them if they are in a logical sequence
- Number the areas as viewed from the front from 'House Left to Right' (Stage Right to Left), e.g. 1–3 across stage and 4–6 behind
- When using a hard patching system, patch the lanterns lighting an area to the same numbered channel fader but check that the total load doesn't exceed the capacity of the dimmer unit
- Record the channel fader number that is controlling the lantern in front of the symbol on the lighting plan
- Record the circuit outlet socket number that is connecting the lantern to the dimmer unit on a hard patch plan so that you can easily identify faults

Points for action

Quickies!

- Try your lighting system out – flash through[5] the lanterns that are hanging and see if you can relate the control channel fader to the lanterns and the areas that they are lighting

Takes longer

- Make a simple sketch plan of the areas that the existing lanterns are lighting and number them according to the channel fader numbers

A proper job!

- Make a lighting plan of the position of the lighting bars, outlet sockets and their numbers
- Mark the position of the lanterns on the plan use the CIE symbols, see Chapter 2 'Lanterns – performance luminaires'
- Flash through the lanterns and record the channel fader number in the lantern symbol on the plan

[5] See 'Lighting jargon – Lighting control desks'

1 FROM LANTERN TO CONTROL **A quick start**

2 Lanterns – performance luminaires

A quick start – Identifying lanterns

Looking at the five types of generic lanterns: Floods, Parcans, Fresnels, PCs/Prism/Pebble & Plano-convex, Profiles, the characteristics of the beams, where to use them, makes of lanterns and models

More info – Adjusting lanterns

Angling and focusing the lanterns, adjusting and shaping beams, lantern accessories and adding colour

Extras! – How do they work?

Looking at the optical system of the five types of generic lanterns

A quick start – Identifying lanterns

There are three groups of lighting units or fixtures: generic lanterns, automated or moving lights and LED fixtures. Generic lantern is a term given to a fixed luminaire, which is a lantern that is manually positioned and focused. There are five different types of generic lanterns and they each have a distinct quality of beam of light that are used for different purposes.

Five types of generic lanterns:
Floods – Parcans – Fresnels – PCs/Prism/Pebble & Plano-convex – Profiles

The lanterns can be divided into two main groups:

- **Fixed beam lanterns** – having a lamp and reflector
- **Focus lanterns** – having a lens system to adjust the focus and or the size of the beam

 Fast Forward on the DVD to **2.1 Five types of lanterns**

Five types of lanterns – five different beams of light

Lanterns can be identified by the:

- Shape of the body housing
- Type of lens system or reflector
- Quality of the beam of light produced

➤ Fixed beam lanterns

⌐ 90° Flood – symmetric

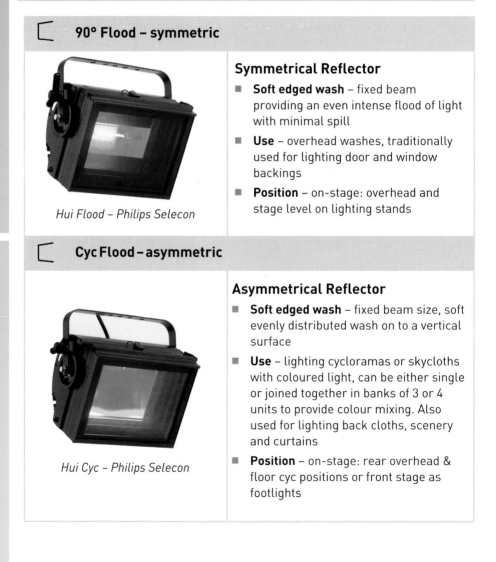

Hui Flood – Philips Selecon

Symmetrical Reflector

- **Soft edged wash** – fixed beam providing an even intense flood of light with minimal spill
- **Use** – overhead washes, traditionally used for lighting door and window backings
- **Position** – on-stage: overhead and stage level on lighting stands

⌐ Cyc Flood – asymmetric

Hui Cyc – Philips Selecon

Asymmetrical Reflector

- **Soft edged wash** – fixed beam size, soft evenly distributed wash on to a vertical surface
- **Use** – lighting cycloramas or skycloths with coloured light, can be either single or joined together in banks of 3 or 4 units to provide colour mixing. Also used for lighting back cloths, scenery and curtains
- **Position** – on-stage: rear overhead & floor cyc positions or front stage as footlights

A quick start

2 LANTERNS – PERFORMANCE LUMINAIRES

⊏ Parcans

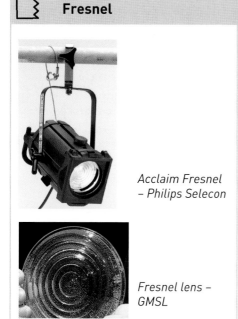

Parcan – Thomas Eng

PAR lamp – GMSL

- **Sealed beam PAR lamp** – a lamp containing a filament with a **P**arabolic **A**luminium **R**eflector and lens in a sealed unit
- **Parallel beam of light** – intense near parallel oval beam of light that can be rotated
- **Use** – narrow or wide shafts of light, downlighting, side and back lighting. Good for use with strong, saturated colours. Light in weight, easy to angle, no focusing required, originally designed for pop concerts
- **Position** – on-stage: overhead, side and rear stage, floor & special effects

➤ Focus lanterns

⦚ Fresnel

Acclaim Fresnel – Philips Selecon

Fresnel lens – GMSL

- **Fresnel lens** – concentric stepped lens, each step having a flat and convex surface
- **Soft edged beam** – evenly distributed, diffused beam having a soft shadow edge producing scatter/spill light
- **Use** – large areas from a short throw distance, used for area, side and back lighting. Soft scatter light helps blend overlapping beams to create smooth washes
- **Position** – on-stage: overhead, side and rear stage
- **Lantern body** – Selecon Acclaim same as PC but shorter

2 LANTERNS – PERFORMANCE LUMINAIRES

A quick start

11

⬭ **PCs**

Prism-convex lens – GMSL

Acclaim PC – Philips Selecon

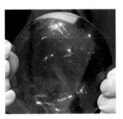

Plano-convex lens – GMSL

- **Prism/Pebble-convex lens**
  – Plano-convex lens cast with a prism/stippled on the flat surface softening the edge of the beam
- **Semi-hard/semi-soft edged beam** – a 'crisp' intense beam with smaller amount of spill light than the Fresnel, soft edged beam is good for blending areas of light
- **Use** – small or large areas of light, long or short throws, used for specials, acting areas or washes and side lighting
- **Position** – on-stage: overhead, side stage
- **Lantern body** – Selecon Acclaim same as the Fresnel but longer

- **Plano-convex lens** having a highly polished flat surface available in 1K, 2K & 2.5K lanterns
- **Sharp edged beam** – zoom beam with no spill light, shaping limited to barndoors
- **Use** – controlled beam of light suitable for projecting over longer throws an alternative to using Profile spots – quick to focus
- **Position** – FOH lighting (mainly used in Europe), on-stage: overhead, side stage

⊂⊃ Profile spot

Acclaim Profile – Philips Selecon

Plano-convex lens – GMSL

- **Plano-convex lens** having one curved and one flat surface
- **Hard edge/soft focused, precise beam** – an optical spotlight having a beam that can be accurately shaped or 'profiled' with very little spill light
- **Use** – controlled beam of light suitable for projecting over longer throws and lighting precise areas, images and patterns can be projected with the use of gobos
- **Position** – Front of House 'FOH', on-stage: overhead, side stage

Basic lantern symbols

$$\sqcup \quad \biguplus \quad \underset{\wedge\wedge\wedge}{\square} \quad \bigcap \quad \textrm{⑧}$$

Basic lantern symbols – GMSL

The CIE basic lantern symbols provide a simple and easy way of recording the type and positions of lanterns on lighting layout plans. The symbols are based on simplified images of the five generic types of lanterns and are easy to use as they can be drawn by hand or reproduced on basic computer drawing programs.

For generic lantern stencils, see 'Quick resources'.

Generic lantern symbol stencil – White Light

Did you know that –

■ Focus Lamps or Lanterns were the first theatre spotlights to be developed in the 1890s by adapting the basic optical system used for 'Limelights' and adding an incandescent lamp. They worked in a similar way to the Fresnel/PC, having a movable light source with a reflector and a Plano-convex lens that gave an uneven distribution of light across the beam creating a rainbow effect on the edge

■ The Strand Patt 43A 1000W Batten spot, Patt 44 500W Baby spot and Patt 45 250W Miniature spot were developed in the 1930s, having a Plano-convex lens and spherical reflector that tended to project the pattern of the lamp's filament

■ The Fresnel lens was first developed by Augustine Fresnel (1788–1827) for use in lighthouses and it is named after its designer and pronounced with a silent s, 'Frenel'

■ The Fresnel focus spot was developed from the focus lantern by changing the lens, adding a reflector to increase the output and the quality of the beam of light

■ In 1981, the PC/Prism-convex lantern was introduced to the new Strand Prelude range of lanterns replacing the Plano-convex lens of the focus lantern with the newly developed Prism-convex lens

■ In North America, PCs are not commonly used or sold by theatre lighting companies

■ PCs with Plano-convex lenses are used in Europe for FOH lighting as an alternative to Profile spots

■ The CIE symbol used for the Profile spot is based on the shape of the original Strand Patt. 23 lantern but that's a bit of history!

■ 'In the film business, PAR lamps are known as "bird's eyes" after the alleged inventor Clarence Birdseye'[6]

[6] A Glossary of Technical Theatre Terms – www.theatrecraft.com

Different makes & models of lanterns

Lanterns are a bit like cars in that each manufacturer produces their own distinctive design model and name for their range of each of the five types of generic lanterns.

➤ **Makes of lanterns**

Some lanterns tend to be mainly used in the country where they are manufactured, while others are used worldwide:

Country of manufacture	Makes of lanterns
United Kingdom	**CCT** (often used in education) – **Strand** (no longer manufacture lanterns but still in use) – **Philips Strand** (now distribute **Philips Selecon** lanterns in the UK) – **Thomas**
Europe	**ADB** (Belgium) – **Robert Juliat** (France) – **Teatro** (Italy)
North America	**Altman** – **ETC** (used in UK & Europe) – **Thomas** **Strand Century** (no longer manufactured but still in use)
Southern Hemisphere	**Philips Selecon** (New Zealand, widely used in UK and Europe)

Lanterns wattage & names

➤ **Power/wattage of lanterns**

The models can also be grouped together by their power/wattage of the lamp used in the lantern which affects the light output, throw and use. Watts are a measurement of electrical energy or power used by the lamp and they indicate the quantity of light produced by the lantern.[7]

- Lantern wattages range from:
  500/650W – 575/600W – 750W – 800W – 1000/1.200W (1/1.2kW) – 2.000/2.500W (2/2.5kW)

➤ **Models of lanterns**

Manufacturers identify their generic lanterns in a number of ways, e.g.:

- Some use the wattage and the generic name – **650W Fresnel**
- Others link the name of the model to the wattage – **Acclaim Fresnel, PC** (650W range)
- Profiles are often identified by their beam angle – **Acclaim Axial 18-34** (8°–34°)
- Some are identified by the diameter of the lens – **Alt. 6" Profile**

[7] See Chapter 4 'Dimmers'

2 LANTERNS – PERFORMANCE LUMINAIRES   A quick start

Wattage	Model name	Throw	Use
500/650 watts	Acclaim, Alt. 6" Fresnel, Coda, Minuette, Prelude, Quartet	Short	Small stages & drama studios
575/600 watts	*Axial Profiles:* Acclaim, Alt. 6" Ellipsoidal, Pacific, SL, Source Four, Shakespeare, Warp *NB The advanced optical system & lamp source produces a powerful beam of light*	Medium	Medium auditoriums & larger stages
750 watts	*Axial Profiles:* Ellipsoidal, Pacific, Source Four *Equivalent output to former 2000/2500W Profiles*	Long	Larger auditoriums & stages
800 watts	*Axial Profile:* Pacific, Warp	Long	Larger auditoriums & stages
1000 watts	*Axial Profile:* Leko, Pacific, Silhouette *Fresnel –* Alt. 8", Lutin, Rama	Long	Larger auditoriums Medium to large stages
1000/1200 watts 1Kw/1.2kW	Cantata, Compact, Europe, Harmony, Rama, R&J 600 R&J SX, Starlette	Medium	Medium to large stages Medium auditoriums
2000/2500 watts 2kW/2.5kW	Alto, Arena, Europe, R&J 700SX2, Starlette	Long	Large theatres

- Some of the above models of lanterns are no longer being made but you may still find them in current use for hire or in educational establishments
- **R&J -** Robert Juliat, **Alt.** – Altman Lighting
- More information can be found in Part 3: 'Lighting Resources – Technical info. – Makes & models of lanterns'

Did you know that -

■ Older lanterns were originally designed to take 500w and 1000 watt lamps; equivalent modern lanterns now use 650w and 1200 watt lamps

■ Strand Electric lanterns originally called their lanterns by their Patent or Pattern numbers

■ In 1953, the Patt 23 was the first die cast 500 watt 'baby Profile' spotlight in the world to be mass produced by Strand Electric, closely followed by the Patt 123 Fresnel

■ 500,000 Patt 23s were produced by 1983 and they can still be found in use worldwide

■ Strand first introduced zoom lenses in 1981 to the 1000w Harmony and then in 1983 to the 500w Prelude Profile spot

■ Strand Electric was founded in 1914 and it is the oldest UK stage lighting company. It was originally formed to service the London West End theatres, having its offices at 29 King Street, Covent Garden

■ Strand Lighting was formed in 1968 with the purchase of the company by the Rank Organisation, also taking over Century Lighting in New York, acquiring Vari-Lite and the Italian Quartzcolour

■ Strand Lighting was bought in the late 1990s by venture capitalists and then in 2006 it was acquired by the Genlyte Group who were purchased in 2008, becoming part of the Royal Philips Lighting group along with Selecon Performance Lighting in 2009

■ Philips Strand Lighting now produce dimmers and controls and Philips Selecon produce lanterns

QUICK TIPS

■ A safety bond must be used when hanging a lantern to provide a secondary suspension

■ Safety bonds have now replaced the use of safety chains in the UK as they are required to be load tested

■ Parcans – to adjust the position of the oval beam, rotate the lamp housing knob on the end of the lantern

■ Parcans are called after the name of the Parabolic Aluminium Reflector (PAR) lamp which is used in the lantern

■ Theatre lamps have a short life and are expensive to replace; don't use them as working lights

■ Protect your lamps by controlling them on a dimmer; switching them on creates an electrical surge that can blow the filament

2 LANTERNS – PERFORMANCE LUMINAIRES   A quick start

Quick resources – go to

www.theatrecrafts.com – Types of lanterns
www.lightingworkshop.com – Info site on lanterns
www.seleconlight.com – Selecon Lighting
www.whitelight.ltd.uk – White Light Ltd – generic lantern stencils

Points for action

Takes longer

■ Make a list of the numbers of different lanterns that you have available

A proper job!

■ Try rigging an example of each type of lantern and explore the difference in the quality of the beams of light

A quick start

2 LANTERNS – PERFORMANCE LUMINAIRES

More info – Adjusting lanterns

Focusing is a term used for adjusting the position, the size, shape and focus of the beam of light projected by a lantern. This is normally carried out at the top of an access system in the dark so you need to become familiar with all the adjustments on the various different types of lanterns.

Focusing – There are two parts to focusing a lantern

➤ **Angling** – directing/pointing the beam of light to hit a required spot
The body of the lantern is held in a 'U'-shaped bracket which allows it to rotate horizontally and pivot vertically. There are two basic terms used for these movements that can be adjusted on all lanterns:

- **Panning,** swinging from left to right, rotating the lantern on the suspension bolt from the hanging clamp
- **Tilting,** angling up and down, pivoting the lantern on the trunion arm or yoke wing bolts

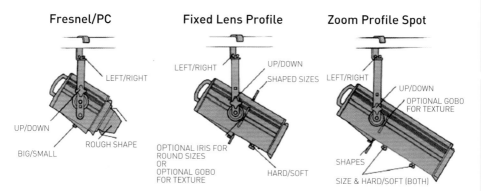

Fresnel/PC   Fixed Lens Profile   Zoom Profile Spot

Adjusting lanterns – Strand Electric

➤ **Focusing** – setting the size and focus of the beam of light on adjustable beam lanterns:

- **Fresnel/PC** – adjusting beam spread from 'spot' (small) to 'Flood focus' (wide spread)
- **Fixed Lens Profile** – adjusting the focus of the beam from hard edged to soft edged (out of focus)
- **Zoom Profile Spot** – adjusting the size and focus of the beam
- **Fixed beam lanterns** – it is not possible to focus or change the size of the beam

Profile spots – shaping & adjusting the beam

The beam of light on a Profile spot can be accurately shaped or Profiled at the 'Gate' of the lantern which is at the central point of focus between the reflector & lamp tray and the lens system.

➤ **Four rotating shutters** or 'Cuts' can be used to produce an accurate angular, rectangular or diamond shape. As you slide the shutters in, they produce a straight edge on the opposite side of the projected circular beam of light. They can be rotated to line up with any obstruction to remove or 'cut' unwanted parts of the circular beam of light overshooting the edge of the stage, the proscenium arch, the edge of a piece of scenery or the masking.

Profile shutters – GMSL

➤ **Gobos** are thin stainless steel discs with a pattern etched through the surface. It is mounted in a gobo holder that is inserted into the gate, a slot in the centre of the body of a Profile spot. Gobos are used to project an image on to the stage floor, backcloth or scenery.
NB The gobo image is mounted upside down as the optical system reverses the projected image.

Inserting a Gobo holder – GMSL

➤ **Irises** are used on fixed lens Profile spots to change the size of the beam of light as the beam size cannot be adjusted optically as on a zoom spot. They are also used in follow spots where the size of the beam needs to be manually controlled by the operator.

Inserting an Iris – GMSL

➤ **Flat light distribution**
The characteristics of the beam of light can be altered from 'peak' to 'flat' beam by finely adjusting the position of the lamp filament relative to the reflector.

■ **Peak beam** gives a central hot spot falling off evenly to the edges of the beam. This setting provides an even cover on the overlap between the areas on a wash of light on-stage

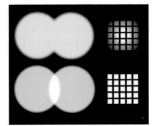

Peak/Flat beam distribution – Philips Selecon

2 LANTERNS – PERFORMANCE LUMINAIRES   More info

- **Flat beam** setting provides an evenly spread beam of light suitable for projecting gobos

➤ **Donuts** are metal masking plates with a circular cut-out that are inserted into the gate of Ellipsoidal spotlights to increase the clarity of projected gobo patterns by reducing halation and sharpening the image.

Donuts – Apollo Design Technology Inc.

➤ **Snoots or top hats** are "devices used in theatrical lighting to shield the audience's eyes from the direct source of the light. It is shaped like a top hat with a hole in the top and the brim being inserted into the colour frame guides on the front of a Profile, Axial or Parcan lanterns. The light passes through the cylinder removing any reflected light from the lantern and reduces any flare or spill lighting from the immediate auditorium architecture.

Tophat – Apollo Design Technology, Inc.

'This is very useful when lanterns are hung near the proscenium arch or other objects that the designer doesn't want to light.' [8]

Did you know that –

■ The shutters on the original profiles Strand Patt 23s, 263 and 16–30s only rotated through 90° unlike the almost 360° on modern lanterns. The Patt 264 and 774 had two sets of hard and soft shutters

PCs & Fresnels – Shaping the beam

➤ **Barndoors** are used to shape the beam of light on a PC or Fresnel. They are inserted into the first set of colour runners on the front of the lantern and held in place by a spring clip or by the lift-up top on the colour runner box. They have hinged metal doors that can be rotated and angled in order to shape the beam, reduce the scatter/spill light or mask the overshoot on to scenery or masking.

Barndoors – Philips Selecon

[8] Wikipedia, the free encyclopedia

2 LANTERNS – PERFORMANCE LUMINAIRES

More info

Adding colour

➤ **Colour frames** are used to hold filters which are inserted into the colour runners in front of the lens to colour the beam of light. As the light passes through the colour filter, it becomes very hot and it reaches the state of plasticity so it is important to use a frame to keep it flat and to stop it from buckling. The colour frame should be inserted in the front set of runners to allow for ventilation; however, when a barndoor is being used, the colour frame is inserted in the rear colour runner.

Inserting a colour frame – GMSL

GLOBAL JARGON

Lanterns:
- **Stirrup, yoke** (UK) – Fork (NA) 'U'-shaped hanging bracket in which the lantern pivots
- **Zoom Profile spot** (UK) – Zoomer (NA)
- **Shutters** (UK) – Cuts (NA) term for four rotating shutters in a Profile spot used to 'cut' or Profile the shape of the projected beam
- **Gobo** (UK) – Patterns (NA)
- **Colour filters** (UK) – Gel (NA)

MORE TIPS

- Always use a colour frame to hold a filter – Gaffer tape is not a suitable alternative!
- Colour frames are expensive to replace; don't leave them lying around to get broken or lost, store them in a portable tool tray
- Take care – lanterns become hot very quickly; always use the handles when adjusting them
- Use gloves to protect yourself when handling lanterns, colour frames, gobos, barndoors and shutters
- Take care when adjusting lanterns or repositioning them when they are still hot as the lamp filament may break

More info

2 LANTERNS – PERFORMANCE LUMINAIRES

> **More resources – go to**
> **www.mts.net/~william5/sld** – *Stage Lighting Design*, Bill Williams
> **www.apollodesign.net/product/donuts/thickLine/** donut – view video

Points for action
A proper job!

- Rig a Profile spot and try using the four shutters, mount a gobo in a holder and insert it into the gate of the lantern
- Rig a PC or Fresnel and fit a barndoor and try adjusting the shape of the beam
- Mount a colour filter in a frame and insert it into the colour runners in front of a lantern

2 LANTERNS – PERFORMANCE LUMINAIRES

More info

Extras! – How do they work?

It is important to know how lanterns work and to understand what is happening when you are focusing a beam of light.

Fixed beam lanterns – Floods, Cycs & Parcans

Fixed beam lanterns do not have an adjustable optical system. They consist of a lamp source with a reflector and have no method of adjusting the size of the beam of light:

Flood symmetric	Overhead 'soft edged' wash
90 Degree Flood – Philips Selecon	▪ **Symmetrical reflector** with a linear lamp positioned in the centre ▪ Barndoors can be fitted on some models to shape the beam of light

Cyc/Groundrow asymmetric	Vertical 'soft edged' wash
Cyc light – Philips Selecon *Groundrow – Philips Selecon*	▪ **Asymmetrical reflector** with a linear lamp positioned off-centre ▪ Cyc light is reversed when used as a groundrow ▪ Lanterns can be linked together in groups of 3 or 4

Parcan	Near parallel 'beam light'
	Beam size depends on the type of lens on the PAR lamp that is fitted into the lantern
Clear PAR lamp – GMSL	The beam angle can be identified by: ▪ **Clear lens** – VNSP 9° x 12° very narrow spot ▪ **Frosted lens** – NSP 10° x 14° narrow spot

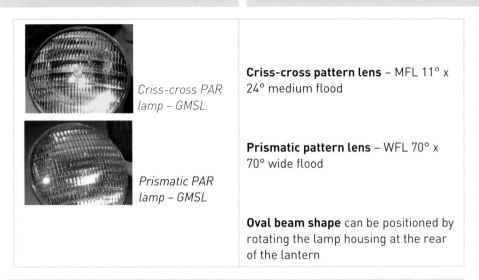

Criss-cross PAR lamp – GMSL

Prismatic PAR lamp – GMSL

Criss-cross pattern lens – MFL 11° x 24° medium flood

Prismatic pattern lens – WFL 70° x 70° wide flood

Oval beam shape can be positioned by rotating the lamp housing at the rear of the lantern

Focus lanterns – lens luminaires

Focus lanterns have an optical system consisting of a reflector, lamp tray and a lens system. The focus and size of the beam can be adjusted.

➤ Fresnels & PCs
The optical system consists of:

- **Fixed lens**
- **Moveable reflector & lamp tray** to adjust the size of the beam of light
- **Base down lamp** (apart from Source Four Fresnel)

Fresnel	'Soft edged' beam
	▪ Fresnel lens ▪ Beam angle, 6–60 degrees* wide variable cone of light

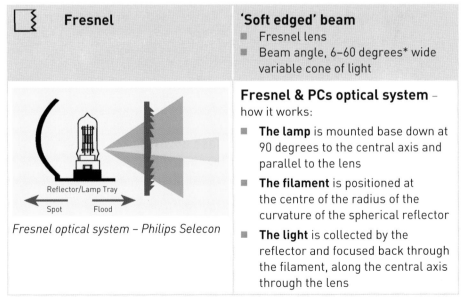

Reflector/Lamp Tray

Spot ← → Flood

Fresnel optical system – Philips Selecon

Fresnel & PCs optical system – how it works:

- **The lamp** is mounted base down at 90 degrees to the central axis and parallel to the lens

- **The filament** is positioned at the centre of the radius of the curvature of the spherical reflector

- **The light** is collected by the reflector and focused back through the filament, along the central axis through the lens

* Beam angles quoted can vary depending upon the make and model of the lantern

▭ **PC – Prism & Plano-convex**	**'Semi-hard/soft edged' beam**
	▪ Plano/Prism/Pebble-convex lens ▪ Beam angle, 4–64 degrees* wide variable cone of light

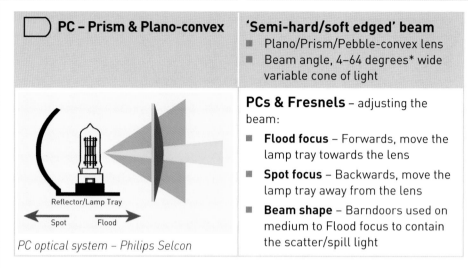

PCs & Fresnels – adjusting the beam:

▪ **Flood focus** – Forwards, move the lamp tray towards the lens

▪ **Spot focus** – Backwards, move the lamp tray away from the lens

▪ **Beam shape** – Barndoors used on medium to Flood focus to contain the scatter/spill light

PC optical system – Philips Selcon

➤ **Profile lanterns**
The optical system consists of:

▪ **Fixed reflector & lamp tray**
▪ **Lamp tray adjustment** – to produce a peak or flat beam
▪ **The gate** – to Profile the shape of the beam
▪ **Moveable lenses** – to focus and adjust the size of the beam (zoom beam lanterns)
▪ **Interchangeable lens tubes** – to change the size of the beam (fixed beam angle lanterns)

⊶ **Base down Profile spot**	**'Hard edged/soft focus' precise beam**
	▪ Plano-convex lens ▪ Zoom Profile, long throw beam angle 18–34 degrees* ▪ Zoom Profile, short throw beam angle 24–44 degrees*

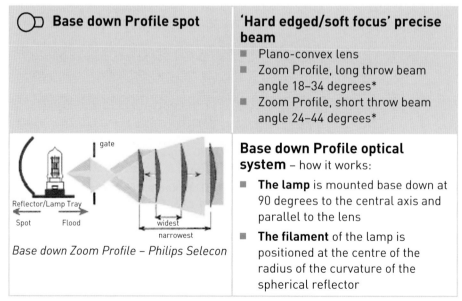

Base down Profile optical system – how it works:

▪ **The lamp** is mounted base down at 90 degrees to the central axis and parallel to the lens

▪ **The filament** of the lamp is positioned at the centre of the radius of the curvature of the spherical reflector

Base down Zoom Profile – Philips Selecon

* Beam angles quoted can vary depending upon the make and model of the lantern

2 LANTERNS – PERFORMANCE LUMINAIRES | **Extras!**

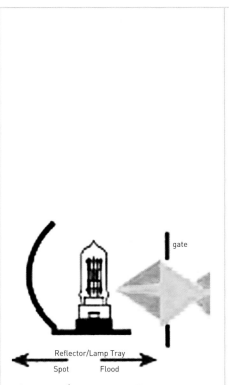

Reflector/Lamp tray – Philips Selecon

- **The light** is collected by the reflector and focused back through the filament, along the central axis through the gate to the lens system
- **The gate** aperture accurately shapes the circular beam with the addition of four masking shutters, a gobo to project a pattern, or an iris to alter the beam size as used on fixed beam angle lanterns

Profile lanterns – adjusting the beam:

- **Beam focus** – hard or soft by adjusting the position of the lens
- **Beam shape** – 4 integral rotating shutters, an iris or gobos can be inserted into the gate
- **Flat/Peak light distribution** – fine adjustment of the position of the lamp tray to the lens system. Peak field move the lamp tray towards the lens system, flat field away

Fixed beam having a single adjustable lens to focus

- **Interchangeable lens tubes** can be inserted, basic narrow, standard, wide angle & other beam angles

Zoom beam having two adjustable lenses

- **Front lens** adjusts the size
- **Back lens** adjusts the focus
- **Wide beam** – moves lenses together
- **Spot beam** – moves lenses apart

2 LANTERNS – PERFORMANCE LUMINAIRES

Extras!

2 LANTERNS – PERFORMANCE LUMINAIRES   Extras!

⊙ Axial Ellipsoidal Profile

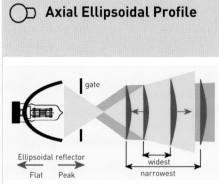

Axial Ellipsoidal optical system – Philips Selecon

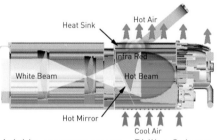

Axial heat management – Philips Selecon

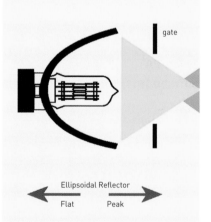

Flat/Peak beam adjustment – Philips Selecon

'Hard edged/soft focus' precise beam
- Plano-convex lens

Axial Ellipsoidal Profile optical system – how it works:

- **The compact filament lamp** is mounted axially, along the central axis of the lantern
- **The filament** of the lamp is positioned at the focal point of a half elliptical reflector
- **The light** is collected by the reflector and directed along the central axis through a hot mirror and to a second focal point beyond the gate of the lantern
- **The hot mirror** is a part of the heat management system at the rear of the lantern that diverts the infrared rays, reducing the heat in the beam and increasing the life of colour filters and gobos. The mirror acts as a selective filter managing the colour balance to produce a 'whiter light'
- **Peak/Flat light distribution** – fine adjustment of the position of the lamp filament in the middle of the reflector by rotating the lamp tray on the rear of the lantern. Peak field: rotate clockwise towards the lens system; flat field: anticlockwise away

Base down Ellipsoidal Profile

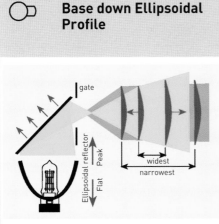

Base down Axial Optical System – Philips Selecon

'Hard edged/soft focus' precise beam

- Plano-convex lens

Base down Ellipsoidal optical system – how it works:

- **The lamp** is mounted base down in a vertical axis
- **The filament** of the lamp is positioned at the focal point of a half-elliptical reflector
- **The light** is collected by the reflector and directed along the vertical axis
- **The cold mirror** turns the light through 90 degrees directing the beam of light along the axis through the gate as with the Axial Profile

Peak/Flat light distribution – adjusting the position of the filament by rotating the gear wheel on the end lamp tray housing at the base of the lantern

Pacific cutaway – Philips Selecon

Advantages of base down Ellipsoidal – Selecon Pacific

- **The cold mirror** diverts the ultraviolet and infra-red heat directing it through the heat sink on the angled back of the lantern
- **The active heat management system** delivers a cool beam of light on-stage. It also directs the heat away from the lantern adjustment knobs, colour filter and other important parts, such as the lamp, internal wiring and lantern cable
- **The cool system** provides the option of projecting plastic transparency images mounted in heat-resistant gobo holders

2 LANTERNS – PERFORMANCE LUMINAIRES

Extras!

Lanterns makes & models – see Part 3: 'Lighting Resources – Technical info.'

Lantern design

The development of the optical systems for lanterns has always been dependent on the production of the appropriate lamp sources. Traditionally in the UK, lamps were designed to be used 'base down' at 90 degrees to the central axis of the lantern.

➤ **1930s** – Elliposidal reflector spotlights were developed using 110 volt 'base-up' lamp. They were widely used in North America but the low-voltage lamps greatly restricted their use in countries where 240 volt power supplies were in use in the UK, Europe and the Southern Hemisphere.

➤ **1960s** – Strand Lighting developed an Ellipsoidal Profile using a 240 volt, T4 1000 watt 'base-up' lamp. The Patt 264 bifocal spotlight had hard and soft edged shutters with a throw of 10M and was widely used in the UK.

➤ **1970s** – Altman Lighting introduced the 360Q Axial Ellipsoidal, the first lantern to have the lamp positioned parallel to the axial plane

➤ **1990s** – Further developments in the development of Axial lanterns with the availability of the compact tungsten filament allowing the lamp to be mounted along the central axis of an elliptical reflector and the optical system.

Patt 264 – Strand Electric

- The 'Cool' lantern concept was created with the development of hot mirror filters, dichroic-coated glass reflector technology and heat management systems
- The 570/600 watt lamp and the efficient optical system produces a more powerful 'whiter' light equivalent to other 1000 watt lanterns using 40% less energy

Did you know that –

- In 1933, the first Ellipsoidal spotlight was developed by Century Lighting in North America and was called 'Leko' or 'Lekolite' after the first half of the surnames of its inventors Joseph Levy and Edward Kook
- In the 1970s, Zoom spots or 'Zoomers' having an adjustable beam size were developed and used in North America
- In 1992, ETC created the Source Four applying the advances in lamp and reflector technology to increase light output with reduced wattage.

This was the first lantern to have interchangeable lens tubes, allowing a single body to use a multiple of beam field angles ranging from 5° to 90°. Source Four is a popular lantern with international lighting designers

■ Zoom Axial Profiles are now more widely used in Europe and the UK, especially in drama studios and medium-sized theatres where flexibility is an important requirement

■ Lighting designers especially in North America prefer to use Axial Ellipsoidal lanterns with interchangeable lenses rather than lanterns having zoom lenses/Zoomers

■ The lamp on a Source Four Fresnel is mounted axially and not like other Fresnels at 90° to the central axis

EXTRA TIPS

■ Flat & peak field adjustment – angle the lantern at a white wall 4–8 metres away, focus light to a narrow sharp focused beam, carefully adjust the position of the lamp tray/housing to move the filament. NB the filament will be burning at white heat and it can be easily damaged

■ 90 degree Ellipsoidal lanterns can be used for back lighting instead of Fresnels. They have a similar light output with the beam control of a Profile and the option to use gobo break-ups

■ ETC Source Four & Selecon Pacific lanterns have a range of 11 interchangeable lens tubes which can be fitted with beam angles ranging from 5 to 90 degrees. The barrel/lens tubes can be rotated for the accurate alignment of projected gobos

More resources – go to
www.altmanltg.com – Altman Stage Lighting: NA
www.adblighting.com – ADB Lighting Technologies: Belgium
www.cctlighting.com – CCT Lighting: UK
www.etcconnect.com – ETC: NA
www.seleconlight.com – Philips Selecon: New Zealand
www.robertjuliat.fr – Robert Juliat: France
www.strandarchive.co.uk – Strand Lighting archive
www.jthomaseng.com – James Thomas Engineering: UK
www.teclumen.it – Teatro Teclumen: Italy

2 LANTERNS – PERFORMANCE LUMINAIRES   Extras!

3 Working with lanterns

A quick start – Rigging lanterns

Good working practice, hanging, angling & focusing, striking lanterns and accessories

More info – Lantern maintenance

Maintaining lanterns, troubleshooting and replacing lamps

Extras! – Electrical safety

Introduction to the requirements of electrical testing, user checks, what to do if you find a fault

A quick start – Rigging lanterns

Good working practices help to create a safe working environment and can save a lot of time when working on-stage so it is worth finding out the right way to do things.

Good working practice

Hanging lanterns

Lanterns are hung from lighting bars on hanging clamps by a suspension bolt that is attached to the lantern stirrup/hanging bracket. The lantern should have a safety bond/wire attaching it to the bar for safety in case the primary suspension fails, e.g. suspension bolt or hook clamp.

Lantern suspension – GMSL

> ➤ **Preparing the equipment – checklist**
> Before you start to rig the lanterns, check the following points:
>
> ✓ **The hanging clamp is correctly fitted** above the hanging stirrup so as not to restrict the movement of the lantern
>
> ✓ **The suspension bolt is tight** in the stirrup to prevent any addition movement once the lantern has been set in position

33

A quick start

3 WORKING WITH LANTERNS

☑ **The safety bond/wire** is permanently attached to the anchor point on the lantern; see 'More info'

➤ Checking the electrical safety of the equipment

A visual check should be made by the user every time a lantern or extension cable is used. This is an important safety precaution as many faults can be identified providing you know what to look for.

PAT sticker – GMSL

Cable socket – GMSL

Damaged cable – GMSL

Check the equipment to ensure that:

☑ **The lantern has been PAT tested** in the last 12 months – check the date on the green test sticker on the lantern[9]

☑ **The lantern cable** is securely held at the point of entry to the body of the lantern and to the cable plug

☑ **Flexible extension cables have been PAT tested**, the cable is free from damage and securely held at the point of entry to the cable plug, socket/ connector. That the live and neutral connections on 15 amp flexible cable socket are protected by red sprung shutters

☑ **Do not use the equipment** if it hasn't been PAT tested or if there are any obvious visual electrical faults

Rigging

It is important to do the things in the right order to hang the lanterns correctly, also to check that the lighting plan is the right way round.

Hanging lanterns – check the following points:

☑ **The lantern stirrup** is hanging in vertical position and not at an angle; see 'Quick tips'

☑ **The hanging clamp is tight** on the bar

☑ **The lantern is hanging the right way up** with the cable entry at the bottom

☑ **The safety bond is attached over the bar** allowing the lantern to fully rotate

☑ **The lantern cable is looped loosely over the bar** allowing the lantern to move freely

☑ **The lantern movement** is free to rotate from side to side and tilt up and down

☑ **The lantern has enough space** – roughly angle it in the right direction to check that it will do what you want it to do and isn't restricted by other lanterns

[9] Portable Appliance Testing, see Chapter 3 'Working with lanterns – Extras!'

Hanging a lantern –
Philips Selecon

✓ **Spot focus the lantern** in preparation for focusing
✓ **Colour frames & barndoors** are safely attached to prevent them falling out when the lantern is tilted
✓ **Open up barndoors and shutters on Profile spots** so that you can see that the lantern is working when it is 'flashed through'
✓ **The lantern cable is not fixed or taped to the bar** to allow easy removal if a fault occurs
✓ **Extension cables being used are the right length**; too long or too short can cause a safety hazard also that they will not be damaged by some mechanical movement, e.g. pinched under a door

>> **Fast Forward** on the DVD to **3.1 Adjusting lanterns**

Focusing lanterns – 'Hitting your spot!'

When you are focusing, position yourself directly behind the lantern.

➤ **Angling the lantern**
- **'Spot focus'** the beam adjustment
- **'Turn, Slacken, Slide & Tighten'** the adjustment knob to move the lens or lamp housing and to fix the setting
- **'Pan and Tilt'** the lantern so the middle of the beam hits between the neck and shoulders of the person standing in the centre of the area to be lit
- **'Lock off'** tightening the hanging bolt and pivoting wing bolts to prevent any further movement

➤ **Focusing the lantern**
PCs & Fresnels
- **Open up the beam** of light slowly to the required size to light the area
- **Shape the beam** of light, adjusting the barndoors to remove any unwanted scatter or spill light from the set or masking

➤ **Profile spots**
- **Zoom Profiles adjust size** – by moving the front lens adjustment knob
- **Hard or soft focus** the edge of the beam as required using the rear lens adjustment on zoom Profiles (on some lanterns it can be easier to adjust both lenses together)
- **Shape the beam** of light using the four rotating shutters or 'cuts' to remove or cut the unwanted light from proscenium arch, front of stage or off parts of the set

3 WORKING WITH LANTERNS   **A quick start**

➤ **Saving your lamps**

Take care when angling and focusing lanterns. The lamps are expensive to replace, they only have a relatively short life and the tungsten filament is very fragile.

- **Set the dimmer level at 90%** or point 9 when focusing to reduce the possibility of the filament breaking
- **Handle lantern carefully** when you are adjusting it as the tungsten filament in the lamp burns at white heat and it can be easily broken
- **'Save your lamps!'** – fade out each lantern when you have finished focusing it to remove unwanted light and to prevent it becoming too hot too handle

De-rigging lanterns

Strike the lanterns in the following order to prevent damage and ending up in a mess.

➤ **Lanterns checklist:**

Step 1
- ✓ **Switch off the lantern**
- ✓ **Unplug the lantern and coil the cable**

Step 2
- ✓ **Profile spots** – close the shutters to prevent them being bent
- ✓ **PCs & Fresnels** – close the barndoors

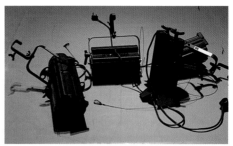

Lanterns before! – GMSL

- ✓ **Swing the lantern into the vertical position**

Step 3
- ✓ **Release the safety bond** from the bar, coil it up and attach to the lantern
- ✓ **Slacken the wing bolt** on the hanging clamp
- ✓ **Lift the lantern off the bar** with the hanging clamp attached and place it lens down on the floor

If you have followed the above instructions:
- ✓ **The lanterns should stand vertically** on its colour runners without falling over
- ✓ **The shutters and barndoors will be protected** and they will not become damaged or bent

- ✓ **The cables and safety bonds will not be trailing on the floor** when the lantern is moved

Lanterns afterwards – GMSL

De-rigging accessories

- ☑ Remove the filter from the colour frame and store in a colour storage folder
- ☑ Store the barndoors and colour frames in an accessories tray

➤ Coiling up extension cables

There is a simple and effective way to coil cables. If you are right-handed:

1 Hold the socket end of the cable in the left hand (or the right hand if you are left-handed)
2 Allow the cable to run through the fingers of the right hand (or vice versa)
3 Extend the right arm out to measure a standard length for the loop
4 As the first loop is made, twist the cable with the right fingers to remove any kinks

Coiling a cable – GMSL

5 Repeat measuring the length of cable for the next loop, twisting to remove the kinks
6 The loops of the coil should now all be the same length hanging free without any twist or kinks
7 Tape the coil together with PVC tape or use tie lines; see 'How they do it in North America'

➤ Organising accessories

Plastic tool trays provide a quick, convenient and portable storage for colour frames, barndoors and spare lamps. They can be lifted out and used on-stage as the accessories are de-rigged, preventing them from being left lying around becoming lost or damaged.

Extension cables – sort into standard lengths, 5M, 10M and 20M and colour code by attaching a small band of PVC tape at both ends to help identify them by their length. Store the cables by their sizes in large plastic boxes or crates marked with the length and colour.

How they do it in North America

Using PVC tape to hold a coil of cable together is considered very bad practice in USA:

'This is bad working practice in North America. As with securing cable to bars, we use "tie line," what would be called "sash" or "sash cord" in the UK. It is the sign of a well-organized and well-maintained theatre to have a piece of tie line attached to the male end of a cable with an overhand knot with long tails extending; that way, when you coil the

3 WORKING WITH LANTERNS

A quick start

UNIVERSITY OF WINCHESTER

cable, you tie the ends in a BOW (always a bow!) around the entire coil, making for easy undoing, no wasted or messy tape on the floor, and no adhesive sticking to the cable! The same is done to secure a cable to a bar, as it allows for more movement slack if pulled, less mess and less waste of tape since the lengths are reusable, and ease of removal from the bar (just pull the end of the bow!).'[10]

Perhaps we should consider adopting this as good working practice in the UK? It would certainly save a lot of waste and could be a green issue.

Cable connectors

Each country use different types of cable plugs and sockets; they can have 2 or 3 pins that are round, flat or shaped.

The size of the connectors and diameter of the pins depends upon the maximum power handling of the cable being used that is measured in amps. See Part 3: 'Lighting Resources – Technical info.'.

➤ **In the UK:**
- **15 amp round pin** cable plugs and sockets are used for generic lanterns
- **16 amp CEE P17** are used for moving heads with discharge lamp sources to prevent them being connected to a dimmer circuit.[11] They are also used for outdoor installations as the circular body of the male and female connector is fully enclosed when joined together providing a waterproof connection
- **CEE P17** 16 amp cable plugs and sockets are part of a larger range used in the UK: 16A, 32A, 63A & 125 amp connectors used for mains power

Lantern reference guide

Wattage, lamps, colour frames, gobos & holder sizes – see Part 3: 'Lighting Resources – Technical info.'.

[10] Ziggy Jacobs – an American Lighting Design student, Central School of Speech and Drama
[11] Moving heads/discharge lamps, see Chapter 6 'DMX fixtures – A quick start – Animated & intelligent fixtures'

GLOBAL JARGON

- **Hanging clamps** (UK & Europe) – are used to hang lanterns on lighting bars
- **Pipe or C-clamps** (NA) – are used to hang lanterns on pipes
- **Hanging clamps and lightweight half couplers** (NZ & Aus) – are used to hang lanterns on **'spot bars'** (NZ) and **'pipes'** (Aus)
- **Safety bond** (UK) – safety wire or 'safety chain' (NA)
- **Plugs & Sockets** (UK) – 'female ends' and 'male ends' connectors on cables
- **Flexible cable** mains lead (UK) – Cord (NA)

Did you know that –

- Electric lanterns were first hung on the 2" gas barrels that supplied the original gas lighting, hence the term 'pipe' used in some countries for lighting bars
- The 48mm diameter is now the standard size for stage lighting bars in the UK which is the same size as aluminium scaffolding bars
- In 1959, the 'hook clamp' was introduced by Strand Electric, having a finger-tightened wing set screw. This revolutionised the rigging of lanterns, replacing the original 'L'-shaped bracket and bolted pipe clip requiring the use of a spanner
- Philips Selecon have added a number of design safety features to their lanterns, including a retractable safety wire and flip-top colour runner boxes, taking lantern design into the 21st century
- **15 amp plugs and sockets** were originally used for domestic power sockets in the UK prior to the introduction of 13 amp ring circuit/ mains and the use of fused plug tops
- **Flat pinned 13 amp connectors** are not used in the UK for stage lighting installations because the plug tops contain a fuse. The circuit protection on stage lighting is provided at the source by a circuit breaker or fuse on the dimmer unit. Therefore, additional fuse protection is unnecessary and would cause confusion in location faults

3 WORKING WITH LANTERNS A quick start

3 WORKING WITH LANTERNS   A quick start

QUICK TIPS

- Before hanging a lantern, make sure that the stirrup/hanging bracket is in direct line with the axis of the lantern so that it will hang in a vertical position when hung on the bar
- Base down mounted lamps are designed to be burnt at an optimum angle of 45 degrees either side of the vertical
- If the lantern is hung upside down or at a side angle, it will greatly reduce the life of the lamp
- Axial lanterns, Parcans and Floods can be used in a vertical position without reducing the lamp life
- Check that the lantern is hanging or mounted the right way up with the cable entry at the bottom
- When mounting a lantern on a stand, remember to reverse the position of the stirrup if it has been hanging to ensure that it is the right way up
- When removing a lantern from a stand, reverse the stirrup before hanging it on a bar
- Save your lamps! Don't use lanterns as working lights
- Domestic linear lamp Flood lights make good working lights
- Tool trays can be purchased from DIY stores
- It is easier to identify the length of extension cables if they are colour coded
- De-rigging cables from a lighting bar – always start from the end with the shortest cables to save ending up with a knot of cables like a pile of spaghetti
- Cables have a mind of their own! Never coil them on your arm round your hand and elbow because the twists will be left in the cable and the coil will not stay together

Points for action

Takes longer

- Check that you have frames to fit all the different sizes of the models of lanterns and replace them where necessary

A proper job!

- Organise the colour frames and barndoors into tool trays and mark them with large labels
- Large labels can be produced on a computer; print and laminate them, and attach them with double-sided adhesive tape
- Colour code extension cables, e.g. 5M – Brown, 10M – Orange, 20M – Green

More info – Lantern maintenance

A lot of time can be wasted when focusing dirty lanterns or faulty equipment with missing parts. Preparing the equipment can save a lot of valuable time when you are lighting the show.

Maintaining lanterns

➤ Cleaning

Lanterns need to be cleaned at least once a year. A build up of dust on the lens can considerably reduce the intensity of the lamp and it can be a safety hazard. Remove the dust from the lens, reflector, inner and outer casing of the lantern with paintbrush and cloth; a face mask should be worn to provide protection.

➤ Friction hanging bolt suspension

Tightening the assembly – GMSL

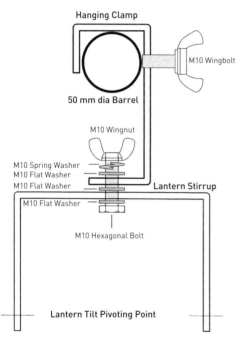

Hanging bolt assembly – GMSL

A friction hanging bolt assembly saves a lot of time when angling and focusing lanterns as it allows the lantern to be rotated but holds it firmly in position after it has been adjusted. The assembly consists of a series of flat washers between each moving surface to allow the parts to rotate under the pressure of a spring washer that maintains the tension and prevents any additional movement. The friction assembly removes the need to use a spanner every time a lantern is repositioned.

3 WORKING WITH LANTERNS

More info

41

➤ **Attaching safety bonds/chains**

Attaching a safety bond – GMSL

The safety bond/wire is a load tested steel cable with a loop at one end and a clip at the other.

- The safety bond should be permanently attached to the lantern to stop it falling to the floor when the lantern is being struck
- On lanterns with anchor points, pass the loop at the end of the cable through the hole, thread the hook end of the cable through the loop and pull tight
- Safety bonds in the UK are marked with the safe working load
- Check that you are using the correct size safety bond to match the weight of the lantern

Troubleshooting

➤ **If a lantern isn't working:**

1 **Isolate the lantern** – switch off the main electrical power supply as there might be an electrical fault and the lantern could be live

⬇

2 **Check the Miniature Circuit breaker trip switch** (MCB) or fuse on the dimmer unit control[12]

⬇

3 **If the MCB is in the on position** or the fuse intact, check the circuit and cabling by substituting a known working lantern and test the circuit

⬇

4 **If the MCB has tripped out** or the fuse is blown, this would indicate that there is an electrical fault or that the lamp has blown

5 **Allow the lantern to cool down** before touching it

⬇

6 **Disconnect the lantern**

⬇

7 **Strike the lantern** – it is always safer to work on it at floor level

⬇

8 **Inspect the lantern** for any obvious visual electrical faults in the wiring. If in doubt, remove the lantern from service and refer it to a qualified electrician

⬇

9 **Inspect the lamp** – if the filament is intact, there could be an electrical fault and remove the lantern from service

⬇

10 **If the filament is broken**, replace the lamp

⬇

---

[12] Dimmer units, MCBs and fuse circuit protection, see Chapter 4 'Dimmers – More info'

3 WORKING WITH LANTERNS   More info

11 **Test the lantern** by using a known working circuit outlet socket on a dimmer rack. If the lantern still doesn't work, there must be an electrical fault

↓

12 **If it works, hang the lantern** and reconnect to the original circuit and test

Replacing lamps

➤ **The lamp housing**
  - On a Profile lantern, the lamp housing is at the rear with the access either from the side or underneath the housing
  - On an Axial Ellipsoidal lantern, the lamp is positioned on the end of the lantern
  - On Fresnels and PCs, the front of the lantern hinges forward or access may be from the side

➤ **Three types of lamp bases used in lanterns**

Bipost lamp – GMSL

  - **Bipost base lamps** as used on modern lanterns have a two pin base. To remove, gently ease out or use the release lever on Selecon lanterns to part eject the lamp
  - **Prefocus cap lamps** as used on older lanterns are held in place by two fins that line up the filament of the lamp in the lamp post holder so that it is at 90° to the axis of the lantern. To remove, press the lamp down against the strung base and turn anticlockwise through 90 degrees
  - **'K' class linear lamps** as used in Cyc and Floods have terminals at either end of the tube and fit into a sprung lamp post holder
  - **When handling tungsten halogen lamps**, always use protective gloves or a soft cloth as grease from your fingers burns on to and through the glass envelope that will affect the halogen cycle and shorten the life of the lamp[13]

✓ **Check the lamp**
  - **Check to see if the filament is broken** by holding the lamp up to the light
  - **Check to see if there are any dark finger-shaped burns** on the glass envelope from where it has been previously touched which will have reduced the life of the lamp
  - **Check the pins on the base of the lamp** to see if there is any sign of burning from arcing caused by poor contacts and a faulty lamp post holder that may need to be replaced
  - **If there is no obvious fault**, it could be an electrical fault in the lantern's wiring

[13] *A Beginner's Guide to Stage Lighting*, Peter Coleman

3 WORKING WITH LANTERNS   More info

✓ **Check the type of lamp and wattage**
Most commonly used lamps:

T18	T26	T11	T29	GKV600	HPL575	HPL750
500 watt	650 watt	1000 watt	1200 watt	600 watt	575 watt	750 watt
Focus lanterns CCT, Philips Selecon & Strand				**Axial lanterns** Acclaim, SPX, Pacific, SL	**Axial lanterns** Source Four	

Check out Part 3: 'Lighting Resources – Technical info.' – Lanterns Reference Guide data sheet

✓ **Fitting a new lamp**
- **Clean the lens** and reflector before fitting a new lamp
- **Remove the lamp** from the top of the box and hold it by its metal base below the glass envelope
- **Use a soft cloth** or gloves when handling the lamp
- **Bipost lamps** – line up the large and small pin with the base of the lamp post holder and firmly push home
- **Prefocus lamps** – line up the large and small fins with the openings on the base of the lamp post holder, press down and turn clockwise through 90 degrees

✓ **Test the lantern**, close the lantern housing and test it on a known working dimmer channel. If possible, always protect theatre lamps by using a dimmer control as a sudden electrical surge from a switched supply can cause the filament to blow which can be an expensive mistake

LAMPS NOT BULBS!

It is important to use the correct terms –
'The lamp produces the light in a lantern; we plant bulbs in the garden!' [14/15]

And as they say in North America:
Q: 'How many techies does it take to change a light bulb?'
A: 'We don't, it's called a lamp, you idiot!' [16]

[14] *A Beginner's Guide to Stage Lighting*, Peter Coleman
[15] 'A Glossary of Technical Terms', www.theatrecrafts.com/glossary
[16] Ziggy Jacobs – American Lighting Design student

Types of lamps

There are two types of lamp sources that are used in theatre lanterns – incandescent and discharge lamps.

➤ **Incandescent lamps**
   - **Tungsten-halogen lamps** have a tungsten wire filament enclosed in a halogen-filled glass envelope
   - **As used in** theatre generic lanterns, some moving lights, also for TV and film lanterns

Types of incandescent lamps

Class	Colour Temperature	Use
T Class	3000 degrees Kelvin	Stage lighting
CP Class	3200 degrees Kelvin – slightly higher	Originally used for television and film
HPL & GKV	3000 degrees Kelvin	Ellipsoidal/Axial lanterns
K Class	lower colour temp than T or CP Class lamps	Floodlights – linear double-ended lamps
ANSI Lamps		PAR fittings – sealed beam lamps

➤ **Discharge lamps**
   - **Metal-halide lamps** have two metal rods separated by a small gap enclosed in a gas-filled glass envelope; the high voltage passed between the electrodes causes the gas to conduct electricity. Discharge lamps emit a higher light output and have a longer life than incandescent lamps. Discharge lamps cannot be dimmed so the lanterns are fitted with shutters to control the intensity of the light. Some discharge lamps do not have the facility for 'hot restrike' and may require up to 15–20 minutes to cool down before they can be restruck again
   - **Colour temperature** of a discharge lamp is significantly bluer than the white of a tungsten-halogen lamp. This can cause problems in using and blending generic lanterns with moving lights, although this is not so much a problem with follow spots
   - **As used in** moving lights, follow spots, effects projectors, also for TV and film and generic lanterns used for display and exhibitions

3 WORKING WITH LANTERNS

More info

3 WORKING WITH LANTERNS   **More info**

Types of discharge lamps

CSI	CDM	HMI	MSR
Compact Source Iodide	Ceramic Discharge Metal-halide	Halide Metal Iodide	Medium Source Rare-earth
Follow spots	**Display fittings**	**Moving lights**	**Moving lights, follow spots**

Did you know that –

■ Safety chains formerly used in the UK have been replaced by safety bonds because they are not load tested and the size and weight of lanterns and moving lights has increased

■ Safety wires are used in North America but they are still called 'safety chains'

■ When the lamp filament blows in a lantern, the circuit fuse may also break or Miniature Circuit Breaker trip out

■ Domestic light fittings use BC – Bayonet Cap, ES – Edison Screw, MES – Miniature Edison Screw lamps. Larger commercial light fittings use GES – Giant Edison Screw lamps, also used on older types of stage Floods

GLOBAL JARGON

■ **Spanners** (UK) – wrenches, 'AJs', 'C wrenches' (NA)
■ **Safety bonds** (UK) – safety chains (NA)
■ **Miniature Circuit Breakers or MCB** (UK) – Ground Fault Circuit Interrupters or GFCI (NA)

MORE TIPS

■ 10mm is the standard size for lantern hanging set screws in the UK

■ A 17mm open-ended spanner fits a 10mm hexagonal nut & set screw

■ A 'Quad' is a reversible ratchet spanner with hexagonal headed socket at either end, 17, 19 & 21mm sockets cover most of the common sizes used for working with lanterns. A lanyard can be attached to the Quad, a must for a technician's tool kit

■ Use a Caritool belt clip karabiner to safely carry the Quad spanner and other tools up to 5kg when working at heights

■ 12mm set screws are supplied as standard suspension bolt with Philips Selecon lanterns and they are also used on heavier lanterns in the UK

■ 12mm set screws are used in Australia and New Zealand with their forked-shaped hook clamps

■ Continuous lamp failure can be caused by arcing on a burnt-out lamp post holder that needs to be replaced

■ Frosted K1 & K4 lamps as used in Cyc and Floods give a better performance than clear lamps

■ Always open the printed end of the lamp box to extract the lamp by the base end

■ If you should touch the glass envelope of the lamp, you can clean the surface with methylated spirit

Points for action

A proper job!

■ Fit your lanterns with friction hanging bolts, you will need a quantity of flat and split washers

■ Check your stock of spare lamps – have you got at least one of each type to match your lanterns?

3 WORKING WITH LANTERNS   More info

Extras! – Electrical safety

It is important to personally check all equipment, lanterns and cables that they are electrically safe to use before using them

'The trouble about electricity is that it gives no warning of its dangers. It is a quiet, unseen, obedient servant who at any time, given the chance, will round on his employer and may even slay him!'

Frederick Bentham, The Art of Stage Lighting

Electrical testing

The line manager of the theatre or studio space is responsible for ensuring the electrical safety of the installation and equipment. In the UK, regular inspection and testing of the fixed installation and the portable electrical equipment is required to satisfy the 'Electricity at Work Regulations' 1989.

➤ **The Institution of Electrical Engineers (UK) (IEE) – Code of Practice**[17] states that every installation requires regular inspection which for theatre spaces should consist of:

- **A periodic electrical test** of the lighting bars, wiring installation, dimmers and control
- **P**ortable **A**ppliance **T**esting, **PAT testing** – theatrical equipment should be inspected and tested by a competent and trained electrician; each item should be marked with the test date sticker, a record of testing and repairs should be kept

➤ **The IEE 'Electrical Maintenance including Portable Appliance Testing'**[18] **recommends:**
The testing of fixed electrical installations – a maximum period between inspections of:

- **Theatres**   1 year
- **Educational establishments**   5 years
- **Emergency lighting**   3 years

Moveable, portable and hand-held equipment that is in regular use – the following good working practice should be carried out:

- **User visual checks**   Weekly
- **Formal visual inspection**   4 months
- **Inspection and testing**   12 months

---

[17] The Institution of Electrical Engineers 'Code of Practice for In-Service Inspection and Testing of Electrical Equipment'
[18] The Institution of Electrical Engineers 'Electrical Maintenance including Portable Appliance Testing'

Checking electrical equipment

Making a formal visual inspection – every 4 months

➤ **Disconnect the equipment before inspecting and check for the following faults:**

✓ **Flexible cables** – cuts in the outer insulation cable or damage covered by tape. The size of cable is suitable for the intended load, 2.5mm TRS should be used with 15/16 amp cable plugs and sockets

Damaged cable – GMSL

✓ **Flexible plug top & cable socket/connectors** – outer covering of the flexible cable is firmly held at the point of entry by the cable grip and that the plug top hasn't been cut, damaged or that there are signs of overheating caused by loose internal connections

Damaged plug top – GMSL

✓ **Wiring of connectors** – check that the live, neutral and earth cables are connected to the correct terminal pins, that the internal wires are fully insulated and are not too long, the terminal screws and outer cable grip screws are tight and that the live and neutral sprung terminal shutters are in place

Correctly wired – GMSL

✓ **NB** The rewiring of flexible cable plugs and sockets/connectors should only be carried out by a competent electrician

✓ **Lanterns** – outer covering of flexible cable firmly held at the point of entry, a fault found on older lanterns

✓ **Old lanterns** – secondary earth bonding between the moving parts can be found on all new lanterns. It is wise to check that older lanterns have been updated to meet the current requirements and that there is earth bonding from the lamp tray to the outer body and to the hinged sides or fronts

Lantern cable entry – GMSL

➤ **Flexible power 3 core cable – colour coding**

Country	UK/EU - IEC	Australia/NZ/ South Africa	US/Canada
(L) Single phase Live/hot	Brown	Red, Brown	Black
(N) Neutral/cold	Blue	Black, Blue	White
(PE) Protective earth/ground	Green/yellow (bi-colour)	Green, Green/yellow	Green

IEC – International Electrotechnical Commission

➤ **If you find an electrical fault**
- **Switch off – do not use the equipment**
- **Disconnect**/unplug it from the mains supply
- **Remove it from use** and immediately report it to the technical manager or chief electrician
- **Label the equipment – 'Electrical fault: do not use'**

Did you know that –

- Flexible cables in the UK pre-1977 were colour coded, Live – red, Neutral – black, Earth – green
- Non-flexible cables in the UK finally changed to the IEC harmonised colours in 1999 in line with the EU

GLOBAL JARGON

- **Single phase Live** (UK) – Hot (NA), Active (Aus)
- **Neutral** (UK) – Cold (NA)
- **Protective earth** (UK) – Ground (NA)

Extras!

3 WORKING WITH LANTERNS

EXTRA TIPS

- Regular user checks are vital for electrical safety
- On the annual PAT test, the equipment is most likely to fail on the visual inspection even before it is electrically tested for insulation and earth continuity
- 13 amp plug tops on non-lighting equipment should have sleeved live and negative pins
- It is also good practice to use sleeved 15 amp plug tops
- TRS Tough Rubber Sheaved is preferred to PVC for flexible cables as it has increased flexibility, easier to coil free from twists and kinks
- Use heavier-duty extension cables on extra-long runs to prevent a voltage drop
- Avoid having thick bunches of cables or coils of cable as they can overheat

Extra resources – go to

www.pat-testing.info – Information on PAT testing, good example of how to wire a connector/plug

Points for action

Quickies!

- Make a visual inspection of a lantern and cable to check for electrical faults
- When were they last PAT tested?

Takes longer

- Check out the dates and records of when the lanterns and cables were last tested
- Carry out a visual inspection of a cable plug or socket and check the connections

3 WORKING WITH LANTERNS

Extras!

4 Dimmers

A quick start – Dimmer racks, packs & patch panels

Looking at the use of dimmer racks, packs and patch panels

More info – Dimmer units

Circuit protection and faults, mains supply and distribution and connecting the light desk

Extras! – Power supplies

Understanding mains power supplies, single and three phase supplies, calculating maximum power handling

A quick start – Dimmer racks, packs & patch panels

A dimmer is an electronic device that controls the amount of electricity flowing to the lamp and the level or intensity of light produced by the lantern.

Dimmer units

Each generic lantern is connected to a dimmer unit that is controlled by a miniature sliding fader on the lighting control desk. In theatres, the dimmer units are usually positioned adjacent to the stage area with a remote control desk at the rear of the audience. On smaller stages or in studios, the dimmer packs may be positioned in the lighting control room.

>> **Fast Forward** on the DVD to **4.1 Dimmers**

Racks, packs & cable patch panels

 Fixed dimmer racks

In theatres and larger installations, groups of individual dimmer units are rack mounted in cabinets and they are directly hardwired to the circuit outlet sockets or patch panels. The dimmer racks are assembled in modules of 12, 24, 48 and up to 96 dimmer units and they are usually powered by a three phase electrical supply.[19]

[19] Three phase electrical supply, see Chapter 4 'Dimmers – Extras!'

> **Portable dimmer packs**

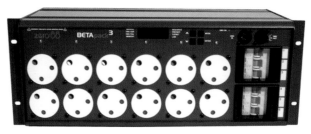

Betapack 3 – Zero.88

Dimmer packs are used for temporary lighting rigs, smaller stage or studio installations in schools and colleges.

Dimmer packs have the following features:

- 6 dimmer units rack mounted in a case that can be used either as a portable unit, wall or rack mounted in a permanent installation
- The dimmer units can be terminated with either a single or a pair of outlet sockets mounted on the front or rear of the pack
- Two lanterns can be plugged or 'hard patched' into each dimmer unit, providing the total wattage doesn't exceed the dimmer rating. This is referred to as 'pairing' or a 'paired circuit' which will be controlled by the same channel fader
- Two-way adaptors can be used to pair circuits where there is single outlet socket on the dimmer unit
- The connection to dimmer units can be made via a multipole Socapex socket connecting the lanterns via multicore cable
- Each dimmer unit has its own circuit breaker or fuse to provide protection against overload or electric shock

- The mains supply to the dimmer pack may be permanently 'hardwired' from the main distribution board or in the UK connected via a 32 amp or 63A CEE cable panel socket and plug
- Each dimmer pack is controlled by an isolation switch mounted in the distribution board which needs to be switched on before the dimmers will work

Distribution board & sockets – GMSL

> ## Cable hard patch panels

The numbered outlet sockets on or above the lighting bars are individually wired back as a circuit to a central patch panel being terminated in a flexible cable with a corresponding numbered cable plug. The patch panels are mounted below the dimmer packs and the cables run through holes in the comb to keep them organised, making it easier to find each numbered plug top and reducing the tangled 'spaghetti' of cables.

Cable patch – GMSL

Dimmer units – power handling

It is important to know the maximum power handling of each dimmer unit before connecting the lanterns to prevent overloading.

> ### Measuring power/load

Electricity can be measured either as:

- **Watts** the electrical energy or power produced or required
- **Amps** the rate of flow of the electrical current
- **Volts** the electrical pressure of the mains supply affects the rate of flow in amps and the power produced in watts

For further explanation, see 'Extras!'

> ### Global dimmer ratings

Dimmer units are rated in either watts or amps depending upon the country and the manufacturer.

Country	Voltage	Rating	Dimmer ratings
UK	230 volts	Amps	**10A, 16A, 25A**
Europe	230 volts	Watts	**2.5kW, 3kW, 5kW, 12kW**
Australia/New Zealand	230 volts	Amps	**10A, 13A, 15A, 25A**
		Watts	**2.5kW, 3kW, 5kW, 12kW**
North America	120 volts	Watts	**600W, 1.2kW, 2.4kW**

Lanterns are rated in watts, so when the dimmer units are also rated in watts it is relatively easy to work out how many can be controlled without overloading.

4. DIMMERS   **A quick start**

55

➤ **A quick guide to dimmer power-handling capacity**
When the dimmers are rated in amps, it is necessary to calculate the safe working load, see 'Extras!'

UK, Europe, Australia, New Zealand – 230 volts supply

Mains supply – 230 volts	Dimmer rating amps	Max power watts	Approx load kilowatts	Safe working load no of lanterns
Dimmer units	10 amps	2300 watts	2kW	3 x 650W lanterns 2 x 1000W lanterns
Dimmer units & sockets	13 amps	2990 watts	3kW	4 x 650W lanterns 2 x 1200W lanterns
Dimmer units & sockets	15 amps	3450 watts	3kW	5 x 650W lanterns 3 x 1000W lanterns
Dimmer units & sockets	16 amps	3600 watts	3.5kW	5 x 650W lanterns 2 x 1200W lanterns
Dimmer units	25 amps	5750 watts	5.5kW	4 x 1200W lanterns 2 x 2000W lanterns

For 230 volts, a safe 'rule of thumb': 10 amps = 2kW; 15 amps = 3kW; 16 amps = 3.5kW

North America – 120 volts supply

Mains supply – 120 volts	Dimmer rating amps	Max power watts	Approx load kilowatts	Safe working load no of lanterns
Dimmer units	10 amps	1200 watts	1kw	2 x 575W lanterns
Dimmer units	20 amps	2400 watts	2kw	4 x 575W lanterns 3 x 750W lanterns

For 120 volts, a safe 'rule of thumb': 10 amps = 1kW; 20 amps = 2kW

A quick start

4 DIMMERS

GLOBAL JARGON

■ **Two-way adaptors** – Grelcos or **'Twofers'**! (NA)

Did you know that –

■ Early electric lighting was controlled by switchboards, hence the term 'control board' or 'on the board' or 'board operator'
■ Liquid salt solution pots were the first dimmers to be used; the electrical resistance was created by parting the submerged electrodes operated on tracker wires
■ Wire wound slider resistance dimmers superseded the liquid pots

QUICK TIPS

■ Always switch off the isolating switch (MCB) supplying the dimmer packs after use, otherwise the control desk will remain live and the lanterns can be left on at a low level thus creating a safety hazard

---

Quick resources – go to

www.adblighting.com –	ADB Lighting Technologies
www.etcconnect.com –	ETC
www.jands.co –	Jands Ply Ltd
www.lsclighting.com –	LSC Lighting Systems
www.strandlighting.com –	Philips Strand Lighting
www.Zero88.com –	Zero.88

Points for action

Quickies!

■ Check the make and specification of the dimmer racks/packs installed
■ Check the amperage of the dimmer units and find out the power handling capacity

Takes longer

■ Obtain technical information from the manufacturer

4 DIMMERS   A quick start

More info – Dimmers units

Electronic dimmers work in a similar way to a tap controlling the flow or the power of the water from a full-on Flood to a slow dribble. The dimmer controls the power of the electricity flowing to the lamp by adjusting the voltage. As the voltage from the dimmer is reduced, the wattage and the intensity of light decreases.

Dimmer units

Dimmer units have a number of features:

Dimmer module & MCBs – Zero.88

➤ **Circuit protection**
Each dimmer unit is controlled by a Miniature Circuit Breaker (MCB) to isolate (switch off) the electrical current to the individual dimmer unit. The MCB is a combined circuit breaker and trip switch providing electrical protection against overload, electrical faults and shocks. The electrical protection on some older dimmer modules is provided by a cartridge fuse mounted in a panel holder with a neon indicator showing that the circuit is live or the fuse is blown.

➤ **Restoring a fault**
The trip switch or fuse is the weakest link and it automatically breaks the circuit when a fault occurs.

To restore the fault:
- Identify and repair the fault before resetting the trip switch or replacing the fuse
- A common fault can be a blown lamp in the lantern
- When the fault has been repaired, reset the dimmer module MCB or replace the fuse

To replace a fuse – this should only be done under supervision by a competent technician:
- Isolate/switch off the mains power to the dimmer packs
- Remove the cartridge fuse holder by turning the top anticlockwise by a quarter turn
- Replace the fuse with the correct size and rating in amps of the fuse. Always check the manufacturer's specification, as there are many different types and sizes of fuses and they all tend to look the same

More info

4 DIMMERS

➤ **Circuit test buttons** are a special feature and can be found on some dimmer packs.

They are designed to 'flash through' the circuit, to test that the lantern is working. The test buttons are a latch type of switch that can be easily left locked in the 'on' position. This overrides the circuit fader on the control desk and the lantern will remain at 'full'.

If you lose control of a lantern, check the circuit test button before declaring a fault as this button can easily get knocked into the 'on' position, especially when patching, also 'little fingers like pressing buttons!'

Betapack 2 test buttons – Zero.88

>>> **Fast Forward** on the DVD to **4.2 Dimmers, patch panels & power supplies**

Dimmer modules – each dimmer unit has three connections:

- **Mains supply**
- **Lighting control desk**
- **Lanterns via the outlet sockets**

Mains supply – distribution

The dimmers are connected to the main electrical supply via a switch/distribution board positioned near to the dimmer packs or racks. The main electrical supply has a mains isolation switch and the power is distributed via individual isolators to each dimmer pack or groups of dimmer modules in a dimmer rack.

➤ **The distribution board contains:**

MCB – GMSL

- **MCB** – Miniature Circuit Breaker is the main isolation switch for the incoming mains supply and they are marked with the maximum current rating of the supply 63, 100 or 125 amps
- **Miniature Circuit Breakers** are designed to provide protection from current overload and short circuit. If it detects a fault condition, it will break the flow of electricity by tripping the switch to the 'off' position. It works in a similar way to a fuse but the MCB switch can be reset once the fault has been cleared
- **RCD – Residual Current Device** provides protection against electrical shock but not overload or short circuit. The RCD detects the current imbalance between the energised (positive) conductor and the return (neutral) conductor.

4. DIMMERS   More info

An imbalance can be accidently caused by touching an energised part of the circuit, creating a current leakage through the grounded body of a person. The sensitive nature of the RCD is designed to quickly disconnect and trip the circuit to prevent a lethal electrical shock

RCBO – GMSL

- **RCBOs** – Residual Current Breaker Over-current protection switch acts as an individual isolator for each dimmer pack or rack and is marked with a maximum current rating in the UK of either 32, 63 or 100 amps
- **Residual Current Breaker Over-current** combines the functions of a **Miniature Circuit Breaker** protection from current overload and short circuit with a **Residual Current Device** providing the added protection from electrical shock
- **It is important to check the size of the MCB controlling the incoming main electrical supply** and to calculate the maximum power measured in watts that is available to all the dimmer packs or racks. When pairing lanterns to dimmer units, it is important that the total wattage doesn't exceed and overload the maximum mains supply

A quick guide to the main electrical supply power capacity

UK, Europe, Australia, New Zealand

Mains supply – 230 volts		Max power watts	Approx load kilowatts	Safe working load no of lanterns
Main electrical supply	32 amps	7360 watts	7kW	10 x 650W lanterns 6 x 1200W lanterns
Main electrical supply	63 amps	14490 watts	14kW	20 x 650W lanterns 12 x 1200W lanterns
Main electrical supply	100 amps	23000 watts	20kW	35 x 650W lanterns 19 x 1200W lanterns

*(left margin: **4 DIMMERS** | **More info**)*

North America

Mains supply – 120 volts		Max power watts	Approx load kilowatts	Safe working load no of lanterns
Main electrical supply	30 amps	3600 watts	3.5kw	6 x 575W lanterns
				4 x 750W lanterns
Main electrical supply	60 amps	7200 watts	7kW	12 x 575W lanterns
				9 x 750W lanterns
Main electrical supply	120 amps	14400 watts	14kW	24 x 575W lanterns
				19 x 750W lanterns

Lighting control desk – control systems

There are two types of control systems used to connect the lighting control desk to the dimmer racks: Analogue and DMX 512.

➤ **Analogue** system uses a single wire per dimmer control channel. Each dimmer pack is connected to the control desk by a separate eight-way multicore cable that interconnects the multipole socket on the control desk to a dimmer pack, one wire per dimmer unit and the remaining two supplying the control voltage. The channel fader on the lighting control desk sends a low-voltage control signal to the dimmer module which controls the power supplied by the dimmer to the lantern in proportion to the voltage. The control voltage is between 0 and 10 volts where 0 or zero volts represents no light and 10 volts maximum light supplied by the dimmer unit. Most control desks operate on a positive + 0–10 volts, whereas there are others that use a negative – 0–10 volts system. The pin configuration on the multi plugs varies depending upon the make; therefore, it is important to match the same make of desk and dimmer units.

➤ **DMX 512** – Digital Multiplexing uses a computerised data system in place of the low-voltage analogue system. The control information for the dimmer unit is sent at high speed from the control desk by a series of pulses called 'bits' down a single data cable. A binary code is used which is a group of eight pulses or bits; each bit can be either 'on' or 'off' and they represent part of a total number. The dimmer module recognises the number as a lighting level between zero 'no light' and 255 'full light' and it controls the output voltage sent to the lantern and the level of light produced.

DMX uses a two-core screened data cable that is capable of handling 512 separate control channels to connect the control desk to the dimmer packs or racks. They are connected together in a loop or 'daisy chain' via the DMX 'in' and DMX 'out' sockets on the dimmer packs by DMX cables that are terminated in 5 pin XLR plug and sockets.

4. DIMMERS

More info

Other digitally controlled equipment can be linked into the chain, such as moving lights, colour scrollers, smoke and mist machines, so that they can be controlled by a single lighting control desk. Each dimmer pack, rack or item of equipment has to be set up with its own DMX 'start address' so that it can receive the control data.

DMX address – Zero.88

➤ **DMX addresses** – The DMX address of each unit is set either by a digital keypad or a miniature rotating switch that is turned by a small screwdriver. The first dimmer pack in the chain will be assigned with a start address beginning No.1. If there are six dimmer units in the pack, then the start address of the next pack will be No.7 and so the sequence continues.

DMX rotary switches – Zero.88

Patching & hardwired systems

➤ **Hard patching** to the dimmer units via a patch panel provides the flexibility to connect the lanterns to any dimmer unit and the corresponding channel control or slider fader.[20] On a small lighting rig, it can be convenient to patch the lanterns lighting a particular lighting area to the same number channel control fader as the area number, making it easier to identify. However, it is important to check the wattage of the lanterns and that dimmers are not overloaded. Once the lantern has been patched, it is always called by its control channel fader number and never by the outlet socket number that the lantern is plugged into. In North America, patching is called 'hooking up'.

➤ **Hardwired system** does not provide the same flexibility, as each outlet circuit socket is connected directly back to a designated dimmer unit. When using this system, the lanterns will initially be called by the channel control fader number which may be the same as the dimmer and outlet socket number depending upon how the lighting control desk has been set up. See 'soft patching', Chapter 5 'Lighting control – Extras!'.

---

[20] On some memory lighting desks, the circuits can be controlled via a keypad by inputting the channel number and level which is displayed on a monitor without any physical control of a fader

62

On a hardwired installation, the most logical sequence for easy identification of the outlet sockets for the lanterns is to have them distributed and numbered from front to back and from left to right as viewed from the lighting control desk when positioned in front of the stage.

For example:

- **FOH advance bar** numbered 1–10 operator's left to right (stage right to stage left)[21]
- **On-stage No.1 bar** numbered 11–20 operator's left to right
- **On-stage No.2 bar** numbered 21–30 operator's left to right

When the outlet circuit sockets are arranged in this way, the lighting control desk operator is able to easily identify the groups of channel faders on the desk that are controlling each lighting bar in a logical sequence. If they have not been connected in this way, it is possible to reconfigure the layout by soft patching electronically the control channel fader to the DMX address of the dimmer unit; see more information in 'Extras!'.

MORE TIPS

Common faults

- **Lantern isn't working** – check the lantern to see if the lamp filament is blown – see Chapter 3 'Working with lanterns – More info'
- **Is the circuit working?** – test the circuit with a lantern that is known to be working
- **Circuit isn't working** – check MCB trip switch and reset; or check the fuse and replace. On dimmer packs, check the circuit by patching a lantern known to be working directly into the dimmer unit
- **Two lanterns work together** – both lanterns are patched/paired to the same dimmer module
- **Lantern is on but cannot be controlled by the channel fader** – check that the circuit test button is not latched in the 'ON' position on the dimmer pack
- **Group of lanterns aren't working** – check the RCBOs supplying the dimmer packs, DMX connection and address
- **All lanterns are off** – check that the MCB on the incoming mains supply is on and that it hasn't tripped out due to an overload
- **Analogue control cables** in the UK are terminated with 8 pin Din plugs at either end (pins to pins)
- **DMX control cables** in the UK are normally terminated with 5 pin XLR plugs and sockets to differentiate them from sound cables. Some moving lights have 3 or 5 pin DMX sockets

4. DIMMERS   **More info**

---

[21] See Part 2: 'Lighting Designer – Lighting the Performance Space – Lighting jargon – Stage directions'

More resources – go to

www.theiet.org – The Institute of Electrical Engineers – UK

www.hse.gov.uk/pubns/indg247.pdf – Electrical safety for entertainers – Health & Safety Executive – UK

GLOBAL JARGON

- **Residual Circuit Device or RCD** (UK) – Ground Fault Circuit Interrupter or GFCI or Appliance Leakage Current Interrupter or ALCI (NA)
- **RCDs** (UK) – 'Safety Switches' (Aus), 'Salvavita' (life saver!) (Italy)

Extras! – Power supplies

It is important to understand the nature of the electrical mains power supply and to be able to calculate the maximum safe working load.

Power supplies

Voltage is the measurement of the electrical pressure or force of the main power supply. In the UK, Europe and Southern Hemisphere the nominal generated supply is rated at 230 volts and in North America and Canada 120 volts.

➤ **Three phase supply**
- Electricity is generated by continuously rotating a magnet in a coil of wire. Each revolution induces three separate currents that are 120 degrees out of phase; therefore, the pressure or voltage of each of the three currents generated is on a different time phase with each other. Should a fault occur between two of the phases, the potential voltage is doubled
- **230 volts** (Europe and Southern Hemisphere). On a three phase supply, there is a potential danger of 400 volts across the phases which would provide a lethal electrical shock! Therefore, it is important to maintain a safe working distance or separation between the equipment powered by the different phases. This is not a legal requirement but it is regarded as good, safe working practice
- 230 volts is the nominal generated voltage in Europe, formally 240V in the UK and 220V in the rest of Europe. The 'harmonised voltage limits' in Europe are now specified as 230V –10% + 6%, i.e. 207V–243V. However, manufacturers still rate their equipment at 240 volts
- **120 volts** (North America and Canada). On a three phase supply, the difference between two of the phases is reduced to 208 volts which is less than voltage on a single phase on a 230 volt supply and not such a hazard as 400 volts!

➤ **Single phase 230 volts mains supply** is mainly used for small installations, drama studios, small or medium stages to power the dimmer packs with the circuit outlet sockets hard patched to the dimmer units.

➤ **Three phase 230 volts mains supply** is used for theatres with larger installations to supply the power required for a larger number of lanterns.

- A three phase supply provides three separate power supplies to the dimmer racks and the dimmer units are connected and powered as three separate groups
- One group of dimmers is powered by phase 1 and the outlet sockets from these dimmers will be used in a specific area of the theatre. Phases 2 and 3 supply different groups of dimmers with the outlet sockets in different areas providing a safe working distance between them

4. DIMMERS

Extras!

An example of distribution of a three phase supply:
- **Phase 1** – front of house lighting positions
- **Phase 2** – overhead stage bars
- **Phase 3** – stage 'dips' floor sockets

➤ **Using a three phase installation**
- It is important that you understand the distribution on a three phase 230 volts supply and have a clearly marked plan showing the outlet socket numbers and phases
- Mistakes can be easily made by using an extension cable from one bar to provide an additional outlet circuit, thus 'crossing the phases' and creating the danger of receiving a 400 volts electric shock should a fault occur
- NB. Three phase supplies are sometimes used on smaller installations, as the electrical engineers prefer to have the potential load of the lighting system equally balanced across the three phases
- In North America and Canada, phase separation is not an issue as the danger of electrical shock across the phases with a 120 volt three phase supply is greatly reduced and the lanterns can be freely patched or 'hooked up' to any dimmer
- The circuit outlet sockets are usually marked according to the phase of the supply, L1, L2, L3 or colour coded Brown, Black and Grey in the IEC[22] harmonised colours. Previously in the UK, before 2004, Red, Yellow and Blue were used. For other countries, see Part 3: 'Lighting Resources – Technical info.'

Maximum power capacity

When using electrical equipment, it is important to be able to calculate the maximum power available in a circuit and the total power requirements of the lanterns being used.

➤ **Electricity – how does it work?**
Imagine electricity as water flowing in the hot water circuit in your house which is circulated by a water pump.

- **Volts** – the constant pressure the pump exerts in pushing the water around the circuit
- **Amps** – the number of litres of water flowing around the circuit per hour
- **Watts** – the number of litres of water you are actually using and will be charged for drawn off from a tap
- **Resistance** – how difficult it is for the water to move around the circuit; an increase in the number of bends or a reduction in the size of the pipe will increase the resistance

[22] IEC – International Electrotechnical Commission

If you increase the diameter of a pipe, more water will flow; if you increase the core diameter of the conductor in a cable, more electricity can flow.[23]

➤ Three components of electricity that can be measured
- **Volts** – measurement of the constant **electrical pressure** or force of the mains supply
- **Amps** – measurement of the **rate of flow** of the electrical current in the circuit
- **Watts** – measurement of the amount of **energy or power**

➤ Safe working load
- **The rating in amps** of the mains supply, circuit breakers, dimmer units, plugs and sockets defines the maximum electrical current or capacity that the component can safely handle without being overloaded, the possibility of damage occurring or the circuit protection tripping out
- **The rating in watts** of lamps and lanterns defines the amount of electrical power required or the load
- **Calculating a safe working load**
  The safe working load can be calculated by using the relationship between the three components of electricity that is based on Ohms law. This can easily be remembered as the West Virgina Formula; see below 'Global jargon'.

Power in **Watts** = **Voltage** x Current in **Amps**

The voltage is a constant in the formula so the power available in watts is directly related to the size or capacity of the current in amps. If you compare the pin sizes of a 16 amp and a 32 amp connector, the larger amperage has thicker pins in order to safely handle an increase in the electrical current

➤ Calculating a safe working load/power requirements in watts

Voltage x Current in **Amps** = Power in **Watts**

Northern Europe – Mains supply 230 volts			
		Max power capacity	Safe working load
Dimmer units	230 **volts** x **10 amps**	= 2300 **watts/2.3kW**	3 x 650W lanterns
Extension cables	230 **volts** x **16 amps**	= 3600 **watts/3.6kW**	5 x 650W lanterns

A simple safe 'rule of thumb' – estimated power available @ 230 volts

10 amps = 2kW
16 amps = 3.5kW

[23] David Whitehead, *Stage Electrics*

4. DIMMERS   Extras!

➤ **Further data on safe working loads** – see Part 3 Resources – 'Technical info.'.

➤ **Calculating current requirements in amps**
The **Watts = Amps x Volts** formula can be reconfigured to calculate the current required

$$\frac{\text{Power in } \textbf{Watts}}{\textbf{Voltage}} = \text{Current in } \textbf{Amps}$$

Northern Europe – Mains supply 230 volts		
Load – Wattage of lantern		**Current required**
■ 650 watt lantern	$\dfrac{650 \text{ watts}}{230 \text{ volts}}$	= 2.82 amps
■ 1200 watt lantern	$\dfrac{1{,}200 \text{ watts}}{230 \text{ volts}}$	= 5.21 amps

The diversity factor

- In a large production, not all the lanterns will be in use at the same time, some may be used for different scenes or they may not all be used at full intensity
- With careful planning, it is possible to increase the total number of lanterns and the potential maximum load. Therefore, the total power consumption can be greater than the maximum mains electrical power supply. This is what is called the **'diversity factor'**
- It is important that you know the size of your incoming main electrical supply and calculate the average and total load of the lanterns
- Remember not to switch all the lanterns on to full at the same time for rehearsals or working lights as the overload protection switches will trip out
- **This method should only be used with caution and by an experienced technician**

Resistance in a conductor

This is the fourth component of electricity that can be measured:

- **Ohms** – measurement of electrical resistance in a conductor
- **Ohms law** shows the relationship between amps, volts and resistance

$$\text{Current in } \textbf{Amps} = \frac{\textbf{Voltage}}{\textbf{Resistance} \text{ in Ohms}}$$

➤ **Voltage drop on extension cables**
Resistance occurs as an electrical current (amps) passes through a conductor causing a reduction in electrical pressure (volts). The reduction in volts affects the power (watts) that is supplied and the safe working load.

Extras!

4 DIMMERS

- The resistance increases depending upon the length of the conductor or cable
- The voltage drop on a 15 amp cable becomes critical on lengths over 50m, reducing the size of its safe working load as can be seen below when the voltage drops from 230 to 210 volts

Length of cable	Voltage	Max power capacity	Safe working load
Short/medium cables	230 volts x 15 amps	= 3450 watts/3.4kW	5 x 650W lanterns
Long cable with 20 volt drop	210 volts x 15 amps	= 3150 watts/3.15kW	4 x 650W lanterns

- A drop to 210 volts reduces the safe working load from 3.4kW to 3.15kW and the number of 650W lanterns that can be used without overloading the cable
- For longer distances, the size of the cable rating (amps) needs to be increased

Global differences

North America – Mains supply 120 volts

		Max power capacity	Safe working load
Dimmer units	120 volts x 10 amps	= 1200 watts/1.2kW	2 x 575W lanterns
Extension cables	120 volts x 20 amps	= 2400 watts/2.4kW	4 x 575W lanterns 3 x 750W lanterns

A simple safe 'rule of thumb' – estimated power available @ 120 volts

> 10 amps = 1kW
> 20 amps = 2kW

North America – Mains supply 120 volts

Load – Wattage of lantern		Current required
575 watt lantern	$\dfrac{575 \text{ watts}}{120 \text{ volts}}$	= 4.79 amps
750 watt lantern	$\dfrac{750 \text{ watts}}{120 \text{ volts}}$	= 6.25 amps

Comparing current requirements 230 volts (Northern Europe) **& 120 volts** (North America)

The electrical current (amps) required to power a 120 volt lamp is almost double that required for a similar 230 volt wattage lamp as can be seen below. The examples of lamps used reflect the typical wattages used in the UK and North America.

Mains voltage	Lamp/lantern wattage	Current in amps
230 volts Northern Europe	650 watts	**2.82 amps**
120 volts North America	575 watts	**4.79 amps**

The increase in the amperage or current requirements of a 120 volt system requires a larger core size of the conductors, resulting in the use of thicker cables and pins on connectors.

Did you know that –

- Wire wound resistance dimmers replaced the liquid pots. These consisted of two formers wound with resistance wire mounted side by side with a central contact slider in between. As the slider is lowered, the electrical current passed through more of the turnings of resistance wire. The amps flowing are reduced as the resistance is increased and the energy is converted into heat
- The Grand Master and the Sunset boards provided a mechanised way of operating slider dimmers by a master control
- Resistance dimmer boards were usually situated in a raised perch position on the side of the stage
- 'Dip traps' originated from the days of gas lighting for the connection on-stage of portable gas Floods. The gas point was positioned at the bottom of a small tank of water mounted under the trap below the stage, providing a leak-proof connection

GLOBAL JARGON

- **The West Virginia Formula** is an easy way to remember watts = volts x amps
- **W = VA**, where **W** = West and **VA** is the abbreviation of the US state of Virginia[24]

[24] Larry Wild, Northern State University, Aberdeen, USA

Extras!

4 DIMMERS

EXTRA TIPS

■ Electrical manufacturers in the UK rate their equipment at 240 volts

Extra resources – go to

■ www.aged.ces.uga.edu/Browswable_Folders/Power_Points/Mechanics/ Electricity_Principles.ppt –'Calculating power' – Virginia Tech. Demonstrates the application of the West Virginia Formula W=VA
    Google West Virginia Formula

Points for action

Quickies!

■ Calculate the power capacity of a 15 amp 230 volt extension lead
■ Work out a safe load of lanterns on a 15 amp cable
■ Calculate the power available from a 32 amp 230 volt supply
■ Work out a safe load of lanterns on a 10 amp dimmer unit
■ Check your results with the information in Part 3: 'Lighting Resources – Technical info. – Lanterns, Dimmers & Control – Safe working loads'

5 Lighting control

A quick start – Manual lighting control desks

Looking at the functions and ways of operating a manual lighting control desk

More info – Memory lighting control desks

Looking at the functions and ways of operating a memory lighting control desk

Extras! – DMX Digital multiplexing

An introduction to the DMX 512 control system

A quick start – Manual lighting control desks

The lighting control desk is the centre of the stage lighting system. Understanding the function of the manual lighting desk provides the basis of knowledge and understanding for moving on to memory control desks.

Manual lighting control desks

➤ **Manual desks consist of:**

- **Channel faders** which control the level of the dimmer unit and the light produced by the lantern. The fader has a graduated scale; as it is raised from 0 to 10 the light increases and from 10 to 0 the brightness decreases. This is called the 'Raise' and 'Fade'

- **Scene presets** – there are two banks of independently controlled channel faders. Each scene preset can be used independently

Level12 – Zero.88

to set up a separate scene or picture of light that can be saved as a written plot or saved in the lighting desk memory as a lighting cue

- **Preset Masters** – each preset has a master fader that controls the maximum output levels of the channel faders allowing two scenes of lighting to be set up and crossfaded from one to the other

■ **Control desks** which are powered by a local mains power socket that needs to be switched on before it can be used. Some analogue desks are powered directly from the dimmer packs

➤ **Overview of a 12-way 2 preset control desk**

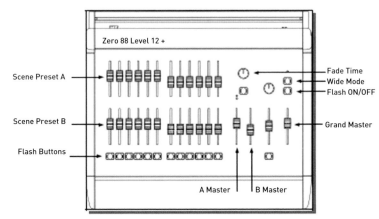

2 preset control desk – GMSL

■ **Scene Preset A** – 12 channel faders controlling the output levels of the dimmer channels
■ **Scene Preset B** – 12 duplicate channel faders controlling the same dimmer channels
■ **Channel faders** – numbered 1–6, 7–12, are each graduated with a scale of 1–10
■ **Master A** – controls the maximum output levels of the Scene Preset A channel faders
■ **Master B** – controls the maximum output levels of the Scene Preset B channel faders
■ **Grand Master** – controls the maximum output levels of all channels on both presets and channel flash buttons
■ **Crossfading** – Master A scale works from 10 to 0 top to bottom
   Master B scale is reversed 0 to 10 top to bottom
   When the master faders are moved together in tandem:
   Master A fades down from 10 to 0 and Master B rises from 0 to 10
■ **'Dipless' crossfade** – channels having the same intensity on both presets will stay at a constant level of intensity
■ **Fade time control** – sets the time taken to crossfade between the two scene presets
■ **'BO'** – Black Out button overrides the master faders switching everything off

- **Channel flash buttons** – flashes the channels to the level set on the Grand Master
- **Wide mode** – 12/24 control desk can be used as a 12-way 2 preset or set in wide mode to a 24-way single preset control desk; the preset B faders are marked with dual numbers 1/13, 2/14–12/24
- **Sequence effects memory** – basic memory feature to program and play back a chase of repeated sequences of patterns or flashing lights
- **Basic memory functions** – on some manual desks, it is possible to record and play back a limited number of sequence effects or stacks of scenes of light/lighting cues

---

>> **Fast Forward** on the DVD to **5.1 Manual Control Desks**

Using a two scene preset control desk

➤ **Setting the lighting scenes:**
- **Masters A & B** – set Preset Master A to level '10' and Preset Master B to level '0'
- **Live preset A** – set the circuit fader levels for the first scene of light (Cue 1)
- **Crossfade Masters A & B** – Master A to level '0' and Master B to level '10'
- **Live preset B** – set the circuit fader levels for the second scene of light (Cue 2)
- **Crossfade Masters A & B** – Master A to '10' and Master B to '0'
- **Live preset A** – set the circuit faders for the third scene of light (Cue 3)

A written plot will need to be made of the channel fader levels on the preset for each lighting cue

➤ **Running the lighting scenes:**
When the master fader is at '0', the preset it controls is 'Dead' and the channel faders can be set without affecting the levels of light on the 'Live' preset.

- **Masters A & B** – set to level '0'
- **Preset A 'Dead'** – preset the circuit fader levels for Cue 1
- **Master A** – Cue 1, raise to level '10', preset A 'Live'
- **Preset B 'Dead'** – preset the circuit fader levels for Cue 2
- **Crossfade Masters** – Master A – '0', Master B – '10', preset B 'Live'
- **Preset A 'Dead'** – preset the circuit faders for Cue 3
- **Crossfade Masters** – Master A – '10', Master B – '0', preset A 'Live'
- **Crossfade times** – can be done manually or preset using the fade time control. Set the control to the required time sequence and activate on cue by quickly moving the master faders together. The fade time control can be adjusted to override the time during the cue to speed it up or slow it down

5 LIGHTING CONTROL   A quick start

QUICK TIPS

- When flashing through lanterns, set the Grand Master at a lower level to protect the filament in the lamps
- If the control desk isn't working, check the blackout switch is off and the preset and Grand Master is at level 10
- If the masters don't appear to work on a crossfade, check that the fade time control is set to manual and not 5 minutes!
- To override a live timed fade, turn the speed control to speed up or slow down

Points for action

Quickies!

- Check out your lighting control desk and see what facilities are available

Takes longer

- Set up a lighting scene on both presets and use the manual crossfade
- Use the fade time control and see the effect of various lengths of time

More info – Memory lighting control desks

With the developments in technology, many features that were originally provided in the advanced memory controls can now be found on the basic memory lighting desks. Some have the provision to control a small number of moving lights.

Memory control desks

They have a built-in specialist computer that can save and play back all the information for the lighting of a show. Lighting scenes can be preprogrammed and played back with timed crossfades.

Three types of memory functions:

- **Scene memory stack** – 'scenes' or 'states' of lighting are set up on a scene preset and saved as cues in a numerical sequence as used for a conventional drama production
- **Sequence memory** – recording a sequence of running 'steps' or changes of individual levels of light from lanterns used to produce a 'chase' or flashing effects as used to create special effects as in pop concerts
- **Sub-masters** – assigning scenes or states of lighting to a dedicated channel fader/sub-master. This is particularly useful where there are natural sequences and repeated states of lighting as used in concerts, pop music events or dance shows. The desired scene of lighting can instantaneously be recalled by raising the sub-master fader, allowing the operator to 'busk' the show and to make a more spontaneous response for live shows

> **»)**   **Fast Forward** on the DVD to **5.2 Memory Control Desks**

Basic memory lighting control desk

Memory control desks have a number of common features; however, there can be variations depending upon the make and model. The basic memory desk has a similar layout to the manual desk but has additional sections for memory, control and other functions.

Jester desk – Zero.88

➤ **Generic lighting controls**
- **Channel control faders** – 12 or 24 channels on two scene presets or in wide mode 24 or 48 single channel control faders
- **Sub-masters** – Scene preset B channel faders can be selected to double up as sub-masters. The sub-masters can be increased by selecting memory pages, e.g.

2 pages x 12 channels = 24 sub-masters, 2 pages x 24 channels = 48 sub-masters

- **Masters** –
  Preset Masters A & B controlling the maximum level of output from the individual preset channel faders and crossfading facility
  Grand Master controlling the maximum output level of the flash buttons on both presets

➤ **Memory controls**

Jester program mode – Zero.88

- **Program mode** – selecting scene memory, sequence memory, sub-master memory
- **Sequence/chase control** – run modes
  Direction:
  - Forwards
  - Backwards
  - Auto reverse
  - Random
  Attack:
  - Snap on/Snap off
  - Snap on/Fade off
  - Fade on/Snap off
  - Fade on/Fade off

- **Editing** – clear, reset, cut & paste
- **Page selection** – A & B, 12 x 2 pages of memory 24 scenes, 24 x 2 pages memory 48 scenes
- **Store/program**

➤ **Play back**
- **'Go'/'pause'** button
- **Fade time** control
- **Memory master** controlling the overall level of memory output
- **Sequence speed** control
- **Auxiliary buttons** – triggering simple DMX controlled devices, scrollers, smoke machines and strobes

➤ **Screens, monitors & storage**
- **LCD desk screen** – small screen displaying basic functions and information on cues
- **External monitor** – displaying the output levels and memory information
- **USB storage** – USB port to back up the show on an external memory device

5 LIGHTING CONTROL   **More info**

Advanced memory control desks

These control desks have a larger number of control channels than the basic memory lighting control and an advanced memory effects engine that provides additional control for moving lights, LED fixtures, scrollers and effects, smoke, mist machines and strobe lighting. They are mainly used for structured programming and playback as used for theatre productions.

➤ **The DMX control channels are assigned to:**
- Manually operated channel faders controlling dimmer units and the generic lanterns
- The attributes/functions of automated fixtures, moving lights, LED fixtures, scrollers, mist machines and other effects

LeapFrog – Zero.88

➤ **DMX controls for moving lights/fixtures**
Fixture attribute/selection buttons
- Intensity/brightness
- Colour
- Beam shape – pattern/gobo
- Position

➤ **Control wheels assigned to fixture personality**
- Brightness – 0–100%
- Colour – Cyan, Magenta, Yellow
- Pattern – gobo wheel 1, gobo wheel 2, Prism, prism rotation, speed
- Beam shape – shutter, focus
- Position – pan, tilt, speed

LeapFrog – Zero.88

➤ **Other features**
- Additional pages of memory increase the size of the scene memory stack, number of sequences and sub-master states that can be saved
- External desk monitors to preview, edit scenes and plot 'blind' cues on the monitor using the desk without the dimmers or lanterns being connected
- Fixture libraries provide the facility to select the preprogrammed attributes/personalities of all the standard DMX fixtures when setting up the fixtures control
- Colour picking – colour pallets providing precise selection from the standard ranges of colour filters to be reproduced by DMX controlled fixtures. The pre-loaded colour pallets of the Apollo, GAM, Lee & Rosco ranges of colour filters can be selected by make and number, e.g. Lee 106 or on screen colour display
- Effects engines provide preprogrammed effects that can be used with all fixtures/attributes, Fly Ins, Can Cans, Rainbows and Iris Pulses[25]

[25] Zero 88 Product Guide – Leap Frog

5 LIGHTING CONTROL

More info

Integrated lighting consoles

These desks have a larger number of control channels and are capable of controlling an increased number of automated fixtures. The number channel faders are reduced or replaced by a numeric keypad or touch screen selection to input the control information which is displayed on monitor screens.

Live control desks

Live memory desks are designed for fast hands-on control of moving and generic fixtures, as well as LEDs and media servers. They are highly suited to the mix of structured and unstructured playback that is often required for festivals, concert tours, product launches, television and awards shows.

Ion Control – ETC

Jands Vista control desk range, the concept is *'Think visually – Work visually'*. The consoles have a central screen providing a graphical display of the lighting units with the progression of the cues and the relationship between the programmed information being shown as a timeline. The screen provides a direct interaction with the control console, by using a highly accurate Wacom pen tablet on the Vista 'T' series, a pen tablet or touch screen on an i3, or a laptop screen with a Vista 'wing'. The software uses a 'generic fixture model' to make fixture control both fast and simple for the operator; for example, if you want 10 different types of moving light that make colour in 10 different ways to change to red, then you select the graphical representations of those fixtures, click red on the colour picker and the console will work out the mechanics of making each of those fixtures get as close as possible to that red.[26]

Vista T2 – Jands Pty Ltd

Vista i3 touch screen- Jands Pty Ltd

[24] Neil Vann Jands Europe

Did you know that -

- In 1933, General Electrics Radio City Music Hall, New York was one of the first to have multi-scene preset controls and to be mounted in front of the stage
- In 1949, Strand Electrics Light Console was based on the design of an organ console and it was the first lighting control desk to be mounted in a front of house position at the London Palladium theatre
- In the 1960s, preset control desks were developed using the thyristor electronic dimmer
- Prior to memory controls being available, three scene presets were developed to manage the longer setting-up time from a manual plot where there were a large number of faders were being used
- 'Strand Three Set' had three presets and each preset had three group masters. Individual channel faders could be assigned to and controlled by a group master within the preset
- 'Board Op' and 'On the Board' are terms still used from the days when there were resistance dimmer control boards

Lighting control desks makes & models – see Part 3: 'Lighting Resources – Technical info.'

Extra resources – go to

www.avolites.org.uk –	Avolites
www.adblighting.com –	ADB Lighting Technologies
www.chamsys.co.uk –	ChamSys
www.etcconnect.com –	ETC
www.highend.com –	High End Systems
www.jands.com –	Jands Pty Ltd
www.lsclighting.com –	LSC Lighting Systems
www.malighting.de –	MA Lighting International
www.strandlighting.com –	Philips Strand Lighting
www.Zero88.com –	Zero.88

5 LIGHTING CONTROL

More info

Points for action

Takes longer

■ Check out memory facilities of your lighting control desk and learn how to use them

A proper job!

■ Program a small stack of lighting scenes and play them back using the fade time

■ Program a simple sequence of lighting/chase, play it back and experiment with the direction and attack controls

Extras! – DMX Digital multiplexing[27]

DMX 512 is the standard international 'electronic language' used in the theatre industry to allow lighting control desks to send instructions to the equipment used in a production for dimmers, moving lights, LED fixtures, scrollers and effects, haze, smoke, fog machines and strobe lighting.

➤ DMX 512

- Any piece of electronic equipment that can understand this DMX electronic language will be able to receive instructions from the control system on what to do at a particular time within a performance
- It is called DMX 512 because there are 512 separate 'control channels' in each separate DMX universe, which means at any one time 512 separate instructions can be sent out from the control system on one universe
- Many lighting control desks can operate more than one universe, which provides an additional sequence of control channels
- Each piece of electronic equipment you want to control also has to have a name or, in the case of the electronic world, a number called the DMX address. The control system needs to 'address' the piece of equipment to tell it what to do

➤ DMX addresses

- Some pieces of equipment only need one name, like a dimmer which just needs a single instruction 'to fade' and therefore will have only one name or DMX address number
- Other pieces of equipment need lots of names or DMX address numbers. For example, a moving light needs to know when to change colour, to move left, to iris in and to black out, etc. so it will have multiple DMX address numbers, one for each command
- The first universe control channels are numbered 1/001–1/512 and the second 2/001–2/512[28]

➤ DMX – how it works

- One of the many advantages of using DMX commands is that all the 512 separate channel commands can be sent along one piece of cable, which normally links in a daisy chain fashion in and out of each piece of equipment with a buffer at the end of the chain to effectively terminate the cable
- In a more complex lighting rig, you can use a DMX splitter which allows you to split the one DMX 512 output from a control desk to multiple cables linking the equipment in a spider fashion
- Another advantage of using DMX is that you can assign one set of DMX address numbers to multiple items. For example, four 6-way dimmer packs

[27] Information written and contributed by David Whitehead
[28] DMX Universe, see Chapter 6 'DMX fixtures – Extras! – DMX 512 setting it up'

5 LIGHTING CONTROL Extras!

can all be set to receive DMX address numbers 1 to 6 so that dimmer unit 1 on each pack will be controlled by the same dimmer channel

➤ Lighting control desks – soft patching

DMX also allows you to 'soft patch' or connect a control channel on the lighting desk to any DMX address.

- A control channel fader number on the control desk can be assigned to a different dimmer number
- This allows you to plug each lantern into its nearest socket for ease of rigging and patch them to the control channels in the same logical numbered sequence as the lighting areas on the lighting plan. For example, the lanterns on the number Lx No.1 bar may be plugged into dimmers 6 to 10. The DMX addresses of these dimmers can be soft patched to control channels 1–5 so that the lanterns are controlled by the desk channel faders 1–5

Soft Patch – 1:1 default		Example of a Soft Patch	
Control Channel Fader No.	DMX Address No.	Control Channel Fader No.	DMX Address No.
1	1	1	6
2	2	2	7
3	3	3	8
4	4	4	9
5	5	5	10
6	6	6	
7	7	7	
8	8	8	
9	9	9	
10	10	10	

Extras!

5 LIGHTING CONTROL

6 DMX fixtures

A quick start – Animated fixtures

Animated and intelligent light sources, scanners, moving head fixtures – how they work

More info – LED fixtures

LED light sources and fixtures

Extras! – DMX 512 – making connections

Connecting and setting up a DMX system

A quick start – Animated fixtures

The use of colour scrollers and moving fixtures increases the flexibility when lighting a show and reduces the need for additional generic lanterns and the number of dimmers used.

Animated and intelligent fixtures

There are a number of fixtures that can be controlled by DMX from an advanced memory lighting control desk.

➤ **Scrollers – colour changers**

Colour scrollers fit in the front of a conventional lantern replacing a single colour frame with a continuous scroll of colour filters. The colour change is achieved by 'scrolling' through the colours at high speed, which is controlled by the memory in the lighting control desk along with the levels of lighting for the cue. Scrollers remove the need to duplicate lanterns where changes in the colour of the lighting areas and washes are required.

Rainbow Scroller – Stage Electrics

➤ **Moving lights/fixtures**

Moving fixtures can be used as a replacement for fixed generic lanterns or to produce dynamic and exciting lighting effects. They can provide greater flexibility and they can reduce the number of lanterns that are required in the lighting rig; however, they require a far longer time to program than it takes to angle and focus generic lanterns.

➤ Effects

The use of effects, haze, smoke, low smoke, confetti dispensers, snow machines and strobe lighting can be controlled by the lighting control desk. Pyrotechnics cannot be controlled as they require a locally operated key switch system for safety.

➤ LED fixtures

Fixtures using light-emitting diodes provide a low-energy light source. Initially, they were used in the theatre for decorative effects due to limited light output, but with the developments in technology they are now being used as light sources in generic lanterns and moving fixtures. They require a DMX control desk that supports LED fixtures to control the colour mixing, intensity and effects.

Moving lights/fixtures

Moving lights are remotely controlled lanterns that can be operated live and programmed to adjust the size and focus of the beam, change the colour and follow a fixed movement sequence or move to an exact position on cue.

Three types of moving fixtures:
➤ Automated yoke lanterns

The automated yoke is based around a conventional tungsten source generic lantern giving remote pan and tilt control. The Profile models can have auto iris or zoom beam size control, remote frame shuttering, gobo rotation and an integrated colour scroller. The Fresnel and PCs have a motorised beam control.

Automated yoke lanterns combine the precision of a generic lantern with the automated features of a moving head. They are virtually silent, having no need for built-in fans as used in the moving heads, and also use a tungsten light source matching the colour temperature of fixed generic lanterns. They require a dimmer supply for the lamp and an independent supply for the moving parts.

Warp M-3 with Source Four Revolution – ETC

➤ Scanners/moving mirror fixtures

A moving mirror or scanner consists of a fixed lantern body and head with a moving mirror, having a rotating, pan and tilt mechanism to direct the beam of light. The beam is manually focused and the lantern

T-Rex Scanner with Golden Scan 3 – Clay Paky

contains rotating colour and gobo wheels that can produce a variety of moving coloured beams and patterns. The beam can be moved very quickly as the moving mirror can be repositioned almost instantaneously. They are far quicker than moving head fixtures which have a slower response and are used in the theatre to provide effects rather than illumination.

➤ Moving head fixtures

Moving head fixtures are hybrid lanterns with a compact, fully automated micro-mechanic head mounted in a motorised yoke. The fixtures house an array of optical and graphical devices, rotating gobos, colour wheels, CMY subtractive[29] Colour Mixing System, zoom and electronic focus, strobe effect, mechanical dimmer/ shutter system and, on some models, internal electronic dimming. They can be programmed to be reset in between cues. There are three types of moving head fixtures:

- **Profile light** (effects lantern) that has control of the beam size, colour and multiple graphics devices, rotating gobo and animation wheels capable of producing dramatic and spectacular moving effects

MAC2000 – Martin Professional

- **Wash light** – using a Fresnel or PC lens, the size and colour of the beam can be changed. Wash lights are also available with tungsten lamp sources

- **Beam light** is a variation of the wash light. It is capable of producing a 'super concentrated near parallel light beam' that will project over a long distance and cut through the brightness of stage washes creating 'fantastic mid-air effects'. The beam size, colour and gobo patterns can be changed and the addition of diffusion filters provides a sharp to soft focus[30]

MAC3 wash light with BVL300 Wash – Philips Vari-Lite

Moving heads fixtures can be used to provide moving and dramatic effects; they have greater flexibility and can replace and reduce the number of generic lanterns required. Their powerful optical systems allow lower-wattage lamp sources to be used with the obvious energy savings depending upon the lamp source being used. Moving heads are widely used for musical theatre productions often to create spectacular effects. They are also used in opera houses and by national theatre companies to cope with the demands of presenting a repertoire programme of productions and the constant changeovers which require the resetting of the lighting rig.

Alpha Beam – Clay Paky

[29] See 'Lighting jargon – Other abbreviations & terms'
[30] Clay Paky product guide – Alpha 300/700

6 DMX FIXTURES A quick start

A quick start

6 DMX FIXTURES

Animated and intelligent fixtures – how do they work?

➤ **Moving fixtures** are controlled by a series of 'stepper' motors that can accurately position all the moving parts working in a similar way to the movement of the print head and paper feed on a computer printer. The rotating shaft on the 'stepper' motor turns by a fixed amount each time it receives an electronic pulse; the direction of rotation can be reversed by reversing the order of the pulses. The motors are used to pan and tilt the moving head or mirror, to rotate and select the colour, and gobo, to focus or zoom the lens, and to adjust the iris or shutters.

➤ **Fixture libraries** are included in the memory of advanced lighting control desks containing the data of all makes of fixtures. This allows the DMX 512 controller to map the attributes or functions of the fixture to be used and to assign the DMX channels to control the fixture in a common way. The built-in programming allows any fixture to be instantly controlled by the lighting desk.

➤ **Three lamp sources** are available for use in moving head fixtures.
- **Discharge lamps** are commonly used in moving lights for feature lighting and effects. They work by passing a high voltage between two electrodes to create an arc of bright light and require a short warm-up time to reach their full intensity. Once the discharge lamp has been struck, it has to be left running continuously for the entire length of the performance, as when they are switched off they require a cooling-off period before the arc will restrike. They cannot be controlled by electronic dimmer units so a mechanical shutter mechanism is used to control the intensity of the light. Discharge lamps have a colour temperature of around 6000 degrees K
- **Incandescent lamps** can be used in some types of moving lights. The tungsten-halogen lamps used have a colour temperature of 3200 degrees K which matches those of the generic lanterns and can be controlled by a dimmer with the same dimming curve. Therefore, they can be seamlessly integrated into the lantern rig for theatre productions
- **LED** light-emitting diodes are used in some smaller moving head fixtures
- **Carbon footprint** – LEDs have very low power consumption; however, it is difficult to compare discharge and incandescent lamp sources. Discharge lamps use less electricity but are running continuously throughout the show, whereas tungsten lamps consume more power but only when they are in use

➤ **Colour scrollers** use two stepper motors to reel the band of colour filter backwards and forwards in front of the lantern.

➤ **Effects** – smoke machines are triggered by a single channel control with a second channel to control the pump pressure and the quantity of smoke.

Did you know that –

■ Pole operated lanterns were originally developed for use in Television studios and were the forerunner of moving lights

■ In 1981, the first automated lights were developed by a small North American company for the Genesis tour and they were named VARI*LITE by the band's manager; see www.Vari-lite/com

■ One of the first uses of moving heads in the UK was in the original production of the musical *Miss Saigon* at the Theatre Royal Drury Lane when lighting designer David Hersey found that there was very limited space left in the overhead stage rig for conventional lighting with all the flying pieces which included a working replica of a helicopter

■ Moving heads are sometimes called 'nodding buckets' and moving mirrors 'wiggles'

Moving heads makes & models – see Part 3: 'Lighting Resources – Technical info.'

More resources – go to

www.adblighting.com – ADB Lighting Technologies
www.claypaky.it – Clay Paky
www.etcconnect.com – ETC
www.highend.com – High End Systems
www.martin.com – Martin
www.vari-lite.com – Philips Vari-Lite
www.robelighting.com – Robe Lighting
www.qmaxz.com – Qmaxz Lighting

6 DMX FIXTURES   A quick start

More info – LED fixtures

The development of the light-emitting diodes has provided a new low-energy light source for the design of theatre fixtures. LEDs have the advantage over traditional light sources in that they have a low energy consumption and longer lamp life, and they are smaller in size and reduction in heat output as compared with theatre lanterns. These are important considerations in the 'green economy'.

LED sources of light

LEDs were originally available in only two colours, red and green, followed by yellow and orange. Initially, they were used as indicators on electronic equipment. The eventual development of a blue LED made it possible to produce white light by combining it with a yellow phosphor lens coating. White light can also be produced by the mixing of red, green and blue LED emitters located close to each other.[31]

➤ **Single-colour LEDs RGB** – individual red, green and blue LEDs emit the three primary colours that can be added together and mixed to produce white light.

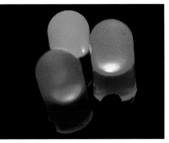

RGB LEDs

➤ **TriColour (TC), Multi-colour (MC)** – single-point source consists of three LED colour emitters combined in a single unit with a small fixed lens having an electro-optical control system that can be controlled by a DMX signal, providing an accurate means of colour mixing and control. The multicolour single point source produces a clean source of coloured light without the rainbow shadows; see 'LED strips'.

➤ **Variable White (VW)** – these fixtures combine cool and warm white phosphor-based LEDs which are capable of adjusting the colour temperature.

➤ **RGB + VW LEDs** – the combination of LEDs in fixtures can provide softer colour combinations of pastel colours, and skin tones can be produced. With 16.7 million colours available, there are endless possibilities for colour mixing from pastels to deep intense saturated colours. The intensity of LED fixtures are controlled by DMX and they can be programmed to create chases and strobe effects.

[31] Pixel Range website, Thomas Engineering

LED fixtures

A range of fixtures and luminaires are being developed using light-emitting diodes.

➤ **LED strips** consisting of a single line of coloured LEDs, red, green and blue, provide linear colour mixing. They are not really suitable for general illumination as the single colour sources can reflect off surfaces producing rainbow shadows. LED strips can be used as decorative features on a set for a musical without dazzling the eyes of the audience.

Easypix – Martin Professional

➤ **LED blocks, battens, bars and banks** are wider units than the strips being made up with either TriColour single-point sources or single RGB + VWs units providing various possibilities of use. The blocks and battens have a double line of LED units with the wider banks having a more patterned arrangement. The battens made up with single-source TC units provide a suitable linear colour wash for frontal illumination as a low foot-level fill light or for a backing surface behind a window, especially where there is limited space for conventional Floods.

Stagebar – Stage Martin Professional

➤ **Light wall** units provide a low-energy alternative to conventional cyc lighting providing greater control over the total surface to paint a seamless colour mix by back lighting a screen or cloth. The space required for using Cyc lights above and below can be dramatically reduced from 2.000m to less than 500mm by using a light wall.

➤ **Martin EventLED wall** consists of one metre square panels, each containing 16 super wide-angled RGB Multicolor LEDs. The lightweight panels can be clipped together as a column or assembled as a wall behind a plastic back projection screen to diffuse the LED sources. The white surface of the EventLED panels acts as a bounce surface providing a very even distribution of the coloured light. A very wide range of colours can be produced from primary to pale tints, and graduated cyc colours, rainbows, sunsets, dissolves and wipes can be produced by having the ability to control the colour and intensity of each LED source.

EventLED – ABTT Sightline

➤ **LED Luminaires**

■ **QPar – Thomas Pixel Range § QPar –** Par 56/64-type luminaries use high-intensity QUAD colour RGBW multicolour LEDs producing an accurate standard 10° beam angle that can be varied with the use of light-shaping diffusing lenses, focusing the light output to 17° and 23°. The accurate soft edged Fresnel-like beam of light provides a shadow-free colour wash

QPar Thomas Eng. Pixel Range

■ **Selador wash lights** provide high-wattage brightness equivalent to 575 watts and their unique 7 colour system is able to reproduce colour mixing to match the conventional ranges of colour filters. They are 90% more efficient than conventional wash lights without the loss of intensity experienced with saturated colours, e.g. 2.5 times brighter than 575W Source Four with Roscolux 68 Sky Blue.[32] Fire & Ice effects are also produced in the Selador range

Fire & Ice – ETC

■ **Asymmetrical Cyc Floods** – ADB Lighting Technologies ALC4 'Combines the equivalent light output and colour rendition as conventional tungsten halogen 1000W lighting fixtures'[33]

■ **Moving head LED wash light** provides both the combined opportunity of movement and colour change with a low-energy source. With the development of moving optical lens systems, it is possible on some models to control the beam size and zoom from a wide wash to a tight spot that can be projected over a good distance

VLX Wash –Vari-Lite

■ **Moving head LED profile** – Martin Professional have developed a hard edged light source providing an alternative to traditional HID source moving heads

Mac Entour – Martin Professional

■ **Profile spots** – Robert Juliat have developed the first Profile spot Aledin to have an LED light source inserted into the optical system of their 600 Series Profile luminaire

[32] ETC website
[33] ADB website

Aledin – Robert Juliat

6 DMX FIXTURES   More info

Use of LED fixtures

LED fixtures were initially used in the theatre for special effects and dressing the set with decorative lighting and also widely used for architectural features and entertainment lighting. The light output from the moving heads and focusable luminaires are starting to match that of generic lanterns and are now becoming more suitable for use on smaller to medium stages and educational drama studios.

There are a number of advantages over the use of LED luminaires:

- Low heat, low energy and no UV IR emissions
- Plastic gobos can be used in LED Profile spots
- No 'colour shift' constant colour temperature when unit is dimmed
- Low power requirement ideal for venues with limited power supply
- Dimmer unit not required as controlled by DMX, therefore no need for extensive installation cabling
- Instant ability to call up any colour
- Colour created by additive mixing of individual LED colour sources with no reduction in the intensity of the light or wastage as with the subtractive nature of colour filters in generic lanterns or moving fixtures. See Chapter 8 'Colour filters – Extras! – Colour filters – How they work'

The development of an LED light source to replace the tungsten lamp in a Profile spot is a further breakthrough in the development of LED luminaires for use on the stage. The LED technology is developing very fast so it is a question of watch the manufacturers' websites for latest developments.

Did you know that –

- LEDs began to be developed in the late 1950s
- The first LEDs emitted infrared light and were first used for TV channel controllers
- Blue LEDs were finally developed in Japan in the 1990s[34]
- Philips Vari-Lite wash luminaires were first used for HD broadcasting of America's Got Talent
- Robert Juliat produced an LED lamp source-based Profile spot Aledin 630SX in 2010

LED fixtures makes & models – see Part 3: 'Lighting Resources – Technical info.'

[34] Pixel Range website, Thomas Engineering

Extra resources – go to

www.adblighting.com –	ADB Lighting Technologies
www.chroma-q.com –	Chroma-Q
www.etcconnect.com –	ETC
www.gekkotechnology.com –	Gekko Technology Ltd
www.glp.de –	GLP German Light Products
www.highend.com –	High End Systems
www.martin.com –	Martin
www.vari-lite.com –	Philips Vari-Lite
www.pulsarlight.com –	Pulsar
www.robelighting.com –	Robe Lighting
www.robertjuliat.fr –	Robert Juliat
www.pixelrange.com –	Thomas Engineering

Points for action

Quickies!

■ View the products on the websites

Takes longer

■ View Selador Fire & Ice demo video, go to www.etcconnect.com

A proper job!

■ LED Lighting – for a brief history of LEDs and future developments, go to www.pixelrange.com

■ Information on LED technology – www.wikipedia.org/wiki/Light-emitting_diode – Wikipedia

Extras! – DMX 512 – making connections

It is important to understand how the DMX chain works and to connect up DMX units in a logical way.

DMX 512 – making the connections and setting the addresses

➤ **DMX – Quick connections**
- Dimmers and fixtures are connected together in a 'daisy chain' with DMX data cable terminated in 5 pin XLR connectors
- Each dimmer pack, rack and fixture has connection sockets marked DMX 'In' and DMX 'Out'
- The control desk is linked to the dimmer rack and fixtures in the following way – see diagram on page 96
- A cable is taken from the 'DMX Out' on the desk to the 'DMX In' socket on the dimmer rack. The next cable is taken from the 'Out' socket on the rack to the 'In' socket on the next fixture and continues through all the fixtures
- A terminating connector should usually be fitted at the end of the chain in the final fixture 'DMX Out' socket, although some DMX fixtures have built-in terminating switching devices
- If the desk has two 'DMX Out' sockets, then it will have two universes of DMX 512. The two daisy chains are run separately and it is good practice to use one universe for the dimmer units and the other for fixtures

➤ **DMX – Control channels**
Each DMX controlled unit requires a specified number of control channels to operate all of its functions. Examples are listed below:

Luminaires & Fixtures	No. of control channels	No. of attributes	Personality/functions
Dimmer/Generic lantern	1	1	Intensity
Dimmer/Lantern + Scroller	2	2	Intensity, colour
Smoke machines	2	2	on/off, pump pressure
6-way dimmer pack	6	6	Intensity
Moving Head	10–36	10–36	Intensity, colour, pattern/gobo, position

➤ **DMX – addresses**
- Each dimmer pack, rack, fixture and effect requires a dedicated DMX start address
- The start address of the next unit will depend upon the number of control channels being used by the previous unit

- The start addresses do not need to be in the order that the units are linked together and spaces can be left in between the address numbers
- It is good practice to leave a space in between the sequence of the individual addresses. If the addresses overlap, the control of some of the functions will be lost
- It is best to set up the start addresses in a logical pattern by grouping the different types of equipment together, e.g. dimmer packs, moving heads, scrollers, LED fixtures, effects

➤ DMX – connections and assigning the addresses

The diagram shows an example of DMX connections and addresses.

- The 48-way dimmer rack is set with a start address of DMX 001, each dimmer unit requires a single control channel so the address will run from 001 to 048
- The next moving fixture in the chain can be set with a start address of DMX 050 for convenience. It requires, say, 25 control channels, so the address will run from 050 to 075
- The next fixture is a colour scroller and it is set at start address of DMX 076; it requires only two control channels with the addresses running from 076 to 077
- The next fixture or effect could be given a start address of DMX 078 or 080 for convenience
- The DMX data from the control desk is received from one channel address to the next onwards until it reaches the required address; it is then separated and series of 8 pulses or bits are passed on to the control function of the unit

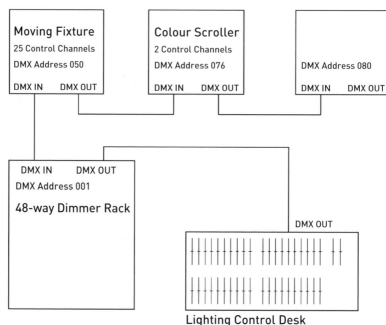

Diagram showing control desk and connection of dimmers and fixtures & start addresses

Extras!

6 DMX FIXTURES

QUICK TIPS

■ If some of the fixtures are not working, check the chain of DMX connections

■ Dimmer modules, packs or racks can be paired together by using the same DMX address and operated by the same channel fader

Quick resources – go to

www.onstagelighting.co.uk – DMX Stage Lighting Systems

6 DMX FIXTURES

Extras!

7 Health & Safety

A quick start – Good working practice

Safety checks when working with lanterns, using access systems and working at heights

More info – Access equipment

Using access systems, portable step ladders and platform equipment

Extras! – H&S policies & risk assessment

Understanding and carrying out a risk assessment

A quick start – Good working practice

There are many potential hazards when working with lighting equipment. It is important to use safe working practices and to be aware of the dangers when working on the stage or in the studio.

> **›› Fast Forward** on the DVD to **7.1 Safety when working at heights**

Safety checklists

The following checklist is provided as a guideline for safe working practices and user awareness. It is not a replacement for the current legislation and relevant health and safety recommendations which are the responsibility of the manager of the theatre space to enforce.

➤ **Electrical safety** – check that:

- ✓ **Portable Appliance Tests** have been carried out on all the lanterns and cables in the last 12 months.[35] Check the date on the green test stickers usually attached to the plug top or on the equipment
- ✓ Regular visual 'user checks' have been made on all the lanterns and cables. Look for the common faults; damage to outer cable insulation and exposure of internal cables at the point of entry to lanterns, plug tops and cable sockets

[35] IEE Electrical Maintenance including Portable Appliance Testing

✓ **Periodic Electrical Test** of the installation including the lighting bars has been made during the last year (Places of Entertainment) and within the last five years (Educational Establishments)[36]

If the equipment and installation hasn't been checked or is faulty, don't use it; refer it to your technical manager or chief electrician.

➤ **Safety when working with lanterns** – check that:

✓ The hanging clamp is correctly fitted to the lantern and that the top bolt is tight

✓ A safety bond is permanently attached to the anchor point or hanging bracket of each lantern to prevent it falling off when being unclipped from the lighting bar

✓ The safety clip is used to prevent the colour frames and barndoors from falling out of the colour runners

✓ The shortest length of cable is used without creating any obvious hazards, as a long cable has the risk of compromising the earth impedance which could be fatal

✓ Extension cables are not coiled as they can overheat

➤ **Safety when working at heights**

✓ Wear strong, non-slip rubber-soled shoes and have no loose clothing to catch on obstructions

✓ A Bump Hat should be worn for protection when working under hanging equipment

✓ A hard hat should be worn when working in the area below an access system

✓ Tools should not be carried in a pocket but carried on belt clip, held in a 'tool belt' or attached to a lanyard around the neck

Bump Hat – GMSL

✓ If you drop anything, shout 'Heads', as this is a recognised signal

✓ Equipment should be rigged on flown bars at stage level and then raised into position

✓ On fixed bars lanterns can be raised and lowered by using a strong rope over the bar

✓ Use a karabiner to clip on to the lantern; always use a bowline knot to attach it to the hauling line[37]

✓ Wear a hard hat and use protective gloves when raising and lowering equipment on a rope

✓ Never carry lanterns single-handed up a ladder

Hard hat – GMSL

---

[36] IEE Electrical Maintenance including Portable Appliance Testing
[37] Karabiner & bowline, see 'Lighting jargon – Rigging'

➤ **Using access systems**

The following points should be checked by a trained supervisor but as an operator it is always worth checking these points for your own personal safety:

✓ **It is suitable for the intended work** providing a safe working height to reach the lanterns and supports the upper body without overreaching

✓ **It is correctly erected** and 'signed off' by a certified trained operator

✓ **It is correctly positioned** to prevent overreaching sideways so that the operator's 'belt buckle' stays within the width of the ladder or access system when working

✓ **The work area** below is clear of obstructions and additional people who might cause distractions

➤ **As the operator** – when using the access system:

✓ **A supervisor should be present** who has received relevant training on the equipment

✓ **You should have received adequate training** over the safe use of the access equipment before being allowed to use it

✓ **Never work alone** – always have somebody working with you to assist in raising and lowering equipment and to summon help if there is an accident

Above all, use your head when working at heights and be safe

QUICK TIPS

■ Electrical safety and testing is the responsibility of the manager of the facilities

■ **If you haven't been trained, don't use the access equipment**

■ Wear a Bump Hat when rigging, angling and focusing to protect your head

■ Never leave tools on the platform of an access system as they could fall when it is moved

■ Wear a hard hat when working below a ladder, tower or access system

■ If you hear 'Heads!', don't look up but just get out of the way

Points for action

Quickies!

■ Check out the Health & Safety policy for your performance space

UNIVERSITY OF WINCHESTER LIBRARY

More info – Access equipment

It is important to understand the safety requirements and to establish good working practice when using access systems.

The following information is provided purely as a guideline for safe working practices and user awareness. It is not a replacement for the current legislation and relevant health and safety recommendations which are the responsibility of the technical manager of the theatre space to enforce.

Portable ladders – Step, extension & combination ladders

Designed to be used to provide access for light maintenance work and not as a working platform.

The following points need to be considered before using a ladder:
- The type of the work that is to be carried out on the ladder
- In the UK the Work at Height Regulations 2004 (WAHR) states that:
  'ladders can be used as workplaces when it is not reasonably practicable to use other potentially safer means and the Risk Assessment shows that risks are low'
- Check that the ladder meets the European standards: BS EN 131 for Light Trade use, a BS 2037 Class 3 Domestic ladder sold in shops for DIY work should not be used
- The ladder must be the right height for the job to prevent overreaching, and to provide support for the upper body, observe the belt buckle limits; see 'A quick start'
- **Three points of body contact should be maintained at all times:** that is, both feet and one hand, which limits the safe working use of a ladder mainly to adjusting lanterns but not rigging

Three types of portable step ladders

➤ **Step ladders** provide a stable free-standing A-frame. When using a step ladder, the upper body should be supported at all times by the ladder or hand rail; therefore, it is important not to stand on the two steps immediately below the top. The step ladder should be positioned at 90 degrees to the work and never used sideways-on as it will be unstable.

➤ **Extension ladders** should be used on a firm level floor with the top resting on a stable, strong surface and not against a lighting bar. It should be inclined at the safe vertical base angle of 75 degrees using the one-to-four rule, 1 unit out at the base for 4 units high, and secured to prevent slippage by anchoring at the top or 'footing' at the bottom by another person.

Step ladder – GMSL

➤ **Combination ladders** – Zarges Skymaster is a three-part extension ladder, which can be assembled to provide a free-standing braced A-frame with an overhanging extended section providing additional access. However, the safest position is to stand either on the apex of the 'A' frame or one rung up with the upper body supported by the extended ladder. Therefore, it is worth considering the average working height when purchasing a Zarges ladder. Footing the A-frame will provide extra stability and reassurance for the user.

Zarges Skymaster

Platform equipment – Towers, Tallescopes & ESCA

A working platform system provides safe access for angling and focusing and rigging of lanterns on lighting bars.

➤ **Towers & Tallescopes**
- **Stabilisers/outriggers must be used at all times** to provide adequate stability and the brakes set before the equipment is used
- The stabilisers and brakes need to be released before they can be moved; therefore, the equipment should not be moved with an operator on the working platform. This means the operator must climb up and down every time the equipment is to be moved
- Equipment to be rigged should only be lifted within the footprint of the equipment and not be hauled up outside
- Tallescopes are not particularly suitable for rigging lanterns as distinct from focusing[38]

The Health and Safety Executive in the UK considers the movement of occupied Tallescopes to be unsafe. This directive is being reviewed by The Association of Theatre Technicians.[39]

➤ **Mobile towers** – Single-width 1.2m or 1.5m wide rectangular ladder frame aluminium tower can be easily positioned alongside lighting bars and take up less space than the double-width square platforms. All towers should be fitted with internal ladders, a full-width platform deck having a trap door access, kickboards and safety rails. Stabilisers/outriggers should be used on towers where the working platform is over 2m, i.e. one unit high. It should never be moved while there is an operator on the platform over 2m high.

[38] David Adams, Chairman ABTT Safety Committee
[39] ABTT Sightline, Autumn 2009

Mobile tower – Instant UpRight UK

103

7 HEALTH & SAFETY

More info

➤ **A Tallescope** is a telescopic aluminium manually operated work platform which is supported on a wheeled base and accessed by a vertical ladder. It should only be used with stabilisers/outriggers in place and not moved with the operator on the work platform.

➤ **An ESCA mobile access platform** has a wide, stable wheeled base that doesn't require the use of outriggers. It can be driven and manoeuvred by the operator from

Tallescope – Aluminium Access Products Ltd

the work platform, saving time and the need to climb up *ESCA – ESCA UK* and down as with other systems, and is a safe system to use only on a flat stage. The ESCA is compact and is easily stored ready for use.

MORE TIPS

- Always use stabilisers/outriggers on mobile towers with a working platform over one unit or 2m high
- Never climb up on the outside of a tower as this can make it unstable
- Never move a mobile tower or tallescope with an operator on the work platform

Technical info. – in the UK

'Code of Practice – working at heights in theatres' ABTT – Association of British Theatre Technicians

'Health and Safety Regulation ... a short guide': HSE – Health and Safety Executive

'Safe Use of Ladders & Stepladders: an employers' guide': HSE

HSE information sheet on tower scaffolds: HSE

'Use Your Head for Heights stay within the Law': The Ladder Association – http://ladderassociation.org.uk

'Operators' Code of Practice for prefabricated towers': PASMA – Prefabricated Access Suppliers' & Manufacturers' Association

More resources – go to

www.abtt.org.uk –	ABTT
www.hse.gov.uk/pubns –	HSE
http://ladderassociation.org.uk –	The Ladder Association
www.pasma.co.uk –	PASMA
www.zargesuk.co.uk –	Zarges Skymaster ladder
www.escauk.co.uk –	ESCA UK
www.airborne-ind-acc.co.uk –	Instant UpRight Span towers
www.instantupright.com –	Instant UpRight
www.tallescope.co.uk –	Tallescope
www.scottint.com –	Scott Health & Safety Bump Hats

7 HEALTH & SAFETY

More info

105

Extras! – H&S policies & risk assessment

The Health & Safety legislation in the UK requires that a risk assessment should be made before taking part in any activity that presents a potential hazard.

Health & Safety Policy

There should be a Health & Safety Policy for the use of the equipment and working practice on the stage or in the drama studio. The health and safety policy should outline: **'Who can do What, Where, When & How'**.

It is important to know:

- What the H&S policy is for working on your stage or studio, especially for working at heights and the use of access equipment
- If you have received adequate training

If in doubt, ask your line manager or the Health & Safety Officer.

Risk Assessment

A risk assessment should be carried out before taking part in any activity that presents a potential hazard. It is a careful examination of what in the workplace could cause harm to people working in that environment, so that an assessment can be made as to whether sufficient precautions have been taken or more should be done to prevent harm. **The aim is to prevent accidents.**

Two factors to consider:

- **Hazard** – anything that can cause harm (e.g. chemicals, tools, electricity, working at heights)
- **Risk** – the chance, great or small, that someone will actually be harmed by a hazard

➤ **5 Steps to Risk Assessment[40]**

The first stage in controlling the risk is to carry out an assessment in order to identify what needs to be done. In the UK, this is a legal requirement for all risks at work.

Step 1	**Look** for the hazards
Step 2	**Decide** who might be harmed and how
Step 3	**Evaluate** the risks arising from the hazards (High, Medium or Low) and decide whether existing precautions are adequate or more should be done
Step 4	**Record** your findings
Step 5	**Review** the assessment from time to time and revise it if necessary

[40] Information from '5 Steps to Risk Assessment' HSE (UK)

Extras!

7 HEALTH & SAFETY

➤ **Risk assessment when working at heights**
This should cover:

- **Possible dangers** and the level of risk involved
- **Suitability of the equipment** available to carry out the job
- **Risk of incorrect assembly** of the access system
- **Positioning and use** of the equipment for all aspects of the space
- **List of who is trained** to use the access systems

Conducting a risk assessment – there are four stages:

1. **Identifying the hazard/risk – Before assessment**
   - List the hazards/risks
   - Assess each hazard/risk identified, the probability of an accident occurring and the severity of an injury on a 1 low–5 high scale
   - Calculate the risk factor – probability x severity

2. **Recommending precautions**
   - Assess the risk factors – low, medium, high
   - Identify items to be improved, where further action is required and immediate action needs to be taken
   - Recommend and list the precautions to be taken

3. **Reviewing the hazard/risk – After assessment**
   - Assess the recommended precautions
   - Assess the probability of an accident occurring and severity of an injury based on the recommended precautions to be taken on a 1–5 scale
   - Calculate the risk factor – probability x severity
   - Identify any further improvements, further action or immediate action to be taken
   - List further action required

4. **Feedback and communication**
   - Review the 'Further action to be taken'
   - Ensure that those supervising and undertaking the work know and act on the recommended precautions

7 HEALTH & SAFETY **Extras!**

HEALTH & SAFETY – *Risk Assessment*	Venue: Sundial Theatre Cirencester College [41]				
Activity	**Fit-up** – *Alice in Wonderland*				
Description of operation	**Stage** – Using mobile tower to rig lanterns over stage 5m height				
Who is affected by this operation?	Staff	X	Students	X	Public		Others	

Description of hazards/risk – Before	Probability Accident 1–5	Severity injury 1–5	Risk Factor P x S
Assembly	3	5	15
Stabilisers	3	5	15
Hazards on-stage	4	2	8
Edge of raised stage	3	5	15
Climbing access equipment	3	4	12
Danger of low-hanging equipment	3	2	6
Raising lanterns/luminaires	4	3	12
Carrying tools	4	3	12
Working below access system	4	3	12
Moving access system	5	5	25

Probability	1 Very unlikely	2 Unlikely	3 Could occur	4 Likely	5 Will occur
Severity/injury	1 Very minor	2 Minor	3 Serious	4 Major	5 Fatal
Risk Factors	Multiply Probability x Severity to obtain Risk Factor				

Risk factor **Low 0–6**	Risk factor **Medium 7–14**	Risk factor **High 15–25**
Above 5 – improve if possible	**Above 10 – further action required**	**15 + immediate action required**

Recommended precautions

1 Tower to be assembled and signed off by certified operator
2 Outriggers to be in position and used at all times while operator is on the platform
3 Stage to be cleared of any minor or major obstructions
4 Edge of stage to be marked with hazard tape
5 Internal ladders to be used to access platform

[41] Based on an H&S model from Central School of Speech and Drama

6   Bump Hat or hard hat to be worn by operator

7   Lanterns/luminaires to be passed hand to hand to the operator by technicians using the internal ladders

8   Tools to be clipped to operator's belt

9   Area below access system to be kept clear and hard hats to be worn

10   Tower to be moved by min two operators and third to direct passage

Description of hazards/risk – After	Probability Accident 1–5	Severity Injury 1–5	Risk After 1–5
1 Assembly	1	1	1
2 Stability	1	1	1
3 Hazards on stage	1	1	1
4 Edge of raised stage	1	1	1
5 Climbing access equipment	2	5	10 *
6 Danger of low-hanging equipment	3	1	2
7 Raising lanterns/luminaires	2	3	6 *
8 Carrying tools	2	3	6 *
9 Working below access system	2	2	4
10 Moving access system	2	3	6 *

Further action to be taken *

5   Climbing access equipment – ensure that the students are supervised by qualified staff at all times

7   Raising lanterns/luminaires – ensure that the students are supervised by qualified staff at all times

8   Carrying tools – ensure that students are supervised by qualified staff at all times

10   Moving access system – ensure that students are supervised by qualified staff at all times

7 HEALTH & SAFETY

Extras!

Lighting jargon – What's it called?

The language of stage lighting is a combination of electrical terms, practical descriptive words and historical theatre terms that have been drawn together over the years. It is important to become familiar with the terms as they are the common form of communication in the theatre industry.

➢ Lanterns – performance luminaires

Adjustable Focus	Lanterns that can be focused and the beam size adjusted
Axial Ellipsoidal	Adjustable focus lantern, semi-hard/soft edged precise beam, lamp mounted along the central axis of the lantern
Cyc – asymmetrical	Fixed focus Flood, soft edged even wash directed downwards by an asymmetrical reflector
Ellipsoidal lantern	Adjustable focused lantern having an elliptical reflector
Fixed Focus	Lanterns having a reflector and a lamp but no lens system
Flashing through	Checking that all the lanterns in the rig are working
Flood – symmetrical	Fixed focus lantern, soft edged even wash having a symmetrical reflector
Fresnel	Adjustable focus lantern, soft edged diffused beam with more spill light than a PC
Generic lanterns	Non-automated lanterns often referred to as Generics
Grid	The area above the stage from which lighting bars and scenery are suspended or flown
Instrument	Performance lighting unit, a term commonly used in North America
Lantern	Performance lighting unit, a traditional term used in the UK; see Luminaire, Instrument or Fitting
LEKO (NA)	Common name given to Ellipsoidal lanterns in North America
Luminaire	International general term used by lighting engineers for lighting equipment
Movers	Moving lights, automated fixtures
Multicore cable	A flexible cable having a number of singly insulated cores that can carry a number of mains lighting circuits or sound signals
Parcan	Fixed focus lantern, intense near parallel oval beam of light which can be rotated
Patching	The process of temporarily linking one circuit to another
PC/Plano-convex	Adjustable focus lantern, sharp edged beam of light, no spill light, used in Europe
PC/Prism/Pebble	Adjustable focus lantern, hard/semi-soft edged intense beam with less spill light than a Fresnel
Profile spotlight	Adjustable focus lantern, semi-hard/soft edged precise beam
Socaplex	A 19 core multicore mains extension cable providing six lighting circuits

Spider	A multicore plug or socket having six cables terminated in either plugs or sockets
Spotlight	Lantern that can control the size and focus of the beam of light
Zoom spot	'Zoomer' (NA) having an adjustable optical system to change the size of the beam of light

➤ Lantern accessories

Barndoor	Four-door rotatable hinged flaps used on Fresnels and PCs for shaping the beam central axis of the lantern
Colour runners	Three small lugs projecting from the front of a lantern which holds the colour frame
'Cuts' (NA)	'Shutters' (UK) – thin metal plates that fit into the gate of a Profile spot to shape the beam
'Dips'	Outlet sockets at floor level usually mounted beneath a trap below the stage
Fresnel lens	Lens with a series of concentric steps having a flat and a convex surface
Gate	The centre of the optical system of a Profile spot where the shutters are positioned and the iris and gobos can be inserted
Gobo	Thin steel disc with an etched pattern used in a Profile spot to project patterns
Iris	Adjustable circular diaphragm used to alter the beam diameter of a fixed Profile spot
Lamp	The light source within a lantern
Lamp post holder	The holder in which the lamp is mounted in a lantern
Lamp tray	The lamp post holder is mounted on the adjustable lamp tray at the rear of the lantern
Pan	Rotating the position of a lantern on the horizontal plane
PAT Testing	Portable Appliance Testing carried out on lanterns and cables in the UK
Plano-convex	Lens having one flat surface and a curved surface used in Profile lanterns
Prism-convex	Plano-convex lens having a prism stippled surface on the flat side
Shutters	'Cuts' (NA) – thin metal plates that fit into the gate of a Profile spot to shape the beam
Spill/scatter	Unwanted light on the edge of a soft edged beam of light
Stirrup/yoke	'U'-shaped hanging bracket that allows the body of a lantern to tilt
Tilt	Swinging the lantern up and down in the vertical plane
Trunion arm	'U'-shaped hanging bracket that allows the body of a lantern to tilt

LIGHTING JARGON

What's it called?

111

➤ Rigging

Bar/Barrel/Pipe	Horizontal aluminium bar on which lanterns are hung
Bowline	Knot used to create a loop at the end of a rope used for sailing or climbing
Bump Hat	Baseball-style hat providing bump protection to the head from overhead hanging equipment in low-risk situations
'C' Clamp (NA)	Hook clamp (UK) that is tightened by a spanner or wrench
C-wrench (NA)	Crescent wrench – an open-ended adjustable spanner (NA) originally produced by the Crescent Tool Company[42]
Carabiner	Metal loop with a sprung screwed gate opening used for climbing
Hard hat	Safety helmet providing head protection from falling items in high-risk situations
'Heads!'	Warning shouted when something has been dropped overhead
Hook clamp	Hook-shaped clamp used to suspend a lantern from a lighting bar or barrel
IWB	Internally Wired Barrel, having outlet sockets mounted on the bar internally wired to an end box
Lanyard	Cord around the neck for attaching spanners or wrenches when working at heights
Lighting rig	A general term for the lanterns hanging on the lighting bars
Patch panel	Hardwired outlet circuits terminated with flexible cables and numbered plug tops passing through a holed comb panel mounted below the dimmer units
Patching	Process of temporarily linking or 'hooking up' lanterns via outlet sockets to dimmers
Practical	Domestic light fitting that appears to be operated by an actor on-stage
Rigging	Term used for hanging lanterns and equipment
Safety bond	Load tested steel cable used to prevent a lantern falling if the suspension fails
Spigot	Short threaded rod that is bolted on to a lantern or clamp to fit into the top of a lighting stand
'Signing off'	Certification by a trained operator that the equipment has been safely assembled
Strike	To take down or remove a lantern or a piece of scenery

➤ Dimmers

Amps 'A'	Measurement of the rate of flow of the electrical current in a circuit
Dimmer	Controls the amount of electricity going to a lamp and the intensity of the light
Dimmer pack	Six dimmer units with outlet sockets mounted in a portable pack

[42] A Glossary of Technical Terms – www.theatrecrafts.com/glossary

Dimmer rack	Dimmer units mounted in a rack; the outlet circuits are usually hardwired
Hard patch	Connecting the circuits from the lanterns to a dimmer unit via a hardwired socket distribution box or direct to a socket mounted on the dimmer
Voltage 'V'	Measurement of the electrical pressure or force of the mains supply
Watts 'W'	Measurement of the amount of electrical power, e.g. the power of the lamp in a lantern
Wattage	Power consumption of a lamp providing a rough guide to the intensity of light produced
Ohms	Measurement of resistance in an electrical conductor

➤ Lighting control desks

Analogue	Low-voltage control system connecting the control desk to the dimmers
Black Out – BO	Switch everything off
Chase	Continuous repeated sequence of flashing lights produced by the effects function on a lighting control desk as used on neon signs
Channel fader	Part of a control desk that operates an individual dimmer channel
Control desk	Controls the power supplied by the dimmers to the lanterns
Dipless crossfade	Channel levels, set at the same level on both presets, remain at the same intensity and are not affected by the crossfade
DMX 512	Digital Multiplex – a high-speed data control system connecting the control desk, dimmers and fixtures
Flashing through	Raising each control channel in succession to check that the lantern or fixture is working after rigging and before each performance
Master Fader	Having the overriding control of a group of channel faders
Scene Preset	Group of individual faders on a lighting control desk that control the dimmers
Soft patch	Assigning a control channel on the lighting desk to the DMX address of a dimmer unit or piece of equipment

➤ Other abbreviations & terms

CIE	Commission Internationale de L'Eclairage produced the international lantern symbols
CMY	Cyan/Magenta/Yellow secondary colour filters used together for subtractive mixing to produce additional colours
Cyclorama/Cyc	White rear wall or backcloth used to mix coloured light & create sky effects
FOH	Front of house, the area used by the audience in front of the curtain or stage
NICEIC	UK's electrical contracting industry's independent voluntary body for electrical installation contractors

LIGHTING JARGON

What's it called?

Colour, Gobos & Effects

Some useful additions – *looking at using colour, gobos, projecting slides and moving images, creating special effects, flashes and bangs!*

8 Colour filters

A quick start – Working with colour filters

Establishing good working practice when cutting and storing colour filters

More info – Filters, diffusion & reflection materials

Looking at the range of colour, technical filters and materials used in the theatre, film and television industries

Extras! – Coloured light

How filters work, colour temperature, correction filters and the effects of mixing coloured light

A quick start – Working with colour filters

Colour is created from white light by filtering out all the other colours from the spectrum. A colour filter inserted in a lantern doesn't colour the light; it filters out and absorbs all the other colours from the white light, allowing the single colour to project through.

Identifying colour filters

Colour filters are identified by a reference number and name, e.g. 002 – Rose Pink. Lighting designers and technicians refer to them by their number for ease of use.

➤ **Colour swatches**
Samples of colour filters can be obtained from the manufacturers in the form of a colour swatch. Some manufacturers, LEE and Rosco, include correction filters, diffusion and

*e-colour+
– Roscolab*

reflective materials that are used for film, video and TV with the colour effect filters in their swatch books.

> ## Two types of colour swatches:
The filters are organised in two ways:

- **Numeric edition:** arranged in the order that each filter has been produced and not in a colour order. Very useful for identifying colours by the reference number when working from a lantern plan
- **Chromatic/Designer editions:** arranged in their colour order grouped together in bands of colour making it easier to select colours

Cutting and storing filters

It is important to establish an organised method of cutting and storing colour filters as there are a large number of colours and many different sizes required to match all the lantern colour frames. Colour filters need to be accurately cut to fit the size of colour frame. Too small and the filter will buckle and distort under the heat; too large and it won't fit the frame.

> ## Colour filter sheet sizes:
- Small sheets – 53cm x 61cm
- Large sheets – 53cm x 122cm
- Rolls –   122cm x 762cm

> ## Identifying filters:
- The sheets of colour filters are usually marked with the colour number on a sticker on the right-hand edge of the sheet. Also the number is often printed on the tissue backing paper
- Sheets of colour filters are difficult to identify so always make sure that they are clearly numbered
- Mark the colour name and colour number on the sheet with a chinagraph or grease pencil

> ## Cutting filters:
- It is important to know the exact dimension of the frame that fits the appropriate lantern
- Always cut from the opposite edge to the number marked on the sheet
- Mark the colour number in the top right corner of the cut filter for ease of identification
- Do not mark the number in the middle as this can affect the life of the filter

➤ **Three methods of cutting:**

- Templates will help to cut the filter to the correct size; allow 5mm clearance in each direction to fit the colour into the frame
- Finger sheet cutters are a quick way to cut the pieces
- Use a paper trimmer when cutting a large number of pieces
- Never cut filters using an open-bladed knife and a steel rule, as the knife can easily slip off the steel rule and cut the supporting fingers or hand. This is a potential safety hazard

Sheet cutter – LEE Filters

➤ **Storing filters:**

- Store in single folders clearly marked with the colour number and name
- **It is easier to find colours if they are grouped together**

Neutrals –	Lavenders, Lilac, Pale Violet tints, Chocolate
Tints and Pastels –	Light Blues, Greens, Golds, Pinks & Roses, Ambers
Saturated Colours –	Deep Blues, Reds, Greens

- Use either a filing cabinet or a large-sized (A4) ring folder with clear plastic envelopes and white backing sheets for smaller-sized colours

➤ **Cutting filters with a paper trimmer:**

Paper trimmers provide a safe and accurate method of cutting filters. They are good for cutting single pieces but it is difficult to measure and cut multiple pieces continuously off a strip using the measuring rule mounted on the trimmer.

A simple extension board can be added on to the right-hand side of the trimmer to provide a way of measuring on the opposite side:

Paper trimmer – GMSL

- Cut a board to fit on the side of the trimmer
- Measure from the cutting edge and mark the distance for each colour frame on the extension board with a suitable marker pen. Draw the sizes of the colour frame on the extension board
- Feed the strip under the pressure bar from the left, measured to size, marked on the right-hand side. Hold down the pressure bar and cut. Continue to cut to feed the strip from the left-hand side, measure and cut

8 COLOUR FILTERS   A quick start

QUICK TIPS

- Use chinagraph pencils to number colour filters
- The most accurate way to match two colour filters is to compare them against a white background
- Use the filter backing card in the swatch to compare and identify an unmarked colour

Quick resources – go to

www.leefilters.com – free colour swatches & sheet cutters
www.rosco.com – free colour swatches, sheet cutters & filter markers
www.gamonline.com
www.apollodesign.net

GLOBAL JARGON

- **Colour filters (UK)** – 'Gel' term commercially used in North America
- **Colour (UK)** – Color (NA)
- **Chinagraph pencil** (UK) – Grease pencil (NA)

Points for action

Quickies!

- Look through a Designer colour swatch at the range of filters available
- Obtain a free LEE and Rosco colour swatch for your own use
- Obtain a free filter sheet cutter either from LEE Filters or Rosco

Takes longer

- Explore the manufacturers' websites

A proper job!

- Make an extension board to fit a paper trimmer and mark the colour frame sizes on it

More info – Filters, diffusion & reflection materials

Colour effects filters are a part of a larger range of technical filters and materials that are used in the theatre, film and TV industries.

LEE, Rosco, Gam, Apollo

There are four main manufacturers of colour filters, diffusion and reflection materials that are used for theatre, film, video & TV. LEE Filters, Rosco and GamColor are available worldwide; Apollo Gel & Roscolux is mainly used in North America.

Each manufacturer produces an individual range of materials:
- **LEE Filters –**   **'Standard'** HT – 'High Temperature', 'Dichroic Glass'
- **Roscolab –**   **'E-Colour+'**, 'Supergel', 'Roscolux', 'Cinegel', 'Perma Colour'
- **Gam Products –**   **'GamColor'**, 'GamFusion/Diffusion', 'CineFilter',
- **Apollo Design & Technology –**   **'Apollo Gel'**, 'Dichroic Filters'

➤ **Filters, diffusion & reflection materials**
- **Colour effects filters** – used in the theatre and TV
- **Colour correction filters** – mainly used for film, video and TV to convert and correct the colour temperature of different sources of light
- **Diffusion filters** – used for film, video and TV to diffuse a light source; also used in the theatre including 'Frosts'
- **Reflection materials** – used for film, video and for theatre effects
- **Rosco Cinegel & Gam CineFilter** provide a dedicated range of filters and materials for film, video & TV

➤ **Three types of filter materials**

Filters are made from different materials which have different properties that affect their use:

- **Surface-coated polyester film** – having a high melting point, good resistance to dye fade in hot lights, resistance to tears, punctures, cracking and impervious to water.

  As used for **LEE Filters standard range, Rosco E-Colour+, Roscolux, GamColor & Apollo Gel**

- **Body colour polycarbonate** – very good colour durability and resistance under intense heat of theatre and TV lighting, eliminating buckling and shrinking, making it highly suitable for building colour strings for scrollers.

  As used for **LEE Filters High Temperature, Rosco Supergel**

119

- **Dichroic glass filters** – long lasting, will not fade, withstanding temperatures up to 371°C, used with metal halide discharge and high wattage tungsten lamps. Also they are used for permanent installations, long runs to save re-colouring lanterns and for inaccessible lanterns. Far more expensive than standard colour filters and the range is limited mainly to saturated colours with some pale tints.

  As used for **LEE Dichroic, Rosco Permacolour & Apollo Dichroic filters**

Ranges of colour filters & materials

➤ **LEE Filters & Rosco E-Colour+**

Designer edition – LEE Filters

- Both ranges use a similar numbering system. They include colour conversion filters, diffusion and reflection materials mixed within their range of colour effects filters, e.g. 117 – Steel Blue, 114 – Hamburg Frost, 216 – White Diffusion, 200 – Double CT Blue (tungsten to daylight conversion), 272 – Soft Gold Reflector
- Colour filters are numbered in a random order, e.g. 002 – Rose Pink, 003 – Lavender Tint, 004 – Medium Bastard Amber, 007 – Pale Yellow, 008 – Dark Salmon
- Most of the colour filters with the same reference number in the two ranges are either exact, close matches or similar colours
- LEE Filters – there are some gaps in the numbering and certain colours are missing from the range
- Rosco E-Colour+ – has an additional series of 25 colours inserted into its range numbered from 5017 to 5499
- Rosco produce both Numeric and Chromatic Swatch book editions

➤ **LEE Filters Designer** chromatic edition colour swatch

The colours are arranged in colour order but at the end of the swatch there is a numerical list of the colours with corresponding page reference numbers. The page numbers are printed on the reverse side of the white backing cards that are placed in between the samples of filters, allowing the colour filters to be found by number using the page reference.

Colour wheel – Gam Products

➤ **GamColor**

GamColor filters are divided into the nine colours of the visible spectrum providing a circular classi-fication by hue. The swatch book is arranged according to this system, making it easy to locate any colour in a logical manner. As new colours are

8 COLOUR FILTERS | **More info**

added, they will be numbered and positioned properly on the wheel and in the swatchbook.[1]

100 – Magenta, 200 – Red, 300 – Orange, 400 – Yellow, 500 – Yellow Green, 600 – Green, 700 – Blue Green, 800 – Blue, 900 – Violet

➤ Apollo Gel

The Apollo Gelbook is grouped in the following way

1000 – Diffusions, 2000 – Color Corrections, 3000 – Violets, 4000 – Blues, 5000 – Greens, 6000 – Yellows, 7000 – Oranges, 8000 – Reds

Gelbook – Apollo Design & Technology

Did you know that -

- Colour filters were originally made from dyed gelatine, hence some still call modern filters 'gels'
- Rosco began producing gelatine filters in 1910 and cinemoid filters in the 1950s[2]
- Cinemoid, a self-extinguishing cellulose acetate material, replaced gelatine
- Colour filters are now made from surface-coated or deep-dyed polyester
- The Cinemoid range of colours Nos.1–59 were produced in the 1950s and were arranged in fairly good colour progression/order
- This original range was renumbered 101-159 and new colours have been added as they have been developed, before and after the first 60 colours, making the colour order far more random
- LEE Filters was founded in the late 1960s to meet the demands of the film industry, pioneering the use of modern polymeric materials to produce filters for film, TV and theatre
- 'A common old theatre joke was to get the "new boy" to wash the dusty "Gels" which would dissolve in the water and leave a colourful mess!'[3] Possibly more of an American practice?

[1] GAM Products inc website
[2] 'Guide to Colour Filters' Rosco
[3] Ziggy Jacobs – American Lighting Design student

8 COLOUR FILTERS   More info

MORE TIPS

- Polyester-coated filters have an approximate life of between 6 and 10 hours
- Never mix different makes or types of colour filters on scroll as they shrink at different rates
- When using dichroic filters, it is important to follow the manufacturer's instructions
- 'No one makes a Chocolate colour filter like GAM!'[4]
- Try LEE 742 Bram Brown, 'Dirtier than 156 Chocolate, good for skin tones. Dims well and doesn't go pink at low light levels.' Designed by Paule Constable[5]

More resources – go to

www.leefilters.com – 'Lighting Filter Comparator' – LEE Filters available to download as a poster

www.rosco.com – 'Colour the Industry Standard' – Roscolab poster comparing the Rosco Supergel, Rosco E- Colour+ and LEE Filters range of colours

www. rosco.com – 'The First Name in Colour' – Roscolab poster comparing the Rosco E-Colour+ and Supergel, also Roscolux, Supergel and E-Colour range of colours

GLOBAL JARGON

- **Colour filter** (UK) – 'Gel' is a commercial term used in North America

Points for action

Quickies!

- Look through the filters in either the LEE Filters or Rosco E-Colour+ range
- Try using the colour number reference system in the LEE Filters Designer edition
- Look at the range of dichroic glass filters on the manufacturers' websites

[4] Ziggy Jacobs – American Lighting Design student
[5] LEE 700 Designer Series

More info

8 COLOUR FILTERS

Extras! – Coloured light

'Light is an energy that travels in a wave form. The human eye responds to certain wavelengths and these make up the visible spectrum that the eye recognises as a colour.'[6]

White light

Light is a combination of seven different colours that can be seen in a rainbow. If white light is passed through a prism, it splits the frequencies of light into the colours of the spectrum, Red, Orange, Yellow, Green, Blue, Indigo and Violet. A single colour is created by filtering out the other colours from the spectrum. White light is the neutral point from which colour can be added and changed.

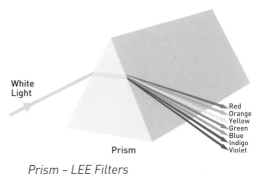

White
Light

Prism

Red
Orange
Yellow
Green
Blue
Indigo
Violet

Prism – LEE Filters

Colour filters

➤ How they work

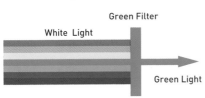

Green Filter

White Light

Green Light

Green filter – LEE Filters

Colour filters work by selectively transmitting and reducing the level of light at certain wavelengths creating or correcting the colour of the light.

- A L089 Moss Green allows the green light frequencies to be transmitted, while blocking the red, orange, yellow, blue, indigo and violet frequencies
- The frequencies of light that are filtered out are converted into radiant heat
- Filters get very hot reaching the point of plasticity, causing it to twist and buckle and therefore should be held in a colour frame
- Colour filter reduces the intensity of light projected by the lantern
- The colour from the filter changes with the intensity of light from the lantern

➤ Two types of filter
- **Plastic filters – polyester/polycarbonate** filters coated with organic dyes that transmit selected wavelengths of light and blocking the rest of the spectrum. The blocked wavelengths create heat, causing the filter to eventually burn or fade when used continuously for long runs

[6] 'The Art of Light' – LEE Filters

8 COLOUR FILTERS

Extras!

- **Glass filters – dichroic durable glass** filters work in a similar way but the unwanted wavelengths are reflected rather than being absorbed. The transmission of light is significantly higher than the plastic filter as virtually no energy is absorbed or heat created, therefore reducing fading and maintaining a constant colour. Dichroic filters are more expensive and are used by lighting designers for long runs or for architectural lighting to maintain a constant colour and reducing maintenance[7]

➤ **Transmitting colours**

The effect of light when shone through a filter can be seen on the Spectral Power Distribution curve. This shows the percentage of light at each wavelength across the visible spectrum and the colours which will be transmitted or reduced. The wavelengths are measured horizontally in nanometres and the transmission factors vertically as a percentage.

- **Neutral colour filter** – 136 Pale Lavender

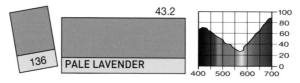

SPD Pale Lavender – LEE Filters

The SPD curve shows a high transmission percentage for indigo, blue and red ends with a reduction in the green, yellow and orange in the centre of the spectrum. The neutral characteristics of this filter can be clearly seen in that the highest transmitted colours will blend with both warm and cool colour filters

- **Blues with green** – 117 Steel Blue

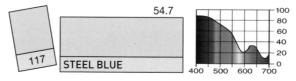

SPD Steel Blue – LEE Filters

The SPD curve shows a high-level transmission of green and great reduction at the red end of the spectrum. This colour filter will not warm the flesh tones of the face but will help maintain a whiter-coloured light when a tungsten lamp in a generic lantern is checked down to a low level

---

[7] 'Guide to Colour Filters' Rosco

- **Blues with red** – 165 Daylight Blue

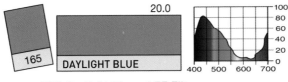

SPD Daylight Blue – LEE Filters

The SPD curve shows a reduction in the transmission in the greens and small increase at the red end, providing a slight warmth to the flesh tones

- **Blues with red** – 174 Dark Steel Blue

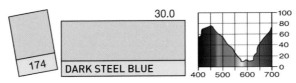

SPD Dark Steel Blue – LEE Filters

The SPD curve shows a considerable reduction in the transmission in the green area and a greater increase at the red end to warm the flesh tones

The SPD curves can assist when selecting colour filters as they provide an indication of the effect that the colour might have on the face, costumes or set.

Designers on colour – *'My filter philosophy is simple. Colour can support and enhance the work of actors, their clothes and the scenic environment. When using filters, I may be removing some parts of the light but I am enhancing those that remain.'* Francis Reid

Did you know that –

- Coloured lighting was first created by using coloured silks in front of a candle mounted in front of a small reflector. Obviously, Health and Safety wasn't such an issue – no wonder so many theatres burnt down!

Sources of light

Each source of light has its own colour temperature that is measured in degrees Kelvin. The colour temperature changes depending upon the intensity – this can be seen in the rays of the sun changing from sunrise to sunset.

➤ **Daylight** – colour temperature 7000° Kelvin

8 COLOUR FILTERS   Extras!

➤ **Incandescent/Tungsten lamps** – 3200° Kelvin

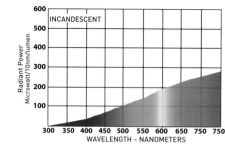

As used in generic lanterns, producing a slightly yellow rather than white light with more energy at the red end of the spectrum.

- The colour temperature of the light changes as the intensity of the lamp is reduced through warm tints to a final rosy glow
- This effect is demonstrated on the 'Fast forward' DVD

Spectrum distribution – Roscolab

➤ **Discharge/ Metal Halide** – 4000°–6000° Kelvin

As used in moving heads and follow spots, producing a whiter light with less energy at the red end of the spectrum and spikes of green and blue.

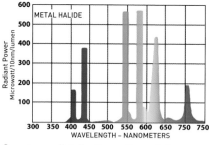

- Discharge lamps cannot be controlled by a dimmer, a dowser or moving shutters are used in the lantern to control the intensity of light without affecting the colour temperature
- Generic lanterns are available with discharge sources and are increasingly being used in the theatre to provide dramatic effects

Spectrum distribution – Roscolab

➤ **Correction filters**

When different light sources are used together in a rig, correction filters can be used to match the colour temperatures:

- **Tungsten light** – using ½ CT Blue correction filter to raise the colour temperature from 3200°K to 4000°K
- **Metal Halide light** – using ¼ CT Orange correction filter to lower the colour temperature from 4000°K to 3200°K

Colour correction is mainly used in the film and TV industry.

Additive mixing coloured light

Colours can be created by mixing the beams of other coloured light, e.g. coloured light from Cyc Floods on a cyc or skycloth.

➤ **Primary colours of light:** Red, Blue and Green

- For primary colours, use LEE/Rosco E-Colour+: 106 – Red, 120 – Deep Blue, 139 – Primary Green

- When the three primary coloured beams overlap, they all combine to produce white light
- Where two of the primary colours overlap, they combine to produce a secondary colour
- A whole series of colours can be created by varying the intensity of light of the three colours

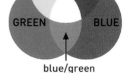

Primary colours – Strand Electric

➤ **Secondary colours:** Yellow, Magenta and Cyan (Blue/Green)

- Yellow produced by combining red and green light
- Magenta produced by combining red and blue light
- Blue/Green by combining green and blue light
- Secondary filter numbers LEE/Rosco E-Colour+: 101 – Yellow, 116 – Medium Blue/Green, 113 – Magenta
- These are also know as complementary colours

➤ **Complementary colours**

The colour triangle shows the three primary colours and the secondary colours that are created by mixing two of the primary colours.

White light is created by mixing a primary colour with the opposite secondary coloured light on the triangle in equal quantities:

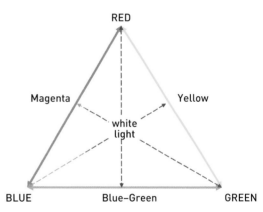

Complementary colours – Skip Mort

- Red + Blue/Green = white light
- Green + Magenta = white light
- Blue + Yellow = white light

This effect works in reverse when a coloured light is projected on to a coloured pigment (paint or coloured material) **turning it black**

- Primary Red filtered light on to a Blue/Green material or painted surface will turn it black
- Blue/Green filtered light on to a primary red pigment will turn it black

Therefore, consideration needs to be given when selecting colours as to the effect that they may have on skin tones, the colours of the costumes, set and the stage surface.

8 COLOUR FILTERS   Extras!

127

Designers on colour – *'The practicalities of my approach are based simply upon realisation that if I take the spectrum apart with filters, then I can put that spectrum together again by superimposing the filter light beams. It is a gloriously unscientific process; not so much a rule-of-thumb as one of crossed fingers. And trusting my eyes.'* Francis Reid[8]

Did you know that -

- The colour reflection effect of red light turning green surfaces black and red light turning green black was first used by Adrian Samoiloff in 1922 at the London Hippodrome to create transformation scenes with costumes and backcloths. It was called the 'Samoiloff Effect' after him[9]
- Strips of colour dipped bulbs/lamps in primary colours were originally used to provide coloured lighting over the stage. They were wired in three or four circuits to give red, green, blue and white light
- The strips were replaced with the development of the three- and four-way compartment batten with clear lamps mounted with a reflector in individual compartments having a slot in front for a colour frame. Coloured lamps were replaced by 'Gels' – gelatine filters
- Compartment battens were used over the stage and as footlights with secondary colours to provide colour washes and to mix white light. A fourth 'open white' circuit was often used to provide additional illumination
- 'Full up to finish'[10] was a common term used in a lighting plot for musicals. On a major musical number, the main singers would be picked with the Limes (follow spots) and the stage lighting would be faded to a colour wash to provide the mood. On the climax at the end of the number, all the stage lighting would be raised to full, followed by the audience's applause
- With the introduction of the use of spotlights and Floods over the stage, the compartment battens were reduced to being used to light skycloths and backcloths
- The cyc colours were originally mixed from primary or secondary colours in a three-way compartment batten. Four-way battens were used to provide an extra set of blue filters to increase the intensity

[8] Rosco Guide to Colour Filters – Designers on Colour
[9] *The Art of Stage Lighting*, Frederick Bentham
[10] David Edmund, Stage Manager, Theatre Royal Exeter

Extras!

8 COLOUR FILTERS

- As the range of colour filters increased, lighting designers started to select individual colours to mix and produce the desired colour on the cyc or skycloth
- Colour cyc lighting on major shows is now produced using LED light walls

GLOBAL JARGON

- **Compartment battens** (UK) – 'Cyc lights', 'Strip lights', 'Cyc strips' (NA)

EXTRA TIPS

- Install glass filters with the coated side towards the lamp as the dichroic coating reflects the unwanted wavelengths of light
- 117 Steel Blue removes the warm tints produced when dimming a tungsten lamp source and it helps to maintain a whiter light
- Always use a colour frame to hold a filter as it will start to buckle when it becomes very hot and reaches the point of plasticity
- Darker/saturated colour filters create more heat and the level of light transmitted by the lantern is reduced

More info – go to

www.leefilters.com – 'The Art of Light' catalogue provides a listing of filters in their 'colour order' with a description of colour and suggestion for use to assist when selecting colours. There are spectral charts that fold out on the side with illustrative SPD curves for all colour samples, making it possible to check the wavelength transmission factors when selecting a colour from the main listing.

'An excellent design resource when planning the colour for a show'

8 COLOUR FILTERS   Extras!

Extra resources – go to

- ■ LEE Filters: www.leefilters.com
- ■ Roscolab: www.rosco.com
- ■ Apollo Design Technology: www.apollodesign.net/Products/View/3242.aspx

Colour packs available:

- ■ LEE Filters colour MAGIC – 'Series of eight individual packs each containing a selection of 12 filters 250mm x 300mm that relate to a particular aspect of lighting. Offers an opportunity to get to know the performance of various colour filters on offer in a cost effective way.' E.g. original, saturates, tint, complementary and light tint packs[11]
- ■ Roscolab – Colour Effects Kit – 12 30cm x 30cm filters, one of each colour, e.g. Cool/Warm, Saturated Colours, Diffusion[12]
- ■ The Apollo Apprentice Gel Kit – 'The purpose of the Apollo Apprentice Gel Kit is to train and educate. It simplifies the color selection process for beginning students, educators in lighting programs, and theater and architectural consultants.' Kit includes: 75 20" x 24" sheets (3 sheets of 25 colours), Apollo Gel Pen, Resource CD, Apollo Gel Swatchbook[13]

Points for action

Quickies!

- ■ Log on to www.leefilters.com to obtain a copy of the 'Art of light'
- ■ Observe the effect of dimming a tungsten halogen lamp and the change in colour temperature
- ■ Compare the transmission wavelengths of some commonly used colours by using the spectral charts in 'The Art of Colour'

A proper job!

- ■ Set up three lanterns and try mixing primary and secondary colours to produce white light and observe the intermediate colours that can be created
- ■ Try out the effect of a range of colour filters on skin tones and coloured materials

---

[11] LEE Filters – The Art of Colour
[12] Rosco – Product Catalogue
[13] Apollo Design inc website

9 Gobos

A quick start – Using gobos

An introduction to working with metal and glass gobos

More info – Projecting and using images

Using gobos to create elements of scenery, add an atmosphere or dramatic effect

Extras! – Other types of gobos

Introducing dichroic break-ups, textured and coloured glass gobos

A quick start – Using gobos

Gobos provide the simplest form of projection and they can be used to create endless effects. An image or pattern can be projected by a Profile lantern by inserting a gobo into the centre of the optical system.

Two types of image projection gobos

- **Stainless steel** – a thin disc of stainless steel having a pattern etched through the surface; fine details of images have to be tagged in order to hold the pattern together. There is an extensive range of ready-made gobos available but custom steel gobos can be made to order from original artwork
- **Glass** – monochrome, black and white photographic or intricate geometric images can be etched on to glass discs. It is possible to project fine details as well as the effect of allowing light around a dark 'island' of image without the need to tag as with the steel gobos. Custom coloured gobos can be made to order. Glass gobos have a far longer life but are much more expensive than stainless steel; therefore, they are mainly used for long-running shows

Steel gobo – GMSL

Glass gobo – Roscolab

131

Working with gobos

Gobos are mounted in gobo holders and inserted into the gate or iris slot of a Profile lantern:

- **The size of the gobo holder** must fit the make of lantern so it is important to check out the manufacturer's information as they all use different sizes; see below
- **The size of the gobo** must match the size of the gobo holder that fits the lantern. The three most common sizes used with generic lanterns are **'A'**, **'B'** & **'M'**

Lantern	Gobo Holder	Gobo Size
Altman – Shakespeare	GH09	B
ADB – Europe Series	GH34	A
CCT – Silhouette	GH01	A
ETC – Source Four	GH61	A
	GH59	B
Robert Juliat	GH58	B
Selecon – Acclaim Axial	GH60	M
Selecon	SPXGHB	B
Selecon – Pacific	GH72	A
Strand – SL	GH46	M

- **Set the lantern to produce a 'flat field'** with equal light distribution across the beam by adjusting the position of the lamp on the lamp tray, see Chapter 2 'Lanterns – performance luminaires – Extras! – Axial Ellipsoidal Profile'
- **Mount the gobo upside down and back to front** with the front side of the image facing the gobo holder. The optical system of the lantern inverts the image the right way up when it is projected
- **Insert the gobo holder into the guides at the rear of the gate slot** with the small raised clips holding the gobo facing the front of the lantern. If the holder is loose in the gate slot, you will be unable to accurately focus the gobo
- **The angle of the image** can be adjusted to compensate for the angle of projection of the lantern. This can be done by removing the gobo holder from the gate of the lantern and rotating the position of the circular gobo. Take care as the gobo will be very hot and gloves should be used or asbestos fingers!

Gobo in holder – GMSL

- **Circular-shaped holders** are produced by some lantern manufacturers which allow a degree of rotational adjustment without having to rotate the gobo disc
- **Rotating lens tubes** – The ETC Source Four and Selecon SPX and Pacific lanterns have a combination gate and lens tube that can be rotated. On the Strand SL the whole body of the lantern rotates within a circular yoke that is attached to the stirrup hanging bracket. The ADB Warp Profile also has a rotating gate feature
- **Using glass gobos** – the manufacturers provide strict guidelines for the use and handling of glass gobos, particularly with respect to adjusting the position of the lamp and lamp tray in the lantern being used

Types of gobo images - there are in excess of over 2,000 gobos available

Gobos can be grouped together under the following headings:

➤ **Realistic projected patterns**
  Boundaries, Clouds, Occasions & Entertainment, Trees & Flowers, The World Around Us, Churches & Heraldics, Fire & Ice, Water, Windows Doors & Blinds, Wildlife, Sky

➤ **Non-realistic patterns**
  Abstract, Break-ups, Foliage break-ups, Graphics & Grills, Rotation

➤ **Graphics**
  Architecture & Retail, Graphics, Text

Realistic gobo –
Roscolab

Leaf break-up –
Roscolab

Ritz gobo –
Roscolab

Did you know that –

- The 'Tadpole' is a customised gobo holder that can be rotated by its long tail that is designed to stay cool to touch and can be secured in the final adjusted position
- 'Goes Before Optics' is a derivation of the term gobo which is a term used in the motion-picture industry where 'flags' or 'cookies' are placed in the beam of a light source to create shadows[14]

[14] Wikipedia, the free encyclopedia

GLOBAL JARGON

- **Gobo** (UK) – Pattern (NA)

QUICK TIPS

- Break-up gobos are often best used slightly out of focus
- Steel gobos are very fragile and they need to be carefully stored when not in use, otherwise they will very quickly become damaged
- M-size gobos will fit into computer 3.5" Diskette pockets that are available in clear A4 plastic sheets from office suppliers. Each one can then be stored in an individual plastic compartment keeping them safe, easy to find and accessible

Quick resources – go to

www.rosco.com –	DHA/Rosco gobo catalogue
www.leefilters.com –	LEE Filters gobo catalogue
www.apollodesign.net –	Apollo Design Technology inc
gamonline.com –	GAM Products inc

Points for action

Quickies!

- Obtain a manufacturer's catalogue of gobos
- Check out the types and ranges of gobos available

Takes longer

- Set up a Profile lantern and try adjusting the position of the lamp to produce a 'flat field' spread of the beam. Take the necessary precautions to protect the lamp, see Chapter 2 'Lanterns – performance luminaires – Extras! – Axial Ellipsoidal Profile'
- Try projecting some gobos and observe the effects of adjusting the focus of the lantern

More info – Projecting and using images

'Lighting plays an important part in creating a theatrical illusion. Projected patterns can add to that illusion by suggesting scenery, creating an atmosphere, add dramatic effect or generally enhancing the visual impact of the lighting design.'[15]

Gobos are used to project images and patterns

➤ **Projected images**
- **Scenic images** projected on to a backcloth to suggest time or place, e.g. moon, cloud effects, tree shapes, skylines, e.g. New York, Eiffel Tower, Broadway theatre scene
- **Scenic elements** projected on to hanging screens suggesting period or place, e.g. window bars, stained glass windows, blinds, bars
- **Scenic effects** shadows projected on to the stage, e.g window bars, jail bars, *Les Mis* grilles, chessboard grid, forked lightning
- **Graphic images** projected on to a backcloth or screens, e.g. music notes, strip of film, clapper board, hats thrown in the air, words and text

➤ **Projected patterns**
- **Foliage break-ups** projected on to the stage to create the effect of shafts of sunlight or the shadows of dappled light through trees, leaf patterns, plants
- **Effects break-ups** – the reflected light from fire or water, snow and rain
- **Pattern break-ups** – blobs, swirls, linear, geometric, grids
- **Abstract break-ups** – geometric patterns, rotating patterns used with gobo rotators

➤ **Projection surfaces**
  Gobos can be used to create patterns and effects by projecting them on to the surface of the stage, scenery, cycloramas, skycloths, backcloths and even drapes. Projection surfaces can also be made by inserting white panels in between curtains on a track or by hanging them from the grid. Interesting effects can be created projecting gobos on to small frames covered in white material hanging at various positions over the acting area. Alternatively, try projecting on to gauze for a softer image. Break-up patterns can also be projected on to actors' costumes. The possibilities are endless and are just waiting to be explored!

> **》   Fast Forward** on the DVD to **9.1 Using Gobos**

9 GOBOS

More info

---

[15] Rosco Product catalogue

Naturally occurring sources of light

An intense source of light produces the effects of shadows as can been seen when using a follow spot. Sun and moonlight produce naturally occurring patterns of light and shade that can be introduced into lighting a scene to break down a flat wash of light and add interest to the lighting.

Lighting in a room

Strong sunlight shining through a window casts a brightly shaped area of light on to the floor or walls of a room, projecting the pattern of the window bars. Similar effects are created as the outside light passes through vertical bars or horizontal Venetian blinds.

These effects can be created on-stage by focusing off-stage lanterns through the window of the set to project a natural shadow or they can be simulated by projecting a gobo pattern from an overhead lantern. The mood, time of day or the change of the effects of the weather can be achieved by subtle changes in the length and position of the shadows and colour of the light.

Scenic projections using realistic patterns

A window effect can be created by projecting a gobo on to a small suspended rectangular screen with the pattern of light passing through the window being projected on to the stage from a second gobo to heighten the effect.

➤ **A window gobo** will add depth to the setting and it can also:

Window gobo – GMSL

- suggest the period of the setting – medieval church, Georgian, eastern or modern window – and it can dramatically change the type of room depending upon the shape, style and angle of projection of the window along with the ambient light
- suggest the changes in time of day by a change of colour, e.g. bright sunlight coming through a shuttered window or moonlight through prison bars
- show the effect of the outside light coming into the room and the shadow that is cast by the light passing through the window

➤ The following effects can be produced by using window gobos and up to four Profile lanterns:

- **Change in the time of day** – crossfade two Profile lanterns projecting the same window bar gobo accurately overlaid on top of each other, each having different colours, one suggesting day, the other night

- **The light coming through the window** – position a Profile lantern with the same window bar gobo to project on to the floor from behind the hanging window projected image
- **Lightning effect** – project a forked lightning gobo on to the window effect with a night-time colour. The lightning can be enhanced by flashing the floor window pattern with the lightning. Remember that we see the lightning before we hear the thunder as light travels faster than sound

Lightning gobo – GMSL

➤ **A stained glass window projection** will immediately create the atmosphere of being in a church; add some organ music and you can create the full effect. The projected gobo will require a break-up of coloured light which can be achieved either by using a split/broken colour filter or a Prismatic gobo; see 'Extras!'

The above effects can be viewed on 'Fast forward on the DVD – Using gobos'.

Stained glass window – GMSL

Light outside

Direct sunlight casts the shadows of building and other objects on to the ground. It is also broken up by branches and tree foliage and reflected by water. Firelight creates moving patterns. These effects can be created on-stage by using break-ups and patterned gobos from lanterns on to the stage surface, scenery or costumes.

Abstract projections using non-realistic patterns

➤ **Forest and woodland effects**
There are various foliage/leaf break-ups that can be used to create bright shafts of sunlight in a dense forest or the dappled effect of light passing through woodland foliage. The shafts of sunlight may be projected from overhead or perhaps more dramatically as back or side lighting. As the actors pass through the wash of dappled downlighting, their faces and costumes will be picked up alternately by the coloured highlights and shadows.

Leaf break-up – GMSL

9 GOBOS

More info

137

➤ Foliage
Tree and foliage break-ups can also be used to project realistic patterns on to scenery.

➤ Abstract break-up patterns
Abstract patterns are best used out of focus to provide textural effects to a surface to break up the stage or scenery. Break-ups can also add another dimension to the visual effect of back lighting, especially when the source of the beam is in view of the audience. This can be done by using a wide-angle Ellipsoidal Profile lantern or a moving head fixture which can be enhanced by a very slow rotation of the pattern. The addition of some haze or smoke will soften and pick up the broken-up beams of light.

➤ **Cloud images** projected on to a sky background can add a more natural effect but they require some movement to make them realistic.

Colour break-ups

A subtle mix of colours can add an extra dimension to both realistic and non-realistic projected gobo effects, e.g. foliage break-ups, window patterns, stained glass windows, sunset, water and flame patterns.

➤ Split colours
The use of split filters is an easy and economic way of producing these effects and they can be made by joining together strips or combining shapes of colour of filters with 'scroller tape' and mounted in a colour frame. The projected shapes of coloured light tend to blend but still retain a degree of separation to achieve some interesting effects. This is a cheap way of producing an effect but the split filter will have a limited life. There are some interesting examples of 'split gels' on GAM Products inc website.

Split colour – GAM Products inc

Fire effect – GAM Products inc

MORE TIPS

- Painters' dust sheets are a good material to use as a covering when making small projection screens for student and amateur theatre productions. It is far cheaper than other scenic materials; however, it does need to be treated with fire-retardant liquid before being used on-stage
- Break-up gobos are more effective when used slightly out of focus
- Scroller tape is heat-resistant tape that is used to make up continuous bands of colour filters as used in scroller colour change units or to make up split colours. It is available from Rosco and possibly local stage lighting suppliers
- An alternative is Scotch Magic or other brands of invisible tape but they will not have the same level of heat resistance as scroller tape. Don't use Sellotape or standard Scotch tape as it becomes very brittle and sticky when subjected to heat

More resources – go to

www.gamonline.com/catalog/splitgel – 'Split gels' – GAM Product inc. website

www.rosco.com/uk – Rosco Gobo Kits – 'Three predefined gobo packs based upon their best selling images. Choose from Break-ups, The World Around Us or Graphics'

Point for action

Quickies!

- Log on to www.gamonline.com/catalog/splitgel – look at the examples of 'split gels'

Takes longer

- Make up a split colour to fit a Profile lantern colour frame. If scroller tape is not available, you could try using Scotch Magic or invisible tape

9 GOBOS   More info

Extras! – Other types of gobos

There are a number of specialist glass gobos that can be used to project colour break-ups, textured shadows, coloured textures and shapes.

Colour break-ups & textured glass gobos

These specialist gobos provide a dynamic range of coloured textured patterns and effects. They can be used on their own, combined with steel gobos to create additional patterns or with rotators to produce moving effects.

Dichroic break-ups

Dichroic glass gobos work in the same way as the glass filters by filtering and reflecting the unwanted wavelengths of light. They are made up of small chips of dichroic glass mounted on either clear or coloured glass gobos that project dynamic multicoloured effects. Dichroic break-ups are also used in moving head fixtures.

➤ **Colorizers/Crushed dichroics** create beautiful, stunning multicoloured projected effects with bits of white light being projected within the colours. The glass gobos are coloured in gentle hues in one of three styles: Stippled, Featherlight and Free Flow

Free Flow colorizer – Roscolab

➤ **Prismatics/Enhanced crushed dichroics** combine intense brilliant colours and intricate deep textures, projecting a spectacular multicoloured pattern without any white light

Glass gobos

➤ **Image glass** 'deeply textured glass that refracts and bends light into intricate patterns of light and greyscale images. Softening the focus of the lantern transforms the image into subtle and complex textured shadows'[16]

Prismatic – Roscolab

➤ **ColorWaves** create vibrant coloured textures and shapes.
Five glass textures:
Sparkelite, Waves, Ripple, Strands, Mosaic
Each coated in one of five brilliant dichroic colours:
Red, Amber, Magenta, Cyan, Indigo[17]

Rain glass – Roscolab

[16] Rosco Product Catalogue
[17] Rosco Product Catalogue

Ripple ColorWave – Roscolab

Using Dichroic Break-ups & Glass gobos

- **Available in** size-B gobos for use in Ellipsoidal lanterns
- **Colorizers** can be used with lanterns lamped to a max of **1000 watts**
- **Prismatics, Image Glass & ColorWaves** can be used with Axial lanterns having a max of **600 watts** or for a short term with **750 watt** lamps
- **Glass gobos** need to be mounted in the special glass gobo pattern holders or in a Universal Iris Slot Holder that is inserted into the gate of the lantern
- **Steel gobos** can be double mounted with the glass gobos
- **Set the lantern to produce a 'flat field'** with equal light distribution across the beam
- **Follow the strict guidelines** for the use and handling of glass gobos, particularly with respect to lamp adjustment of the lantern to be used; careful attention should be paid the manufacturer's instructions

> **》 Fast Forward** on the DVD to **9.1 Using gobos**

Examples of projections

The dichroic break-ups, glass and metal gobos are Rosco products.

➤ **Dapple Woodland effect**
Green and Yellow Featherlight Colorizer doubled with a Medium Leaf break-up steel gobo

➤ **Stained Glass Window**
Kaleidoscope Prismatic doubled with Church Window steel gobo

➤ **Firework effects**
Kaleidoscope Prismatic doubled with Fireworks steel gobo, same prismatic; if you change the gobo, you get a different effect

➤ **Flames**
Ripple/Amber ColorWaves double with a Flames steel gobo

➤ **Water Reflection**
Ripples Image Glass double with Reflected Water steel gobo

Did you know that –

- Dichroic glass was first used by the Romans and it can be dated back to the 4th century AD as can be seen in the Lycurus cup, a Roman glass beaker in the British Museum
- NASA, the US National Aeronautics and Space Administration, developed and used dichroic filters

9 GOBOS

Extras!

EXTRA TIPS

■ Make sure that the steel gobo is mounted in the front of the universal iris slot holder on the lens side of the lantern when combined with a Prismatic or Colorizer gobo so that the image can be accurately focused

■ See the Rosco Product Catalogue for some excellent photographs showing the use of dichroic break-ups and glass gobos

■ There are some good video clips on the Apollo Design Technology website showing how to mount gobos and insert them in the lanterns

Extra resources – go to

www.rosco.com; sales@rosco-europe.com – Rosco Product catalogue, examples of using Colorizers, Prismatics, Image Glass & ColorWaves

sales@rosco-europe.com; www.rosco.com – DHA Rosco Gobo Catalogue

www.apollodesign.net /products/dichroics – Apollo Design Technology

www.apollodesign.net – The Apollo Gobo Tool Kit –

'The purpose of the Apollo Gobo Tool Kit is to train and educate. It introduces the basics of using gobos to create visual effects in general stage lighting applications.' Kit includes: Apollo SuperHolder, Creative Effects Guide, Instructional DVD, Resource DVD, (24) B-Round Metal Standards, B-Round B&W Glass Standard

Points for action

Quickies!

■ Look at the different types of Colorizers, Prismatics, Image Glass & ColorWaves and examples of their use either on the Rosco website or in the Rosco Product Guide

■ Obtain a copy of the Rosco Product Guide

Extras!

9 GOBOS

10 Motion effects

A quick start – Animation, rotating gobos & projections

Introducing the use of animation discs, rotating gobos and projections

More info – Animation & rotator effects

Comparing the range of effects that are available on animation discs and gobo rotators

Extras! – Using the three types of rotators to create effects

Creating gobo effects and looking at three different types of rotators and the manufacturers' variations

A quick start – Animation, rotating gobos & projections

Moving effects can be used to create a theatrical illusion and add an extra dimension to a scene. Effects can be achieved by breaking up the beam of light projected from a lantern with a rotating disc or by rotating a gobo image. Realistic moving images like clouds, rain and snow can also be projected by an optical projector.

Animation discs

Animation discs are simple to use and they provide a low-cost method of producing moving lighting effects. An etched metal disc powered by an electric motor unit is mounted in the colour frame holder of the lantern. The slow-turning disc breaks up the beam of light, creating an illusion of movement. The motor unit has an onboard direction and variable speed controls allowing it to be powered direct from an independent power supply or from a dimmer circuit to provide a remote speed control.

➤ **Moving shadow effects**
Flickering effect similar to the reflected light from a fire or water can be created with a Coarse Radial or Tangential animation disc mounted in front of a PC, Fresnel or Parcan. These lanterns provide a wide beam of light but they project

a very basic direct image which needs to be softened by adding a light frost with the colour filter in the colour frame slot.

➤ Adding movement to projected images

Animation disc – Roscolab

Animation discs can add movement to static gobo images projected by Profiles and Ellipsoidal lanterns. They can convert a projected flames gobo into a burning fire, create moving clouds, falling snow, rain and rippling water. The gobo can be independently focused as the animation disc rotates in front of the lantern and its optical system. The effect can be enhanced by adding split colours in the rear of the colour frame runners or by attaching colours to the rotating disc. 'The key to the system is to choose the right gobo for the base effect.'[18]

➤ Direction of movement

The direction of the movement can be changed by adjusting the position of the motor in the front of the lens tube:

- Side to side – mount the motor position above the lens tube
- Up and down – mount the motor position at the side of the lens tube

➤ Focus and speed

For maximum effect, the gobo should be focused between hard and soft focus:

- Hard focus produces minimal movement and the animation hardly works
- Soft focus produces maximum movement but the gobo pattern is lost
- The animated movement is dependent on the speed of the disc and the type of gobo selected

Gobo rotators

Motion effects can be created by rotating a single or double gobo in the path of the light from a Profile lantern. A whole range of abstract and dramatic effects can be achieved depending upon the choice of gobos, speed, direction of the rotation and the use of other static, textured or coloured gobos in the gobo slot. Add some smoke and colour and some vibrant moving effects can be created.

Rotator drive units

The gobo is mounted in a motorised drive unit that accurately rotates on the central axis of a profile lantern. The unit is inserted into the iris slot in the gate of the lantern, allowing the addition of a standard static gobo holder to be accommodated. A rotator

---

[18] Guide to Motion Effects Rosco

unit can take either one or two gobos that can be independently driven in opposite directions at selected speeds.

➤ **Power and control**
Stand-alone rotators are powered directly from an external mains socket having on-board speed and direction controls.

Vortex rotator – Roscolab

Two sizes of gobo rotator units

➤ **Standard 'B'-size gobo rotator units:**
- **Gobos** – suitable for use with metal or glass gobos or any combination of Colorizer, Prismatics, Image Glass and Colour Waves
- **Lanterns** – 'B'-size gobo rotators will fit ETC Source Four, Strand SL, Altman Shakespeare, Philips Selecon SPX & Pacific; CCT Silhouette, Project & Freedom

➤ **'M'-size gobo single rotator unit** – Apollo 'Smart Move Jr'
- **Gobos** – only suitable for use with metal or glass gobos
- **Lanterns** – 'M'-size gobo rotators will fit ETC Source Four Junior, Philips Selecon Acclaim

Projected effects

Moving visual effects can be produced using an optical effects disc with an effects projector:

- The effects projector uses a powerful lamp 2000W/2500W and a high-quality optical system to provide an exceptional light output. Plates can be used to mask off areas of the projection and beam diverters to project the image through 90 degrees on to the stage[19]
- The optical effects disc unit consists of a rotating etched glass disc and motor contained in a metal casing with an objective lens mounted on the front
- The disc unit is fixed in front of the projector housing so that the effects disc rotates through the focus point of the lantern's optical system. The speed and direction can be controlled by the onboard controls or by DMX

Effects projector – Stage Electrics

[19] The Hire Store – Stage Electrics

- The following effects can be created: fleecy cloud, storm cloud, flame, rain, running water, snow and vapour
- NB the optical effects disc must be rotating when the lamp is switched on to prevent damage to the disc

Moving clouds – Stage Electrics

QUICK TIPS

- Experiment with the focus of the lantern to achieve the best effect
- A Profile or Ellipsoidal lantern needs to be focused mid-point between hard and soft to give the full effect of the animated movement
- Effects projectors and optical effects discs can be hired in for productions
- Effects projectors are far more difficult to set up to create a realistic image
- If you are hiring in or renting an animation disc for a production, remember to allow enough time to set them up and to experiment with them to achieve the best results

Quick resources – go to

Rosco Guide to Motion Effects – Effects ideas

GLOBAL JARGON

- **Hiring equipment** (UK) – Renting equipment (NA). Technicians are hired, equipment is rented from a rental company

Points for action

Quickies!

- Obtain a copy of 'Rosco Guide to Motion Effects' or view online

A quick start

10 MOTION EFFECTS

More info – Animation & rotator effects

Adding a small amount of movement to a projected pattern or image can add to the effect. In real life, clouds slowly move and change shape, branches and patterns cast by the leaves sway backwards and forwards in the breeze.

Animation discs

Many varied effects can be produced from the range of animation discs.

➤ **Choice of gobo**
The gobo is the basis of the projected image. A series of different effects can be created using the same animation wheel but changing the gobo.
  The following effects can be produced using a Spiral break-up disc:

- Blowing flames – Rosco175 Flames 1 steel gobo
- Rosco 176 Flames 2 steel gobo will change the style of the fire
- Driving rain – Rosco 882 Rain steel gobo

Spiral animation disc – Roscolab

Flames 1 gobo – Roscolab

Flames 2 gobo – Roscolab

➤ **Disc patterns & effects**[20]
There are 11 animation break-up discs:

- **Tangential break-up**
  Produces a subtle rippling motion particularly when the movement is parallel to the lines projected by the gobo. Suitable for rising flames, flowing water and effects where a single direction of movement is required
- **Radial break-up**
  Provides a strong regular movement suitable for flickering flames, water ripple, reflected water and shimmer for heat haze or mirage effects
- **Spiral break-up**
  Similar to radial break-up, but it has some movement at right angles to the main motion, as seen in wind-blown rain, snow or flames. Worth experimenting with the angle of the gobo image to the orientation of the disc

[20] Moving Effects catalogue DHA Lighting

10 MOTION EFFECTS

More info

- **Linear break-up**
  Rhythmic movement can be used with gobos to simulate a breeze through the branches of a tree or the undulation of sea waves
- **Triangular break-up**
  Provides a more pronounced rapid rhythmic effect linear break-up, suitable for use with split colour as psychedelic or rough-sea effect
- **Cloud break-up**
  Softer directional movement at slow or very slow speeds, used to create moving cloud effect with gobos or soft flowing stream effects
- **Elliptical break-up**
  Produces bi-directional movement similar to the spiral break-up but with constantly changing direction of movement, good for use for snow or similar effects where 'flurries' of movement would be expected
- **Dot break-up**
  Causes motion while maintaining a more focused projection of the gobo image, suitable for falling leaves or rising bubbles
- **Flicker break-up**
  At high speed creates a passing train, simple strobe and the old silent-movie-style animation effects
- **Coarse radial**
  Similar effects as the radial break-up, particularly effective for animating light from non-focusing lanterns, Parcans, Fresnels and PCs
- **Coarse tangential**
  Creates flickering flame effects when used with non-focusing lanterns, Fresnels, PCs and Parcans

>> **Fast Forward** on the DVD to **10.1 Moving effects & fixtures**

Did you know that-

- DHA Lighting specialised in manufacturing gobos and optical effects and was known for its animation units and rotators
- DHA was originally founded by the famous award-winning lighting designer David Hersey, known for his creative use of gobos, whose productions include *Evita, Cats, Les Misérables*
- DHA amalgamated with Rosco, combining their libraries of gobos and the manufacture of optical effects

'Circular motion forms the basis of all manner of effects found in productions today. Gobo rotators come into their own when creating visually interesting textures and break-ups. A raging whirlpool, moving wheels, a time tunnel or the ticking clock hands are perhaps some of the more obvious uses.'[21]

Three types of gobo rotators

➤ **Single or dual basic rotator units:**
- Single motor drive with both gobos rotating at the same speed in opposite directions with the option of selecting either the front or rear gobo to go clockwise
- Stand-alone 'Plug and play' being powered directly from mains socket having built-in manual direction and adjustable speed controls

➤ **Double rotator units:**
- Two motors providing independent drive allowing each gobo to turn in the same or opposite direction at different speeds
- Power supply from DC dedicated remote control unit with a varispeed control for forward and reverse for each motor
- External power supply from power supply unit (PSU) supplying colour scrollers and other lantern accessories. The speed and direction of the motion controlled by DMX from lighting desk

➤ **Indexing rotator unit:**
- Single or double indexing providing a fixed-speed control that can be stopped and started, suitable for the control of the hands of a clock
- External power supply from PSU, speed and direction controlled by DMX from lighting desk

Gobo rotator effects[22]

There are four variations of moving gobos that can be used to create a range of different effects:

➤ **Rotating one pattern** – what you see is what you get
One rotating gobo: The image appears the same as projected in a standard gobo holder. By adding motion, a moving pattern can be created rotating fast or slow with the image in soft or hard focus. Can be used with break-ups in down or back lighting.

[21] Rosco Guide to Motion Effects
[22] Based on product information GAM website

10 MOTION EFFECTS   More info

UNIVER... ...CHESTER LIBRARY

➤ Add a still pattern – to create animation

One fixed & one rotating gobo: A fixed pattern can be added to the gate of the lantern with a rotating pattern to animate the still image. This can effectively be used to make leaves rustle, flames dance and stars twinkle.

➤ Twin patterns spinning – shimmer and sparkle

Two rotating gobos in opposite directions: Two patterns of the same design rotating in opposite directions create a shimmering or sparkling quality. Rotating at high speeds produces a dazzling effect and slow movement creates a mesmerising, dream-like effect.

➤ Mixed doubles – shapes appear and disappear

One fixed and two rotating gobos: Two different patterns rotating in opposite directions will create a unique moving pattern of changing shapes with areas of light appearing and disappearing. It is important to choose compatible patterns so that one doesn't block out too much light and cancel out the other. The lens of the lantern can be adjusted to focus on one or other of the gobos or in the centre.

➤ Add some colour – for effect

Colour can be added by using coloured gobos or a split colour filter in the frame in the lantern colour runners.

MORE TIPS

- ■ It is important to get the rotator the right way round so that it doesn't restrict or bend the lantern shutters
- ■ Mount the rotator with the motor facing the front of the lantern and the flat mounting plate towards the shutters
- ■ Mount steel gobos so that they are viewed the right way round when viewed from the flat mounting plate side of the rotator and the rear of the lantern

---

More resources – go to

Rosco 'Guide to Motion Effects' – www.rosco.com/uk

More info

10 MOTION EFFECTS

Extras! – Using the three types of rotators to create effects

Rotating gobos can also be used to create the subtle change of the colour of light that naturally occurs, the effect of sunset on the clouds, sunlight reflected on water or firelight reflected in the smoke of a fire.

> **>>** **Fast Forward** on the DVD to **10.1 Moving effects & fixtures**

Examples of rotating gobo effects[23]

➤ **Cloud effect**
The changing colours of the sky reflect the season, weather and time of day. The coloured light on a cyclorama or skycloth can be mixed to replicate these effects but tends to lack the texture and subtlety of a real sky. We can change this and add some depth and reality in the following ways:

Cloud effect – GMSL

- **Project a steel cloud gobo** on to the sky – Alto Stratus Rosco 777278. The focus will need to be slightly softened to blend the image
- **Add some colour** to the cloud by inserting a warm colorizer gobo – Warm Free Flow Colorizer Rosco 6102. This provides a broken colour effect, increasing the three-dimensional appearance as the clouds seem to be catching the setting sun on a late-afternoon sky. The combination of the two gobos will change as the focus is adjusted
- **Slowly rotate the colorizer gobo** to add a gentle movement to the layered look to the cloud
- **Different cloud gobos** and colorizers will produce a wide range of effects
- **Crossfading** from one gobo cloud pattern to another can provide a small degree of change and movement

➤ **Fire smoke effect**
The light from a blazing fire is reflected in the rising smoke.

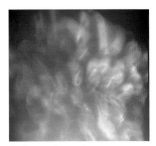

- **Mount a Sphere break-up** steel gobo and an Amber Ripple ColorWave in a double rotator – Rosco 87235 and 33102
- **Rotate the two gobos** in opposite directions to create the effect of firelight reflected in rising plumes of smoke
- **The effect can be changed** by speeding up or slowing down the speed of rotation

Coloured smoke – GMSL

[23] 'Designing with Gobos' Rosco video

Extras!

10 MOTION EFFECTS

➤ **Reflection of sunlight on water**

Crazed patterns of light are created by the reflection of sun on moving water.

■ **Mount a Reflected Water** steel gobo and a Ripples Image Glass in a double rotator – Rosco 79664 and 33619

■ **Slowly rotate** the two gobos in opposite directions to create the patterns of light reflected on moving water

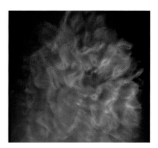

Water reflection – GMSL

Four makes of rotators

Make/ motor	Single Gobo	Dual Gobo	Double Gobo	Double Gobo	Indexing
Apollo	Smart Move Jr (M)	Smart Move		Smart Move (DMX)	
Chroma-Q	Junior FX (B)		Twin FX	Twin FX (DMX)	
GAM		Twin Spin Jr (M) Twin Spin		Dual Motor Twin Spin	
Rosco	Single Rotator	Vortex	Double Rotator	Double Rotator	Indexing Rotator
Control	**Stand alone**	**Stand alone**	**Remote controller**	**DMX**	**DMX**

Gobo controllers

➤ **Built-in controls**

■ **Stand-alone rotators** have direction switches and speed controls

■ **Apollo** – Smart Move rotator has a built-in preprogrammed microprocessor providing an 'array of individual gobo movements ideal for a broad range of applications without the need of a control board'[24]

■ **Chroma-Q** – Junior & Twin FX rotators 'features adjustable dynamic effects including tick-tock, pendulum, shimmer, accelerate, decelerate, fire, water, rotate-pause and shake-pause'[25]

[24] Apollo Design inc – product information website
[25] Chroma-Q – product information website

> **Dimmer control**

Stand-alone rotators with a built-in transformer and power lead can be connected to an electronic dimmer which is capable of handling an inductive load. The rotation speed can be directly controlled from the lighting desk.

- This can only be done on some models: **GAM Twin Spin Jr, Twin Spin & Rosco Vortex**
- **You should check with the dimmer manufacturer before connecting as failure to use a compatible dimmer can result in overheating and/or damage to both the rotator unit and the dimmer**

Extra resources – go to

www.rosco.com.uk – 'Designing with Gobos' – Rosco video
www.rosco.com/uk/lightingequipment/vortex – Rosco video clip
www.apollodesign.net – Apollo video clips detailed instruction over use
www.gamonline.com/catalog/twinspin/index – GAM video clip 4 min plus Virtual Twin Spin
www.chroma-q.com/products – Chroma-Q

Points for action

Quickies!

- View the video clips on the websites

Takes longer

- View 'Designing with Gobos' if available

11 Projected images

A quick start – Projecting plastic slides

Looking at iPro image projection system and slide library

More info – Projecting plastic gobos

Making and using plastic gobo slides with Ellipsoidal lanterns

Extras! – Projecting digital images

Projecting photographic-quality still and moving images

A quick start – Projecting plastic slides

It is possible to project photographic-quality images with the new breed of cool beam lanterns Selecon SPX & Pacific, ETC Source Four, Altman Shakespeare and the Strand SL.

iPro Image Projector

iPro is a gobo slide projection system made by Rosco providing theatrical projection at a budget price. The plastic slide is mounted in the unit protected by an infrared reflecting filter that is inserted in the gate of the lantern. On the top of the unit is a fan box which drives cooling air across the front and back of the plastic slide to reduce the temperature in the gate of the lantern and slow the heat degradation of the slide.

iPro – Roscolab

iPro slides

- There is a library of iPro images available from Rosco on a CD or they can be viewed online
- Professionally made slides cost approximately £30 each
- Custom iPro slides can be made from Adobe Photoshop files
- iPro Slide Film Kits and Printing Packs consisting of iPro slide film and 'One-Time' slide mounts are available to make up your own slides
- The lantern and iPro image projection unit can be hired in for a production

iPro slide – Roscolab

QUICK TIPS

- When printing iPro slides, adjust your printer settings to maximum resolution and select an absorbent paper type such as Double Sided Water Colour Paper to get the best results

Quick resources – go to

www.rosco.com/imagepro/library/ – view the iPro library
www.rosco.com/gobocatalog/imagepro/library/techsupport – detailed advice on printing iPro slides

Points for action

Quickies!

- View the iPro image library online
- Cost out the hire charge for an iPro Projection Unit and a suitable lantern from your local hire company

More info – Projecting plastic gobos

Ellipsoidal lanterns can be used to project photographic images by inserting a plastic gobo in the gate of the lantern.

Plastic gobo projection

The unique heat management system of a 600W Selecon Pacific[26] has a gate temperature that allows the projection of colour images printed on to overhead transparency acetate film mounted in a UV heat-reducing filter. The slides have a limited life but this can be extended by the use of a cooling system like ImagePro.

 Fast Forward on the DVD to **11.1 Gobo slide projection**

Making the slides
- Slides can be created on the computer and printed direct on to OHP inkjet transparency material
- The quality can be increased by printing on to iPro slide film that can be obtained from Rosco or by using a laser printer
- Laser printed slides should be mounted with the printed surface towards the front of the pattern holder to prevent them from melting

Making acetate slides – Philips Selecon

- Laser printed images therefore need to be 'flipped over' from left to right on the computer prior to printing so that they will be projected the right way round
- This is a low-cost system where instant images can be created and tried out as part of the drama development process
- The slides have a very limited life and can easily burn out so it is worth printing duplicate copies of images

Setting up the lantern
- Acetate slides can only be used in a 600W Pacific lantern
- It is necessary to adjust the field setting of the lamp to prevent the slide from burning up

[26] See Chapter 2 'Lanterns – performance luminaires – Extras! – Base down Ellipsoidal Profile'

11 PROJECTED INFORMATION

More info

11 PROJECTED IMAGES   **More info**

- The lamp should be lowered in the lamp module to provide a flat field setting with the light equally spread across the beam with a slight shadow in the centre
- A 90° lens can be fitted to a Pacific which will provide a wide beam spread

Using the slides

- The acetate slides should be mounted in a Selecon heat-reducing slide holder
- Mount the slide upside down in between the UV heat-reducing filter and the glass cover
- The viewing side of the slide should be facing the thick UV filter in the slide holder
- Insert the slide holder in the iris slot in the gate with the UV filter facing the lamp source and the glass cover facing the front of the lantern

Selecon slide holder – GMSL

MORE TIPS

- An acetate slide can melt in front of your eyes if the lantern isn't correctly set up or a laser print is mounted the wrong way round so be sure to make some duplicate copies

More resources – go to

www.seleconlight.com/plasticimages – Information on making and using plastic slides

Points for action

Quickies!

- Investigate making plastic images on the Selecon website

Extras! – Projecting digital images

Digital projection can be used to project high-quality still or moving images that can be integrated as a part of a production.

Digital projection

During the past few years, the technology has improved with the introduction of fine pixel LED screens that can show detail with a precise, bright, quality image. Also the constant development in projector design, with units now being able to produce over 10,000 lumens of light output, has improved image quality. This has allowed designers to use both still and live images in productions. By using audio visual (AV) to create the set, it allows scene changes to happen instantly, without the need of full-size sets that can be expensive to construct and take up huge amount of wing space.

Using digital images

There are a variety of ways that computer-generated or video images can be used to provide virtual reality backdrops, abstracted moving video images, projected images, captions for documentary drama, integrated moving images or effects projected on to the stage. The possibilities are endless but the problem is of creating a seamless integration of the images and effects as a part of the production so that they are developed naturally from the text and drama or a part of choreographed dance or movement.

Projected imagery needs to be a part of the overall design concept and not a bolt-on technical spectacle to add a 'wow' factor to the production. Theatre has different requirements to film or television and therefore video material needs to be specially prepared with this in mind to enhance and blend with the requirements of the production, unless documentary-type material is required.

'There is only one right way to design a play by respecting the text, and not using it as a peg on which to advertise your skills, whatever they may be, nor to work out your psychological hang-ups with some fashionable gimmick.' Jocelyn Herbert, theatre designer[27]

Using digital projection

There are three areas that need to be considered:

➤ **Where is the image to be projected?**
- An area of the set specifically designed to take the projection
- An existing vertical surface rear wall painted white or backcloth
- A commercial projection screen either suspended or incorporated into the set

[27] Designers on Colour – Roscolab Guide to Colour Filters

- The stage floor where this is in view of the audience
- On to moving or static bodies, textured or coloured walls, or other objects either large or small

➤ Reflectivity of the projection surface

Commercial screen material will have a higher level of reflection than a white painted surface and therefore produce a brighter image. The reflectivity on the surface of a back projection screen can be reduced depending upon the type of materials being used. Grey screens provide a wider viewing angle than black.

➤ Projector

The light output of the projector which is measured in lumens affects the brightness of projected image:

- 3000/3500 lumens projector may be suitable for a small to medium space depending upon the amount of ambient/reflected light falling on the screen
- 6500 lumens projector provides a higher light output
- The size of the image and the distance of the projector from the screen will affect the brightness of the image
- As a guide, the standard lens requires the projector to be positioned twice as far from the screen as the width of the projected image
- Interchangeable long throw or wide-angled lenses are available for some projectors

➤ Front projection

There are a number of things to consider when positioning the projector in front of the actors:

- When projecting on to large surfaces, the image may spill on to the actors' faces and bodies and can create quite a surrealistic effect depending upon the image. This can enhance or detract from the action depending upon the requirements of the production
- Projection overspill on to the actors can be balanced out by increasing the front lighting but there is a danger of it washing out the projection
- Projecting above head level providing there is sufficient height will remove the overspill on to the actors. However, the set may need to be extended to fill in the lower vertical area across the stage
- Increasing the angle of projection by mounting the projector overhead on a front lighting bar allows the image to be projected starting at floor level. The overspill on to the actors will now only occur at the rear of the stage creating an up stage 'no go' area and lost acting space
- A 'key stone' effect occurs when projecting on to a screen from an angle and this can be adjusted via the menu function of the projector. Key stone adjustment is a bit like using the shutters on a Profile spot except the shape of the projected image is adjusted rather than the beam being shaped. Zoom facilities are also available allowing the size of the image to be adjusted to

fit the screen. Computer images can be reshaped and masked to prevent overspill when projecting on to non-standard-format-sized screens

➤ Rear projection

Positioning the projector behind the actors to project on to a rear projection screen removes the problem of actors walking through the projected image but there are other considerations:

- The position of the projector and screen will reduce the acting space so this is only possible on a deep stage
- A projector with a wide-angle lens will reduce the depth required for projection
- A special screen made up of back projection material will be required; this could be made as a part of the set or hired depending upon the size required
- The audience views the image from the reverse side but it is possible to reverse this on some projectors and it can also be done on the computer

➤ Controlling the images

- Microsoft PowerPoint can be used as a basic program to produce slide sequences of pictures, text, graphics, video animation and audio
- Other more powerful programs are readily available to produce more sophisticated sequences including video clips, e.g. Modul8, Isadora, Catalyst or Hippotizer
- Media servers provide the facility to play back HD video and sound that can be cued direct from a lighting control desk by using DMX signals via a hardware interface connected to the computer
- Rosco Keystroke provides an interface for video playback programs, PowerPoint, Keynote, Quicktime or Windows Media Player and sound playback programs including ProTools, iTunes, Garageband and SFX

Examples of digital projection

➤ *War Horse* – National Theatre (UK)
Designer Rae Smith, Video designers Leo Warner & Mark Grimmer (Fifty-Nine Productions Ltd)

Tech spec:

Projectors:	2 x PTD10,000, mounted on front of circle rail left and right, edge-blended in the centre
Servers:	1 x main plus 1 x backup Catalyst Media Servers on Mac Pro platforms
Control:	1 x main and 1 x backup High End Hog III PC with control wing, linked via MIDI
Switching:	Remote Kramer DVI switchers

'Rae Smith's designs and superb drawings, the latter projected on to the cyclorama, whisk us vividly from idyllic Devon to the horror of the trenches.' The Telegraph

11 PROJECTED IMAGES   Extras!

11 PROJECTED IMAGES   **Extras!**

War Horse – *National Theatre production – Lighting Design Paule Constable,*
Photographer Simon Annand

The set has an irregular screen resembling a torn strip of paper that is positioned above the action across the full width of the stage. It is used to establish the location and show the passage of time moving from the idyllic rural Devon landscape to the horrors of no man's land of France 1914–18. Note the use of high angles of warm lighting creating the effect of long sunny days associated with Devon.

The scene on the opposite page shows the projected image above of the men rising from the trenches and crossing the barbed wire into no man's land. This is visually linked to the silhouette of the soldiers advancing on-stage lit by intense low-level back lighting from under the screen. Also see Chapter 15 'Other angles of lighting – More info – The effects of layered lighting'.

'The visual language of the screen was carefully developed alongside the stage action during several weeks of rehearsals by Leo Warner and Mark Grimmer the video designers. It combines the use of the designer Rae Smith's black and white drawings of Devon with the stark abstract images created by the war artists of the period, moving images of horses and special effects of water, blood, smoke and explosions. The archival research and bespoke filming was carried out by the video designers who manipulated all the images 'creating textures on screen moving from sepia and faded out paper, through various stages of stained and battered surfaces to photography in the penultimate scene' providing a seamless integration with the lighting and action on stage'. Julie Harper[28]

[28] Based on an article 'War Horse' by Julie Harper, January 2008 in *Lighting & Sound International* (www.lsionline.co.uk)

War Horse – *National Theatre production – Lighting Design Paule Constable, Photographer Simon Annand*

➤ *Alice in Wonderland* – Cirencester College production, Sundial Theatre Designer Andy Webb, Video designs Alex Sharp

Tech spec:

Projector: 1 x 5200 lumen projector with a wide-angle short throw lens located 3.5m behind a 6m x 4m projection screen set towards the rear of the stage

Control: images were run direct from a laptop using video playback software

'Alice is a complicated production as the audience needs to feel that they are travelling through a strange enchanted world from one location to another. Simplicity of the settings was important so as not to interrupt the flow. Using a back projection screen as visual backdrop seemed a logical choice to create a magical look. We used a mixture of still and live images most of which were sourced from the internet.' Andy Webb

11 PROJECTED IMAGES Extras!

Projected scenes as viewed clockwise from top left:

- **Alice in the forest:** The simple addition of a few logs creates the feeling of a magical glade in a forest with the accent lighting catching Alice at the same angle and direction as the natural direction of the light on the projected image
- **The chess board:** The projected perspective image of the squares of the board spreads on to the stage with Source Four Profiles downlighting, shuttered down to create the angular white squares for the game to be played out on-stage

Alice in Wonderland – *Sundial Theatre – Lighting Design Andy Webb, Photographer Nik Sheppard*

- **The sitting room:** The details of the interior are all there to providing a realistic location. All that is needed is to add a rug, table and two chairs and the stage is set
- **The Jabberwocky:** The sinister eyes of the creature visually merge with the shapes of the part-lit bodies. The red uplighting through the grille in the floor creates the feeling of the monster. Alice isolated in front is lit by two narrow focused follow spots acutely angled in from either side with the overshoot of the beam just catching the bodies behind. Add some smoke and evil music and you have created a dramatic setting

11 PROJECTED IMAGES   Extras!

Did you know that –

- Joan Littlewood's Theatre Workshops legendary production of *Oh What a Lovely War* in the late 1950s used projected images to show the horrors of the First World War as part of a documentary-style drama
- Projection in the 1950s used 3½-inch glass slides projected by optical effects projectors
- Kodak automatic Carousel projectors using 35mm slides were also available in the late 1950s, with automatic crossfade between projectors being introduced by the late 1960s

EXTRA TIPS

- 'Front White' screens are used for front projection
- 'Twin White' screens can be used for front or rear projection with no apparent difference in picture brightness
- 'Grey' screens are used for back projection. They provide a neutral-coloured background and have a wider viewing angle
- 'Black' screens are used when there is high ambient light, providing fine detailed resolution when back lit with a strong image[30]
- 'Black' screens have the narrowest viewing angle, that is the reduction in the quality of the image when viewed from the side

Extra resources – go to

www.mesmer.co.uk – 'Mesmer are a collaboration of video and projection designers, with over 20 years experience of integrating video media into performance'[31]

www.fiftynineproductions.co.uk – '59 Productions specialises in design for live performance, often utilising the latest technologies to bring a space to life.'[32] Fifty-Nine Productions were the video designers for the National Theatre's production of *War Horse* and the Cameron Mackintosh national tour of *Les Misérables*

www.rosco.com/uk/screens/roscoscreen.asp – screens

www.rosco.com/uk/software/keystroke.asp – playback interfaces

[30] Rosco Product Catalgoue
[31] Mesmer website
[32] Fifty-Nine Productions Ltd website

Points for action

Quickies!

■ Visit the Mesmer and 59 Productions websites and look at examples of their work for theatre productions

12 Haze, smoke & fog

A quick start – Haze, smoke & fog

Looking at three different types of effects and the machines that produce them

More info – Fluids, maintenance & low-lying fog

Looking at the range of smoke/fog fluids available, maintenance of the machines and different ways of producing low-lying fog

Extras! – Smoke & fog machines

Understanding how the machines work, what to look for in a good machine and the health & safety issues

A quick start – Haze, smoke & fog

Haze smoke and fog are frequently used on-stage and there must be few musicals or pop concerts that do not use one of these effects. 'Smoke machine' is a generic term for what is now a sophisticated range of Mini Mist, Hazemakers, Foggers, Coldflow Fog, Peasouper and even Glacitors!

> **»** **Fast Forward** on the DVD to **12.1 Special effects**

Three types of effects

- **Haze** hangs in the air like a light mist
- **Smoke** rises in the air (it can be confusing as some manufacturers call smoke fog!!)[33]
- **Heavy fog** is dense and hangs at a low level

➤ **Haze machines** – Hazer, Mini Mist, Microfog & StageHazer
Hazers are used to produce a continuous thin mist created by projecting minute water particles into the air.

[33] David Whitehead

- This should be a subtle effect unnoticed by the audience adding an atmospheric haze to the stage
- It has the effect of picking up and softening the airborne beams of projected light and is used by many lighting designers especially when moving scanners or moving heads are being used to project effects
- There are a number of different types and sizes of machines from handheld battery hazers to ones that will fill the size of a stadium

➤ **Smoke/fog machines** – Smoke, Fog & Foggers

Smoke machines produce a white non-toxic smoke. The density depends upon the fluid used from a light to a dense cloud of smoke creating an atmosphere or special effect.

- A dispersal fan will break up the high density at source and distribute the effect around the stage
- Coloured smoke/fog is not available but this can be added by the use of coloured light
- Smoke/fog projected on to the floor will quickly start to rise and disperse

Smoke in the air – GMSL

➤ **Heavy fog/low smoke** – ICE machines

Low-lying dense fog that stays close to the stage can be created by chilling the fog/smoke. There are a number of machines available using different systems for producing and cooling the fog. The ICE machine is the most economical for use on a small to medium stage. It consists of:

- A large-capacity onboard fog machine
- An ice chamber capable of taking 10kg of ice cubes that can be stored for up to eight hours

Heavy fog – GMSL

- The fog is cooled by passing it through the ice chamber providing up to one hour of continuous operating[34]

[34] www.antari.com/products/ice

Controlling the effects

The controls on the machines can vary widely from a basic on/off switch to volume and timer controls that can be mounted onboard, remote or DMX control from the lighting desk.

➤ **Volume control** provides a variation of output to create a variety of effects from dense fog to thin wisps of smoke. The output is controlled by the pump speed and its sensitivity is dependent upon the type and quality of the pump.

➤ **Timers, remote or DMX** control provide a hands-free operation controlling the 'on time', the running time the machine is making smoke, and the 'off time' between the bursts of smoke.

Did you know that –

■ Smoke is most likely one of the oldest effects as it was used in outdoor theatres of the Greeks and Romans. Tar-based substances were burnt to create the gates of hell on the medieval pageants and also in the Elizabethan theatres for battle scenes in Shakespeare's plays

■ Slow smoke used to be produced by burning slow smoke powder on a heated tray; fast smoke was produced as a pyrotechnic effect

■ Originally, the only way to produce smoke effects on-stage was by using a smoke gun that vaporised vegetable oil that was highly toxic and affected the actors' throats

■ The generic term 'smoke' stems from its origins and it is still used as a general term to describe haze, smoke and fog

QUICK TIPS

■ Smoke machines are made for DJs, clubs, small and large theatres, stadiums, theme parks, film & TV studios, so it is worth checking out the manufacturer's specification to match the size of your venue

■ It is good practice to use the manufacturer's compatible fluid for the machine that you are using

12 HAZE, SMOKE & FOG — **A quick start**

Quick resources – go to

www.rosco.com/uk/fog
www.lemaitre.co.uk
www.smoke-factory.de/eng
www.theatrefx.com
www.antari.com – Antari Fog machines

Points for action

Quickies!

■ View the equipment available on the manufacturers' websites

More info – Fluids, maintenance & low-lying fog

It is important to select the right type of fluid to produce the required effect and to regularly maintain the machine. There are also a number of different ways of producing low-lying fog.

Haze, Smoke & Fog fluids[35] [36]

There are a number of different types of fluids available from manufacturers, each having their own specific characteristics from thick clouds of long-lasting fog to effects that disappear very quickly:

- **Haze** – fine air-borne effect (polyethylene glycol & deionised water)
- **Light smoke** – light quick-dispersing smoke
- **Medium smoke** – regular smoke, medium-density slower dispersal
- **High-density smoke** – dense long-lasting air-borne smoke
- **Fog** – medium-dispersing, dense realistic fog without any unpleasant odours
- **Clear fog** – as standard fog fluid without any colorant in the liquid or scent additives
- **Pro stage & studio fog** – lighter and faster dissipating than standard fog, especially useful where the fog must appear and disappear on cue
- **Medium fog** – medium-dispersing low-lying fog
- **Heavy fog** – long-lasting low-lying fog

Maintenance[37]

Regular maintenance of the machine is recommended after use:

- Check the machine's owner's manual for the correct method of cleaning
- Drain the machine by removing the siphon hose from the reservoir and run the machine until there is no haze or fog being produced
- After the machine has cooled down, clean the machine with a clean damp cloth or paper towel to prevent the build-up of dirt and dust that might enter and damage the machine. Only use soap and water and not any solvents
- Before and after storing for an extended period of time, flush the machine through for three minutes by placing distilled water in a clean reservoir tank
- A reduced output from the machine indicates that the heat exchange is clogging up and needs to be cleaned

[35] Rosco technotes/fog products
[36] www.martin.com/productgroup/productgroup.asp?pg=jemsmoke
[37] Rosco technotes/fog products

12 HAZE, SMOKE & FOG

More info

Low-lying fog

If you want to create a *Phantom of the Opera*-type low-lying fog on a large stage, then a Coldflow, Freezefog, Heavy Fog or Glaciator machine will be needed. This can be done in two ways, either by using carbon dioxide or chilling the output of the smoke/fog machine.

Low-lying fog – GMSL

➤ **Low smoke/heavy fog** – ICE machine

The ICE machine uses an ice chamber to cool the output from an onboard fog machine producing low-lying heavy fog.

- 10kg of ice cubes will provide one hour of continuous heavy fog
- Ice can be purchased in bags from local supermarkets and it can be easily stored
- This is a cost-effective and safe option for small venues

Ice machine – GMSL

➤ **Dry Ice** – Peasouper

A Peasouper uses the original method of creating low-lying fog by lowering solid (frozen −78.5°) carbon dioxide in a basket into boiling water which produces steam loaded CO_2 gas providing a low-lying fog.

- Dry ice only lasts a short time, 9kg gives only five minutes of fog production[38]
- The rate of flow can be controlled but once started there is no going back!
- Dry ice is an expensive material, not readily available, very difficult to store and is used up quite quickly

➤ **Liquid CO_2 cooling** – Low Smoke, Dry Icer, Cold Flow

These machines are designed to be used with a standard smoke/fog machine. The machine uses a specially formulated fluid and the output is pumped direct into a cooling unit where it is combines with low-pressure liquid CO_2 making dry ice in the chamber producing a very cold long-lasting fog.

- Continuous flow of low-lying fog from 22 minutes to 50 minutes
- The rate of flow of fog can be controlled and it can be switched on and off[39]
- CO_2 cylinders require safe storage and supervision

➤ **Refrigeration systems** – Glaciator

A self-contained unit consisting of a large vaporising chamber and a refrigeration plant to cool the smoke/fog producing a dry ice-style effect.

[38] Le Maitre Pyrotechnics & Special Effects catalogue
[39] Le Maitre Pyrotechnics & Special Effects catalogue

12 HAZE, SMOKE & FOG | **More info**

- Twin reservoirs allowing the type of fog fluid used to be switched and to vary the effect
- Capable of generating a continuous stream of heavy fog, high volume to cover large areas
- Fog can be controlled on demand by an onboard or DMX control
- The systems are relatively expensive to hire
- Material cost is low and there are no associated Health & Safety problems as with dry ice or CO_2[40]

➤ **Health & Safety**
- Suitable protective gloves should be worn when handling dry ice as it can burn the skin
- 'CO_2 carbon dioxide does not support life, so care should be taken to ensure that small animals, actors etc. are not below the level of the dry ice for more than a few seconds'[41]
- Check out the H&S requirements for storing and handling CO_2 cylinders
- When using dry ice machines, care should be taken with the tank of boiling water

Did you know that –

- Original dry ice machines were pretty basic, consisting of a tank with a heating element, lid and a spout with a shutter
- Cracked oil was originally used to create a thin haze of water droplets; mineral and kerosene fluids were also heated to create effects. These materials were at best unpleasant and at worst dangerous to use

MORE TIPS

- Beware of fake fluids being sold on the internet as they can damage your health and machine

More resources – go to
www.martin.com/productgroup/productgroup.asp?pg=jemsmoke
www.rosco.com/uk/fog
www.lemaitre.co.uk

[40] www.martin.com/general/allproducts.asp
[41] www.theatrecrafts.com – Glossary of Theatre Terms

Extras! – Smoke & fog machines

There have been great developments over the years in smoke machine technology, so it is important to know how they work in order to select the best machine to suit the use and the accessories available and to understand health & safety issues.

Smoke/fog technology

➤ **Smoke/fog machines** – how they work
There are a number of manufacturers of fog machines, each having their own range of models creating different effects, but they all use the same relatively simple system.

■ The smoke/fog fluid is composed of water and glycols that is contained in bottles or aerosols fitted into the machine
■ The smoke/fog fluid is pumped from the reservoir into a heat exchange
■ A high temperature is maintained in the heat exchange to vaporise the fluid – that is known as 'flashing'
■ The 'flashed' fluid expands, forcing the vapour out with the assistance of a fan through the nozzle on the machine
■ As the vapour mixes with the outside air, it cools, creating a plume of opaque smoke or fog effect
■ Each manufacturer calibrates the specific temperature of their machines to match the formula of their fluid to provide the optimum 'flashing' process vaporisation
■ If the temperature is too high, the fluid will burn and decompose, changing its chemical composition which can create harmful by-products and make it unhealthy to breathe
■ It can also cause the heat exchange to clog up and reduce the performance of the machine

➤ **Quality of the machines**
The quality of the machine will be affected by the design, manufacture and material used for the heat exchange unit:

■ **The wattage** – the electrical power used by the machine to create the heat to vaporise the fluid and indicates indirectly the capacity of the machine
■ **The metal used in the heat exchange** – different metals are more efficient at retaining heat:
   Aluminium is commonly used on cheaper machines. It heats up quickly and similarly loses heat, resulting in a large burst of smoke for short periods of time. The casting or extrusion process allows only a straight bore for the fluid to vaporise
   Nickel-steel alloy is less commonly used. It takes longer to heat up but retains its heat providing a continuous output. It can be machined to provide

a spiral bore, making the fluid travel a considerably longer distance when vaporising, increasing the power and providing a continuous heavy output

- **The quality of the thermostat** is important as it controls the temperature of the heat exchange:

    Too low and the fluid may still vaporise but it will leave a wet film over the stage and equipment which can be dangerous

    Too hot and the fluid will burn and the chemical composition may change. A good thermostat will disable the machine to prevent it emitting wet fog

- **The quality of the pump** is critical. If it delivers the fluid too quickly and there is too much fluid passing through the heat exchange, the thermostat will cause the machine to shut down. The heat exchange will then need possibly up to a minute to reheat, which can be very inconvenient

➤ Accessories

Smaller machines are designed to be hand held, others can be suspended in the lighting rig and larger machines are designed to be used at stage level.

- **Ducting** can be used to direct the smoke when it is not possible to position the smoke machine at the source of the effect, e.g. under a raised stage. It should be as short as possible and have a minimum diameter of 100mm to prevent the vapour from condensing back into fluid
- **Dispersal fans** controlled by DMX can also be used to break up the directional nature of the fog, move it around the stage, convert smoke to haze or even produce wind effects. The fan should be placed behind the machine so that the air can mix with the fog

➤ Health and Safety

- 'The vapour from the smoke fluid may be irritating to or cause allergic symptoms in some persons with allergenic sensitivity. **Do not fog in the presence of know asthmatics**.'[43]
- In a recent report, an agency of the US Federal Government, the National Institute of Occupational Safety and Health (NIOSH), recommended 'using only fog fluids approved by the manufacturers of the machines'. (HETA 90-355-2449)[44]

EXTRA TIPS

- Check that the specification of the machine matches the requirements of the production so that it won't let you down under performance conditions
- Always go for the highest specification within your budget

[43] Rosco Product Catalogue
[44] Rosco www.rosco/us/technotes/fogproducts

12 HAZE, SMOKE & FOG Extras!

Extra resources – go to

www.rosco.com/uk/technotes – How fog machines work
www.rosco.com/us/technotes – Materials Safety Data sheets

13 Other effects

A quick start – Strobe lighting, lightning, effects & black light

Looking at the effects and use of strobe lighting, creating lightning effects and using Ultra Violet lighting

More info – Gauzes

Using gauzes to create transformation scenes

Extras! – Pyrotechnics, flashes & bangs

Safe use of pyrotechnic effects

A quick start – Strobe lighting, lightning effects & black light

Lightning is a naturally occurring effect that often needs to be reproduced on-stage, whereas strobe lighting and black light can create some very unusual effects.

Strobe lighting

A strobe lighting unit gives a series of intense pulses of light at fast regular intervals. When used in a blackout, it can create the effect of putting the action into slow motion.

- The speed of the flashes of light can be adjusted by an onboard or remote control
- At a very slow speed, it can be used to simulate camera flashes or lightning effects

➤ Health & Safety

- Strobe lighting should be used with great care and only for short periods of time
- Fast flashes can trigger epileptic fits in susceptible people
- You are advised to check your Local Authority regulations before using strobe lighting in public performances
- Notices should be displayed to inform the audience, cast and crew that 'Flashing strobe lighting will be used during the performance'

Lightning effects

The effect can be simulated by quickly switching on/off an intense light source using the channel flash button on the lighting control desk.

- Parcans with wide-angled lamps or floodlights are good sources to use as the lamps will withstand the sudden surge of the electrical current
- Lanterns with tungsten halogen lamps should not be used as the filament can easily break with a sudden electrical surge
- Strobe or photographic flash units will provide a bright flash
- Gobo patterns of forked lightning that can be projected on to the cyc or backcloth
- Moving head fixtures can produce an excellent effect by opening and closing their shutters

Did you know that –

- The sound of thunder has been traditionally created in the theatre by shaking a hanging metal thunder sheet
- Thunder runs were used in Georgian theatres; cannon balls were rolled down wooden troughs running above the auditorium ceiling

Black light – UV effects

Ultra Violet is invisible to the human eye but in the dark it will pick up and reflect off white surfaces, hence it is called black light. It can also be used with UV paints or fabrics causing them to fluoresce in the dark, creating brightly glowing vibrant-coloured effects. A classic use of UV is in pantomime for fish in underwater scenes or dancing skeletons.

UV effect – GMSL

➤ **Health & Safety**
- Never look at the UV light source
- Do not use UV for long periods of time as it can have a burning effect on the skin

QUICK TIPS

- Remember that lightning is followed by thunder – light travels faster than sound

More info – Gauzes

Transformations provide a way to change what the audience sees before their very own eyes! This can be achieved under the cover of dense smoke/fog, the flash of a pyrotechnic or the age-old scenic technique of using a gauze cloth. They were traditionally used to capture the magic of pantomime.

Gauzes

Gauzes are made from a relatively sheer weave material with very small hexagonal or rectangular holes allowing the light to pass through. When it is lit from the front it appears to be solid, but when the action behind it is lit it becomes almost transparent and all is revealed. Coloured light mixes well on gauze, and projected gobos have a soft edged quality.

➤ **Scenic gauze** is a hexagonal light duty net that creates the effect of softening the focus of the scenery behind, diffusing the lighting and adding the feeling of depth to the setting.

➤ **Sharkstooth gauze** has rectangular or ladder pattern holes, it hangs well and is more expensive than scenic gauze. It is dense enough to provide a surface for projection or to have a scene painted on it with dyes and is most effective for transformations, becoming almost opaque when lit from behind.

➤ **Gauzes**, also called scrim, are available in white, grey or black and made in two widths: scenic gauze 914cm and sharkstooth gauze 1097cm. On a small stage, it is possible to have a small seamless gauze; on larger gauzes, the seams are arranged vertically so they are not so obvious.

Dissolves

The angle of the lighting and the position of the lanterns are important to make the transformation work.

- **Front lighting** needs to be fairly steep illumination down the gauze rather than through it so as to produce a solid surface
- **The stage** behind must be in total darkness
- **The dissolve** is created by raising the illumination on the action and set behind, after which the gauze can be flown out of view
- **Black drapes** behind the gauze will reduce any bleed through of light but they will need to be flown out on cue just before the transformation
- **Painted gauzes** are sometimes used as a front cloth for a play or musical to set the scene instead of using the house tabs

13 OTHER EFFECTS **More info**

An example of a transformation

> ***Swan Lake* ballet** – Director/Choreographer Mathew Bourne, New
> Adventures & Backrow Productions
> Designer Lez Brotherston, Lighting design Rick Fisher, Photographer Mike
> Rothwell

'This was a very traditional gauze (or as referred to in the US scrim) dissolve. The gauze was a painted, sharkstooth gauze and there was a separately flown black cloth on the bar immediately upstage of it.' Rick Fisher, Lighting designer

Swan Lake – *New Adventures & Backrow Productions – Lighting Design Rick Fisher, Photographer Mike Rothwell*

'Front cloth scene of the billboard outside the nightclub'

'In the front gauze scene there was some front light from the balcony profiles or fresnels depending on the distance shaped to the full stage size of the gauze, supplemented by some carefully focused lights that scrape down the cloth and highlight specific parts of the painting of the gauze.' Rick Fisher, Lighting designer

13 OTHER EFFECTS   More info

Swan Lake – *New Adventures & Backrow Productions – Lighting Design Rick Fisher, Photographer Mike Rothwell*

'*As the main characters pass through the door into the nightclub*'

'*Then on cue the lighting is changed, the lights on the front of the painted drop are taken out as the black backing cloth is flown out to reveal the silhouette of the dancers upstage, where the light is carefully focused to not light the gauze itself, and then finally the light builds as the gauze is flown out allowing the dancers to fill the stage space.*'

Rick Fisher, Lighting designer

Swan Lake *club scene – Mike Rothwell*

13 OTHER EFFECTS **More info**

Extras! – Pyrotechnics, flashes & bangs

Pyrotechnics are theatrical fireworks that are especially manufactured for use indoors on-stage. They are specialist effects with the power of an explosive and should be handled and used with care by a fully trained operator.

Pyrotechnics

There are a range of effects that produce a varying amount of light, colour, sound and smoke which can be used to create dramatic effects.

➤ **Some of the main effects that are available from manufacturers:**[45]

■ **Flashes**
'Theatrical Flash – brilliant white flash followed by a pure white mushroom cloud of smoke that rises upwards.' Flashes are also avalble with a loud report (bang) and in red, amber and green

■ **Coloured smoke**
'A small report followed by a thick plume of very dense smoke. Medium 6 to 8 seconds, Large 25 to 30 seconds duration.'

■ **Silver burst or jet**
'A dense column of silver sparks, no bang and very little smoke'

■ **Mini gerb**
'A spray of silver or gold sparks with coloured stars'

■ **Confetti and glitter**
'A bang followed by a cascade of confetti or glitter'

Silver burst – GMSL

■ **Maroons**
An extremely loud bang used for the effects of explosions. They are fired in specially designed bomb tanks made from heavy gauge steel

➤ Control systems

The pyrotechnic cartridges are mounted in pods that are connected by cables to a control system for firing the pyrotechnics.

The control has the following built-in safety systems:

■ Key operating switch to isolate the control and prevent accidental firing
■ Independent control of each effects channel

Pyro controller – Le Maitre

[45] Le Maitre Pyrotechnics & Special Effects

- Channel selection to fire individual effects separately in a double pod
- Test facilities showing firing status
- Fault monitoring system
- Fire button

➤ Setting up the effect

Isolate the control by removing the key switch before connecting the effects. It is good practice for the operator to keep the key hanging around his or her neck.

- The pyrotechnic cartridge is mounted in a pod
- The pods are either single or double independent units
- Variable angle pods can be used to project pyro-flash, glitter and confetti cartridges at an angle
- The pod should be placed in a safe position, clear from the set, curtains and actors. Some larger effects require the pod to be anchored with a safety bond to stop it flying with the effect!
- The pod is connected by a cable to the control system. Make sure that the cable doesn't create a safety hazard for the actors

Angled pod – Le Maitre

- Each pyrotechnic effect has a 'safety zone' specified by the manufacturer
- **The safety zone is a safe radius distance around the effect and a working height**
- These dimensions should be treated as a minimum as pyrotechnics can vary in their performance
- **Always check and follow the manufacturer's instructions**

➤ Firing the effect

Show the actors the position of the pyrotechnics, inform them of the safe working distance and demonstrate the effect before using it in rehearsal and performance.

- Switch on the mains power on the control system
- Place the key in the switch and turn it on
- Select the pod to be fired
- Make a visual check that the area around the pod is clear and not obstructed
- Fire the effect
- Remove the key from the switch

➤ Pyrotechnics are explosives and they are potentially very dangerous to use

There are certain health and safety issues that must be adhered to:

- Read the safety information supplied by the manufacturer
- Pyrotechnics should only be used by a trained operator
- The key must be held by the operator at all times

13 OTHER EFFECTS **Extras!**

- You must be over 18 to fire a pyrotechnic
- Maroons must be used in a bomb tank and should be used with great caution
- Bomb tanks should be positioned off-stage well clear of all personnel and flammable material; warning notices should be displayed
- Make all actors and personnel aware of the positions of the effects and the required safety zones
- A full risk assessment should be carried out to include technicians, performers and audience
- Warning notices should be displayed to inform the audience and cast

Did you know that –

- The original effects were highly dangerous and were made by firing chemical powder on an open tray by passing mains current through fuse wire stretched between two terminals. No health & safety or risk assessment then!
- Flashes were produced by burning magnesium and there were also chemicals known as slow and fast smoke powder
- The safety zone was 'keep it away from the scenery and actors!'
- Bangs – maroons were let off in metal dustbins with chicken wire over the top for safety!!

EXTRA TIPS

- It is good practice to hang the switch key on a lanyard around your neck for security and safety

Extra resources – go to
www. lemaitre.co.uk
www.skyhighfx.com

Points for action

Quickies!

- Compare the range of pyrotechnic effects available on the manufacturers' websites
- Obtain manufacturers' catalogues of effects

Lighting jargon – What's it called?

➤ Colour

Colour	Term used for colour filters
Colour strings	A long string of up to 16 colours joined together used in a scroller to provide remotely controlled colour change on a lantern
'Gels'	The original name for colour filters that were made from dyed gelatine, a term still used by some today
Neutral colours	Colours that will mix equally well with either warm or cool colours
'Open white'	No colour being used
Split colours	Colour break-ups made from strips of colour filters joined together with scroller tape
Transmission factor	The amount of light passing through a filter which varies according to the colour
Two-tone wash	Using different tints of the same colour in a pair of lanterns cross lighting an area

➤ Gobos & motion effects

Animation disc	Rotating effects wheel that fits in the colour frame slot animating the projected image from a gobo
Break-ups	An abstract patterned gobo that gives a textured effect to the light without projecting a specific pattern
Gate	The centre of the optical system of a Profile spot where the shutters, iris and gobos are positioned
Gobo	Thin steel disc with an etched pattern used in a Profile spot to project patterns
Gobo rotator	Motorised drive mounted in the iris slot of a Profile lantern to rotate a gobo
Iris slot	The point where an iris is inserted in a Profile or Ellipsoidal lantern also referred to as the gate
Tags	Small pieces joining together the cut-out sections of a steel gobo

➤ Haze, fog & other effects

AV	Audio visual
Dissolves	Crossfading the light on a gauze from front to back, revealing the scene behind
Fog	Heavy fog low lying close to the stage
Front cloth scene	A pantomime or musical expression where a scene is set in front of a backcloth down stage so that the scenery can be changed behind for the next scene

Haze
A light hanging mist used to soften the effects of lighting and to enhance the projected effects of moving lights

Pod
Unit used to mount and connect a pyrotechnic cartridge to the control system

Pyrotechnics
'On-stage fireworks', electrically fired flashes & bangs, coloured smoke, silver and gold sprays, confetti and glitter

Safety zone
Manufacturer's specified safe radius distance and height around a pyrotechnic effect

Smoke
Light to dense clouds of smoke that will slowly rise and hang in the air. A generic term still used by some for haze and low fog

PART TWO: LIGHTING DESIGNER

Lighting the Performance Space – getting started

14 Angles of illumination
» Fast forward DVD – 14.1: Angles of illumination
   14.2: Three angles of lighting
   14.3: Flat and cross area lighting

15 Other angles of lighting
» Fast forward DVD – 15.1: Focusing lanterns
   15.2: Side, cross area lighting

16 The lighting palette
» Fast forward DVD – 16.1: The lighting palette
   16.2: A touch of colour

17 Using the lighting palette
» Fast forward DVD – 17.1: The language of lighting

■ Lighting jargon

Lighting the Show – from page to stage

18 Preparing to light the show
» Fast forward DVD – 18.1: Designing the show

19 Planning the design

20 The design process

21 The lighting process
» Fast forward DVD – 21.1: Which lantern to use & where

22 Lighting the show
» Fast forward DVD – 22.1: Lighting a scene
   22.2: Lighting the show

■ Lighting jargon

Lighting the Performance Space

Getting started – Looking at different angles of lighting, how they affect the illumination of the face and body when used to light a performance space for drama, dance and musical theatre. Also looking at creating a lighting palette and applying the elements and tools of lighting to lighting a show.

14 Angles of illumination

A quick start – Source & direction of light

Looking at the effects of the direction and angle of light on the face and body

More info – Front lighting

Planning a grid of lighting areas to provide a wash of light

Extras! – Creating a wash of light

Setting up a flat frontal and cross area lighting grid

A quick start – Source & direction of light

The direction, height and angle of the sources of light produce different effects of illumination. The performer on-stage can be lit from an all-round angle of 360 degrees.

> **>>** **Fast Forward** on the DVD to **14.1 Angles of illumination**

Experimenting with a source of light

Take a single source of light and move its position over the head, face and body first from front to back and then from side to side and see how it changes and affects the illumination. You can try this out with a torch, desk light or a lantern mounted on a stand.

A quick start

14 ANGLES OF ILLUMINATION

GMSL

- **Vertical overhead beam:** This produces a tight pool of light highlighting the nose but the eyes and mouth remain in shadow. It creates a very dramatic effect but the light doesn't fully illuminate the features of the face when viewed from the front

GMSL

- **Angled beam from behind:** If the source of light is moved behind, it throws the body into shadow, creating a silhouette and halo effect around the head. The face cannot be seen and a shadow of the body is cast in front of the subject

GMSL

- **Front angled beam:** As the source of light is moved forward in front of the subject, the shadows under the eyes and mouth are reduced. At an overhead angle of 45 degrees, the features of the face are well lit. As the source is lowered, the light spreads backwards and the shadow of the head and body increases

GMSL

- **Front horizontal beam:** When the beam is directly in front of and level with the face, it flattens out the features and produces a large shadow of the body

GMSL

- **Side horizontal beam:** If the horizontal source is moved around to the side of the subject, it will highlight the features of the side of the face and profile the shoulders and body. The shadow is now cast to the side and is less obvious when viewed from the front

GMSL

- **Front low beam:** A low beam of light from the front illuminates under the chin and the eyes that would normally be in shadow from overhead lighting. A low source on its own tends to distort the features of the face, creating a dramatic effect and the size of the shadow is increased, making it larger than life. When used with overhead lighting, it can provide a useful fill light. Footlights used to create a similar effect but they are now not generally used (see 'Did you know that'). Par 16 Birdies are used to create a similar but more controlled effect

GMSL

- **Side low beam:** If the low beam of light is moved to the side, it will provide an alternative angle of floor lighting illumination, profiling the features of the head and body

14. ANGLES OF ILLUMINATION   A quick start

>> **Fast Forward** on the DVD to **14.2 Three angles of lighting**

Lighting the face

For drama it is important to be able to see the facial expressions; being able to see the mouth also assists the audience's ability to hear the actor clearly.

- **Overhead angle of 45 degrees** from the front provides good illumination of the face and upper body, reducing the shadow cast

GMSL

- **Single source of illumination** overhead directly from the front at an angle of 45 degrees produces a tight area of light, reducing the cast shadow of the body. The illumination and profiling of the face tends to be flat; note the single shadow under the chin

GMSL

- **Two sources of illumination** positioned at an overhead angle of 45 degrees and at a horizontal angle of 45 degrees either side of the subject spread the light, increasing the shadows of the body cast sideways

The illumination and profiling of the face is increased and the shadows either side of the nose are reduced; note the lighter double shadow under the chin

GMSL

Three directions of lighting

The stage is illuminated from a range of directions and positions from overhead, the side and from behind.

➤ **Front lighting:**
This is the main source of illumination for the action, being angled to illuminate the face for drama or directly overhead to light the body for dance.

➤ **Side lighting:**
This is a secondary source of lighting used to profile the face and body, illuminating the shoulders and the sides of the face. It removes the shadows created by front lighting and illuminates the moving body for dance. It is used at three different positions: floor, head and high-level cross lighting diagonally across the stage.

➤ **Back lighting:**
This is another secondary light source from behind, it adds depth to the scene by highlighting the head and shoulders. It creates a dramatic shadow-like effect, making the actor stand out from the background.

The different directions and angles of illumination can be combined when lighting the stage to light the face and body or to create special effects.

Points for action

Takes longer
■ Experiment with a source of light to try out the effects as above. You could use a portable light source and a polystyrene head block. If you use a lantern, take care as it will become hot and the lamp can be damaged when it is moved, as the filament is very fragile when burning or when it is still hot

A proper job!
■ Use three lanterns to light an area with a single source and two sources of illumination and compare the difference

14. ANGLES OF ILLUMINATION

A quick start

More info – Front lighting

Front lighting provides the main source of illumination for a performance space. A basic requirement is to be able to light the whole space with an even wash of light. This can be achieved by the careful blending of a series of lighting areas produced by a multiple of lanterns/luminaires.

Creating a wash of light

A wash of light can be created by dividing the performance space into a grid of lighting areas that can be blended together to provide the same quality of light across the space. If the lanterns lighting each area are controlled by separate dimmers, then they can be selected individually to create smaller areas. If the width of the space is divided into an odd number of areas, it will provide a central area which is frequently an important focus for drama that needs to be lit separately.

➤ **Planning a grid of areas**

It is easier to work out a simple plan on paper before starting to hang the lanterns. You will need a lighting layout plan of the space with lighting bars and the positions and circuit numbers of the outlet sockets marked on it. Initially, you may find it easier to plan the position of the areas and positions of the lanterns by walking the stage but with experience you will be able to draw it directly on to the plan.

- **Centre stage** is an essential area and so there will be an odd number of areas across the stage
- **A small stage** or drama studio can be divided up into six lighting areas, three across by two deep
- **A deeper stage** may require an additional row of areas dividing it up into nine lighting areas
- **A wider stage** may need to be divided into five areas across

In a studio or on a small stage, the lighting bars may be hung in a fixed position. To provide an even cover of light from front to back, the lanterns on the first bar need to light the areas positioned immediately under the next lighting bar up stage.[1] The lanterns from the second bar will need to light the areas under the next bar, with the beams crossing over above head height to provide an even cover up and down stage between the two rows of areas. With fixed bars, it may not be possible to maintain a front overhead angle of 45 degrees.

On a larger stage where there is a suspension grid, the position and height of the bars can be adjusted to maintain the optimum angle of illumination when lighting the areas. The positions of the bars can be planned on a side elevation drawing of the stage to provide an overhead angle of illumination of 45 degrees, with the beams crossing over up and down stage above head height to provide a smooth wash.[2]

[1] See 'Angles of illumination – Extras! – Navigating the stage'
[2] See the side elevation drawing on page 200

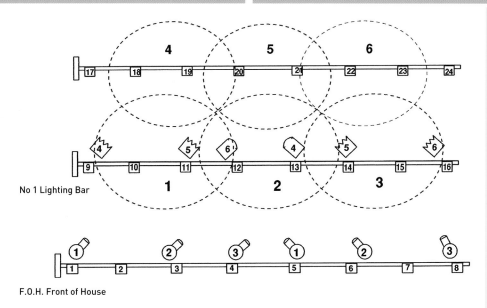

No 1 Lighting Bar

F.O.H. Front of House

Six-area lighting plan – GMSL

- **Planning the areas** – it is easier to walk across the stage to visualise the positions of the lighting areas
- **Draw in the positions** of the areas on the plan, i.e. the positions where the actors will be standing and their faces lit by the beam of light. This is not the position where the beam will hit the floor as this will be behind the lighting area. See the side elevation drawing on page 200
- **Number the areas** in a logical sequence, front line across 1, 2, 3 as viewed by the audience from House Left to House Right (Stage Right to Stage Left) and the second line of areas 4, 5 ,6 as on the plan above
- **A logical sequence of numbering** from 'House Left' to 'House Right' and from front to back will make it easier to remember the area numbers when viewing the stage from the front and directing the lighting or operating the control desk

14. ANGLES OF ILLUMINATION   More info

195

One lantern or two?

The choice of lighting an area with one or two lanterns will depend upon the type of illumination that you want to produce. It is easier to create a wash of light using a single lantern per area especially for the less experienced but two lanterns provide better illumination.

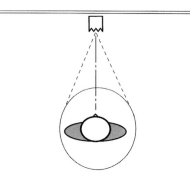

Single source of illumination – GMSL

> **Flat frontal area lighting** – single source of light

This uses a single source of illumination with the lantern positioned directly in front of each area. The angle of the single source creates a tight beam of light with a minimum spread backwards casting a relatively short shadow of the body. The single source of light produces a flat wash and it is necessary to include high cross lighting to provide additional angles of illumination to profile the face and body.

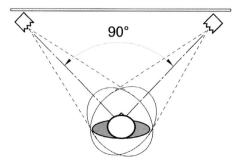

Two sources of illumination – GMSL

> **Cross area lighting** – two sources of light

This method uses two lanterns, one from each side of the area, at an approximate combined horizontal angle of 90 degrees apart. It is more difficult to position the lanterns and to focus them so that the areas overlap to produce a continuous wash. Two sources of light provide a well-balanced illumination of the face but the diagonal angle increases the spread sideways, casting a longer shadow of the body towards the side of the stage. This provides directional illumination that can be used as Key and Fill lighting to create two-tone colour washes as explained in Chapter 16 'The lighting palette – More info – A touch of colour'.

Positioning the lanterns

Initially, it can be quite difficult to visualise and decide upon the positions of the lanterns to light each area using a lighting layout plan. It will be easier to do this when you have gained some experience.

In a studio or on a small stage, a practical way of planning the positions of the lanterns is to stand in the centre of each lighting area and sight the positions of the lanterns on the lighting bar and mark the positions on the lighting plan. This can be done by using the following method:

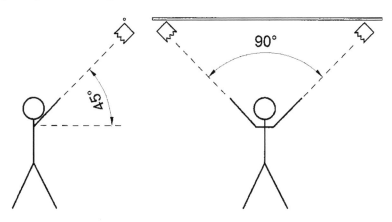

Positioning the sources of illumination – GMSL

- **Flat frontal lighting** – for the position of a single lantern, hold your arm up directly in front of you at an approximate vertical angle of 45 degrees and look along it to sight the position on the bar
- **Cross area lighting** – for two lanterns, hold both arms apart at a horizontal angle of 90 degrees, maintaining the vertical angle of 45 degrees to sight the positions on the bar
- **Mark the positions of the lanterns** on the lighting layout plan with a cross 'X'
- **Fixed position lighting bars** may not always be in exactly the right position so it may be necessary to compromise on the vertical angle in order to overlap the rows of areas
- **Lay out the lanterns** – select the type of lantern to be used to light each area and position them directly under the lighting bar where they are to be rigged. This is a good practical way of planning the types of lanterns to be used and checking the numbers available. If you haven't got enough lanterns, you will need to adjust your plan
- **Mark the types of lanterns to be used in each position on the plan** using the CIE symbols from Chapter 2 'Lanterns – performance luminaires – A quick start'. They can be easily drawn by hand if you haven't got a lantern stencil
- **Now rig the lanterns**

14. ANGLES OF ILLUMINATION

More info

Connecting the lanterns to the dimmers & control

The lanterns are connected via the circuit outlet sockets to the dimmer units and control channel faders on the lighting desk.

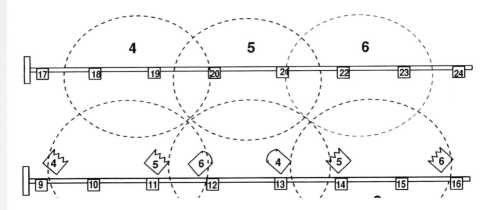

Three-area lighting plan – GMSL

➤ **On the lantern plan**
- **Number each lantern symbol** with the same number as the area that it is lighting
- **For an example** see the above plan:

    Area 4 is lit by two lanterns numbered No.4 connected to outlet circuits Nos. 9 & 13

    Area 5 is lit by two lanterns numbered No.5 connected to outlet circuits Nos. 11 & 14

    Area 6 is lit by two lanterns numbered No.6 connected to outlet circuits Nos. 12 & 16

➤ **Hard patching system with dimmer packs**
On a system with hard patching, the lanterns are connected via a cable patch to the dimmer packs. They can be individually hard patched to the dimmer units so that the lanterns are controlled by the same channel fader number on the lighting desk as the area that they are lighting in the following way:

6-Way Dimmer Pack

Dimmer channel Nos.	1	2	3	4	5	6	
Two outlet sockets per dimmer channel (paired)				9	11	12	Outlet circuit numbers patched to dimmer channels
				13	14	16	

14 ANGLES OF ILLUMINATION   **More info**

- The lanterns lighting area 4 are connected via outlet circuits Nos.9 & 13
- Outlet circuits Nos.9 & 13 are patched to dimmer No.4 which is controlled by channel fader No.4 below
- The lanterns lighting area 4 will now be controlled by channel fader No.4, providing the lighting control desk has been set with a 1:1 soft patch

> ### Hardwired systems with dimmer racks

On a hardwired system, the lanterns are connected via the outlet circuits directly to the dimmer rack. If the lighting desk is set to a 1:1 soft patch, they are controlled by the same channel fader number as the circuit outlet socket number that the lantern is connected to.

The control channel faders on an advanced memory lighting desk can be soft patched or assigned to any of the dimmer units in the rack. The lanterns are controlled by the same channel fader number on the lighting desk as the area that they are lighting in the following way:

- The lanterns lighting area 4 are connected via outlet circuits to the dimmer units Nos.9 & 13 which have the same DMX address numbers
- Control channel fader No.4 is programmed and assigned to the DMX addresses 9 & 13
- The lanterns lighting area 4 will now be controlled by channel fader No.4 [3] [4]

Soft Patching	
Control Channel Fader No.	**Dimmer DMX Address No.**
4	9 & 13
5	11 & 13
6	12 &16

QUICK TIPS

- Lay out the lanterns on the stage directly under the position on the bar where they are to be hung. This is a practical way to plan the distribution of your lanterns
- Check that the lanterns are positioned symmetrically either side of the centre of the bar and up and down stage before hanging them, in order to produce matching angles and an even wash of light

---

[3] See Chapter 5 'Lighting controls – Extras! – Soft patching'
[4] See Chapter 20 'The design process – Extras! – Patching/hook-up schedule'

Extras – Creating a wash of light

To produce an even wash of light, the beams from the lanterns lighting each area need to overlap so that the cones of light blend above head height. It is important to use both a plan and side elevation when planning the positions of lanterns to light the areas in order to try to visualise it in three dimensions.

Side elevation

To create an even wash, the areas of light need to overlap up and down stage.

➤ **Lighting the face not the floor**
It is important to remember that the focal point for most of the lighting areas will be at face level. Therefore, the areas marked on the plan represent the position of the beam to illuminate at the height of the head and shoulders and not the pattern of the beam projected on the floor. The centre of the beam of light from the lantern is usually focused on the actor at shoulder level when standing in the centre of the area to cover the face and lower body.

➤ **Side view/elevation of the stage**
The elevation drawing shows the beams of light from the lanterns on each of the lighting bars crossing over above the head height of the actor at approximately 1.5m from stage level to provide a seamless illumination up and down stage.

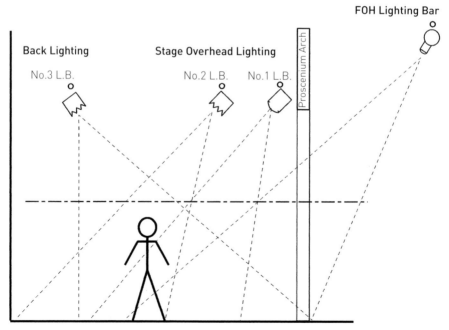

Side elevation drawing of the stage – GMSL

- The actor is standing in the centre of the beam of light from the lantern on the No.2 lighting bar
- If the actor steps back and stands in the centre of the pool of light projected on the floor, the lower body will be lit but the head and shoulders will be in shadow
- If the actor moves down stage towards the audience out of the pool of light on the floor, the face and shoulders will still be lit by the lantern from the No.2 bar and the lower body will be lit from the lanterns on the No.1 lighting bar
- As the actor continues to move forward, he is lit by the beam of light from the FOH advance lighting bar
- The height of the lighting bars affects the angle of illumination and the overshoot or shadow behind the actor. On the stage, this is normally determined by the height of the proscenium arch or the overhead masking, depending upon whether the lighting equipment is to be viewed by the audience or to be hidden
- On a stage with flying facilities, the height and position of the lighting bars can be adjusted and different lighting effects created by changing the vertical angle of illumination
- On a school stage or college drama studio, the height and position of the bars on the grid may be fixed

Choice of lanterns/luminaires

- **Fresnels & PCs** – their variable beam size makes them very suitable for areas of wash lighting. The Fresnel's soft edged beam is good for blending the beams of light and the PC's semi-hard/semi-soft beam is more suited for longer throws. Barndoors are essential to control the overspill of light from the beams
- **Profile spots** – these are more difficult to use for wash lighting but they will be necessary to use for long throws in FOH positions.
- **Zoom Profiles** are ideal in order to adjust the size of the beam to match the areas. More experience is required when selecting fixed beam angle Profiles to match the size of the areas
- **A hard edged beam** of light from a Profile makes it difficult to blend the beams but this can be reduced by soft focusing. Additional brightness will occur where the adjacent beams overlap, which can be reduced by adjusting lantern from the 'flat beam' to a 'peak beam' setting. See Chapter 2 'Lanterns – performance luminaires – More info'

14 ANGLES OF ILLUMINATION   Extras!

Flat frontal area lighting

➤ Six-area front view

On the opposite page, the front view of the stage shows the diameter of the beams of light from the three lanterns on each bar overlapping by about 20% across the stage and from front to back. The beams need to cross over above head height to provide a seamless wash.

- As the actor moves from area 1 to 2 and on to area 3, they should be evenly lit from one beam to the next without passing through any shadows
- The beams from the high-level cross stage lighting can be seen crossing the areas on the diagonal, adding some side lighting to the areas

---

» **Fast Forward** on the DVD to **14.3 Flat area lighting**

➤ Six-area lighting plan

On the plan, the lighting areas are lit in the following way:

- **Down stage areas 1, 2 & 3**
  FOH advance bar in front of the stage 3 x Profile spots positioned directly in front of areas 1, 2 & 3, PCs with barndoors could be used as an alternative.

  If an advance bar is not available, the areas would be lit by cross area lighting using Profile spots positioned on the sides of the auditorium; see Chapter 5 'Other angles of lighting – A quick start – FOH lighting'

- **Centre stage areas 3, 4 & 5**
  No.1 lighting bar, Lx1. 3 x Fresnel lanterns or PCs lanterns as an alternative, 2 x 1.2kW Fresnel lanterns on the extreme ends of the No.1 lighting bar to provide high-level cross stage lighting. The dimmer/channel fader numbers are recorded on the plan in the middle of the lantern symbol

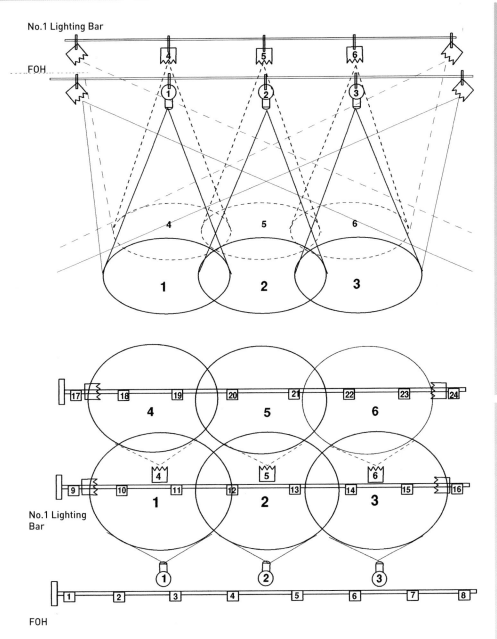

No.1 Lighting Bar

FOH

No.1 Lighting Bar

FOH

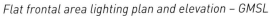

Flat frontal area lighting plan and elevation – GMSL

Cross area lighting

➤ Six-area front view

On the opposite page, the front view of the stage shows the beams from the three lanterns on each bar overlapping above head height across the stage and from front to back to provide a seamless wash.

- The actor standing in area 1 is illuminated by two lanterns lighting down stage right
- As the actor moves towards area 2, they should walk into the beams of light from the pair of lanterns lighting the down stage centre area and on into the beams of light lighting area 3

> **》》** **Fast Forward** on the DVD to **14.4 Cross area lighting**

➤ Six-area lighting plan

On the plan, the lighting areas are lit in the following way:

- **Down stage areas 1, 2 & 3**
  FOH advance bar in front of the stage 6 x Profile spots, two lanterns per area
  Area 2 centre stage is lit by two lanterns numbered No.2 positioned at an angle of 45 degrees either side of the area making a combined horizontal angle of 90 degrees
  Areas 1 & 3 left and right, one lantern is positioned at the extreme off-stage end of the lighting bar and the other is positioned on the opposite side of the centre of the bar, maintaining a combined angle of 90 degrees. Therefore, the beams of light from the two lanterns either side of centre cross over to light areas 1 & 3. If an advance bar is not available, the areas would be lit by cross area lighting using Profile spots positioned on the sides of the auditorium

- **Centre stage areas 4, 5 & 6**
  No.1 lighting bar over stage, Lx1. 2 x PC, 4 x Fresnel lanterns with barndoors, two lanterns per area
  Area 5 centre stage is lit by two Fresnels numbered No.5 positioned at a combined angle of 90 degrees to the centre of the area
  Areas 4 & 6 left & right – Fresnel lantern is positioned at the extreme off-stage end of the lighting bar and a PC is positioned just on the other side of the centre of the bar, maintaining a combined angle of 90 degrees. The Fresnels are used to light the extreme off-stage side areas because of their wide spread over a short distance. The PCs are positioned on the opposite side of the centre of the bar. They are used in preference to a Fresnel as they have a longer throw and a tighter beam, reducing the scatter light on the side of the stage. If PCs are not available, Fresnels can be used but barndoors are essential to contain the spill of light

  - **Patching** – note from the plan that the two lanterns lighting each area are paired together so that they are controlled by the same channel control fader

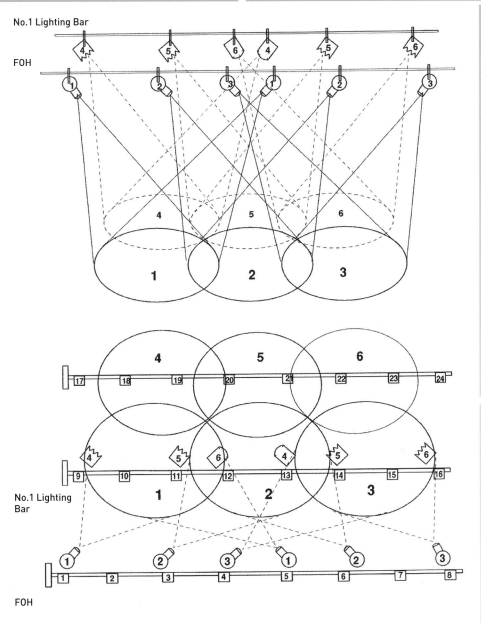

No.1 Lighting Bar

FOH

Cross area lighting plan and elevation – GMSL

Navigating the stage

The stage can be conveniently divided into a grid of areas and standard directions that are useful when directing lighting and for the position of lighting areas. They are primarily used to direct the movement of the actors by the director when facing the action from the front and for the stage manager to record or 'block' the moves.

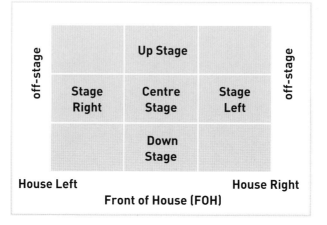

- **Stage left SL & Stage right SR** – actors left and right when facing the audience
- **Centre stage CS** – in the middle
- **Up & down stage US, DS** – away from the audience and towards the audience
- **On- & off-stage** – towards centre stage and away from the centre
- **Front of House (FOH)** – the area in front of the stage used by the audience
- **House left & right** – left and right of auditorium as viewed by the audience

More information on the complete grid of areas can be found in 'Lighting jargon'.

Did you know that –

- The stage directions were devised so that the director could easily direct the moves of the actors in rehearsal. Using stage left and right (the actors' left and right) removed any confusion of whether the instructions given were actors' left or the director's left!
- Up and down stage – this term dates back to when stages in theatre were built with a rake or slope. This was to work with the perspective scenery and also to raise the viewpoint of the actor up stage. Hence the term 'being upstaged' by another actor, causing the other actors to turn away from the audience
- It was said that Laurence Olivier, one of the UK's most famous actors, when playing Shakespeare's Richard III at the London Old Vic always limped with his up stage leg! The Old Vic had quite a steep rake

15 Other angles of lighting

A quick start – FOH lighting
FOH and cross side lighting

More info – Side, cross & back lighting
Floor, head, cross and back lighting

Extras! – Focusing a wash of light
Focusing the lanterns to create a wash of light

A quick start – FOH lighting

FOH lighting is a traditional term for the lanterns mounted in front of the proscenium arch lighting the front of the stage. In some halls or larger theatres, the lanterns are mounted on horizontal and vertical bars on the side walls of the auditorium. These positions provide alternative angles of lighting to an advance bar directly in front of the stage.

Height and angles of illumination

The angle of illumination depends upon the position of the lantern, the height and distance that it is from the area to be illuminated. This can vary for FOH lighting, depending upon the type and size of the venue. The architecture of older theatres was not originally designed for modern lighting with a multitude of lanterns FOH. However, the circles and balconies provide a variation of heights for the positioning of lanterns creating different layers of lighting and angles of illumination that can be used to produce very different effects. A similar effect can be seen in the galleries and lighting positions surrounding the thrust stage of the Swan and the new Royal Shakespeare Theatre.

In many of these theatres, it can be difficult to maintain the optimum angle of 45° to illuminate the face, as the angle of illumination may vary between 35° and 60°. In some theatres, an advance bar has been added in front of the proscenium to provide a suitable angle to light the front of the stage.

UNIVERSITY OF WINCHESTER
LIBRARY

Side auditorium lighting

It is more difficult to maintain a near vertical angle of 45 degrees and to produce an even wash across the stage when the FOH lighting positions are on the side of the auditorium on horizontal bars or vertical booms. Therefore, it is important to use the lanterns in a specific order to try to maintain a steep angle and achieve the best results. In these positions, Profile spots need to be used to throw over a longer distance and it may be necessary to use Axial lanterns or larger-wattage Profiles to achieve an adequate level of illumination.

> **⟫ Fast Forward** on the DVD to **15.1 Focusing lighting**

➤ **Horizontal bars** mounted on the side wall
The beams of light from the three lanterns need to spread like a fan across the stage:

- The lantern nearest to the stage is used to light the off-stage area on the same side
- The middle lantern is used to light the centre area
- The lantern positioned furthest away from the stage is used to light the opposite side

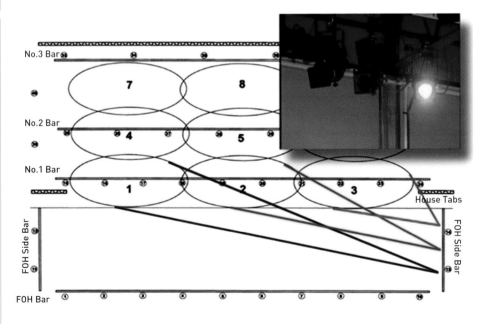

FOH lighting hung on horizontal bars – GMSL

A quick start

15 OTHER ANGLES OF LIGHTING

➤ **Vertical boom bars** mounted on the side wall

The beams of light from the three lanterns need to spread in a similar vertical fan pattern across the stage. They are used in the following order to endeavour to maintain the best possible angle of elevation:

■ The bottom lantern to cover the shortest distance to light the off-stage area on the same side
■ The middle lantern to light the centre area
■ The top lantern to cover the longest distance and to light the off-stage area on the opposite side

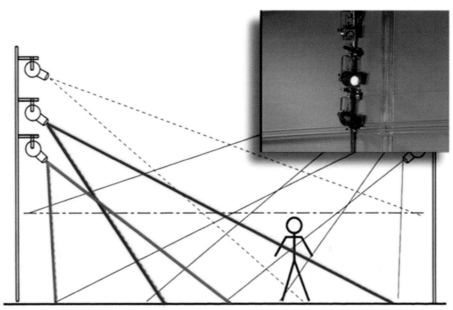

Front elevation of the stage

FOH lighting mounted on vertical booms – GMSL

Cross side lighting

Cross side lighting provides another angle or dimension to the front lighting and is especially used for musicals and dance to produce washes of colour to light the head, shoulders and the side of the face.

Lanterns are hung on vertical booms or ladders positioned on the side of the stage both up stage and in front of the proscenium arch. They are focused in the same way as the vertical FOH lighting positions and angled straight across the stage to provide areas of light; they can also be angled slightly up stage to increase the illumination of the face.

➤ The front elevation view of the stage shows the beams of light crossing over above head height to provide a continuous cover across the stage, reducing the possibility of one actor standing in another actor's shadow.

➤ Profile spots are used for cross side lighting because of the precise control over the beam of light. PCs with barndoors or Parcans with medium to wide angled lamps can be used. The lack of adjustment to the beam size of the Parcan can make it difficult to provide a complete coverage of illumination.

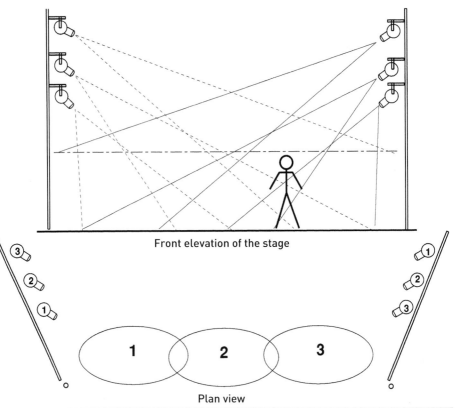

Front elevation of the stage

Plan view

Plan and elevation showing cross side lighting – GMSL

A quick start

15 OTHER ANGLES OF LIGHTING

More info – Side, cross & back lighting

The direction, height and angle of the sources of light produce different effects. The performer on-stage can be illuminated from an all-round angle of 360 degrees. Side, cross and back lighting provide a further dimension to the lighting palette and they are an important part of the lighting rig.

> **»** **Fast Forward** on the DVD to **15.2 Side, cross and back lighting**

Side lighting

This is used to create dramatic effects and to profile the moving body for dance.

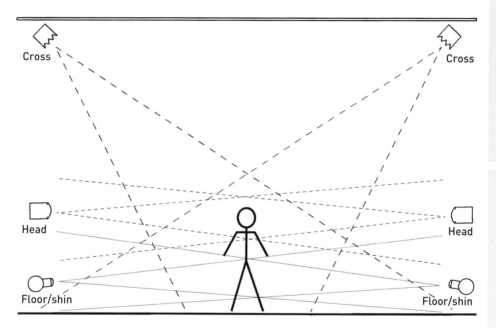

Front elevation showing cross, head, floor & shin lighting – GMSL

> **Floor lighting**
> Floor-level light focused across the stage is mainly used for dance to highlight the legs or to uplight the body and head.
>
> ■ **'Shin busters'** – Profile lanterns mounted on floor stands with a tightly focused beam shaped by the shutters angled directly across the performance area and off the floor to provide lighting on the lower legs to create an illusion of floating, as used for dance

- Fresnel lanterns with barndoors provide a wider spread, highlighting the legs, body and head, and can also be slightly angled up stage to provide a greater coverage where there is a limited number of side lighting positions up stage
- 'Floorlite' Parcans with wide-angled lamps can be used but they lack a degree of control

Shin lighting – GMSL

➤ Head lighting

Head-level light used for drama and dance to illuminate the head and shoulders.

- PCs or Fresnel lanterns mounted on stands or vertical boom bars at head height with the beam adjusted to illuminate the head and shoulders
- PCs provide a more intense and crisper beam than the Fresnel with reduced scatter light
- If floor lighting is not being used, the beam may be widened to cover the whole of the lower body
- Parcans with medium to narrow beam angle lamps can also be used

Head lighting – GMSL

➤ High-level cross lighting

High-level side lighting angled diagonally across the stage to highlight the side of the head, shoulders, raised arms and bodies from above.

- Fresnel lanterns or PCs mounted at the top of boom bars either side of the stage or at the extreme ends of a lighting bar

➤ **Barndoors** are used on side lighting to shape the beam, reduce the overshoot and scatter light.

High-level cross lighting – GMSL

Back lighting

Back lighting is used to highlight the back of the head and shoulders to create a 'halo' effect. Steeply angled lanterns are used to back lighting acting areas or the entire stage.

➤ **Direct back lighting** – lanterns mounted directly behind the acting areas or towards the rear of the stage

Quarter back lighting – GMSL

212

➤ **Quarter back lighting** – lanterns lighting at an angle of 45 degrees from behind either side of the area or from the rear of the stage.

- Fresnels with barndoors are used as they have a soft edged wide beam of light
- A 90 degree Profile will provide the same wide beam coverage as a Fresnel with the added precise control of the Profile spot and the possibility of using a gobo to highlight the effect and to break up the beam
- A small stage or studio can be back lit by three lanterns hanging on the rear lighting bar
- A single 1.2K lantern in the centre can produce a dramatic effect

Gobo back lighting effect – GMSL

Hamlet – The Large Group, Maidment Theatre, Auckland, NZ, 2003 – Director Michael Hurst, Designer John Verryt, Lighting Designer David Eversfield, Photograph © Michael Hurst

'The actor's face is illuminated by quarter back lighting cutting in from stage left creating a dramatic effect.'

War Horse – *National Theatre production – Lighting Design Paule Constable, Photograph © Simon Annand*

'The low-level back lighting captured on this picture cuts in at a shallow angle almost from the side, highlighting the profile of the men on horses.'

- Varying the height of the back lighting can heighten the dramatic effect as can be seen in the Royal National Theatre production of *War Horse.*

The effect of using layers of lighting

In the production of *War Horse*, Paule Constable uses the effect of different layers of back and side lighting to achieve two distinct looks and places in a space of darkness that is defined by light. The hell of the First World War zone is created using low dynamic angles of lighting from under the projection screen of harsh blue white light from discharge source lanterns of a man-made manufactured environment. (See illustrations Chapter 11 'Projected images – Extras!') This is contrasted with the high angles of warm beautiful sunlight for the rural Devon community scenes.[5]

[5] *The Making of War Horse*, More Four

GLOBAL JARGON

- **Cross lighting** (UK) – 'Hi-side' illumination (NA)[6] *'now this is a real American term that we ought to be using in the UK!'*
- **End of bar** (UK) – 'pipe ends' (NA)

MORE TIPS

- In a large show, a greater number of lanterns are used for side, cross and back lighting
- Always try to include some lighting from these angles, even on a small show where the number of lanterns available may be limited, as it will increase the dramatic effect and make your lighting come alive

[6] Ziggy Jacobs – American Lighting Design student

Extras! – Focusing a wash of light

The process of focusing is a precise, lengthy one requiring concentration and the ability to communicate clearly between the team without the interference of any other noise.

> **》》 Fast Forward** on the DVD to **15.1 Focusing lanterns**

Focusing

Ideally, four people are needed to focus the lanterns: two skilled and two assistants to do the following jobs:

1 **Lighting designer** to direct the angling and focusing of the lighting of the areas
2 **Electrician** to adjust the lanterns
3 **Assistant** to operate the lighting control desk
4 **Assistant** to help move and brace the access system

➤ **Good working practice**
- **Work in a darkened space** to see the true effect of the lighting. A torch can be very useful to help read the lighting plan in the dark
- **Focus one lantern at a time** – if possible, disconnect one of the paired circuits at the dimmer patch or direct the beam of light from the spare lantern away from the area to be lit

➤ **Focusing the lanterns**
You need to give clear verbal and visual directions to your team when angling and focusing lanterns

- **Call the lantern to be angled** by its channel fader number from the plan at a fader level of 90%
- **Stand in the centre of the area** to be lit with your back to the light source to avoid being dazzled. Use your projected shadow to focus the light source and to see the area of illumination
- **Call for a spot focus beam**
- **Call for a spot beam** with the centre to hit the neck and shoulders

Focusing the lanterns – GMSL

Sidebar: Extras! | 15 OTHER ANGLES OF LIGHTING

- **Direct the spread of the beam** – indicate with your arms saying *'spread the beam'* or *'close the beam'* to fill the required area and to provide a clear shadow of your head
- **Check that the taller people will be lit** by using the 'Bunny Rabbit' effect, holding your hand above your head to check that you can see its shadow
- **Walk in the beam of light**, watch your shadow to see how far it covers. Use the palm of your hand or a white sheet of paper, e.g. the back of the plan to check the extent of the beam of light; see how the intensity drops off towards the edge. Make any further adjustments to the size of the beam in order to adequately light the area
- **Adjust Profile spots** from 'flat' to 'peak' beam to give a smoother overlap and to increase the light output in the centre of the beam
- **Focus the beam** of Profile spots either hard or soft

➤ Shaping the beam

Remove any scatter light or overshoot of the beam of light on to the proscenium arch, below the front of the stage, the sides or rear of the stage area on scenery or masking:

- **Profile spots** use the shutters to remove any 'overshoot' of the beam. Remember that the shutters work in the opposite way – the right shutter cuts in on the left side of the beam
- **Fresnels & PCs** use the barndoors to remove any scatter light. They work on the same side – the right door reduces the scatter light and cuts the beam on the right side

➤ Flat frontal area lighting

- **Focus each lantern** so that there is an approximate overlap of 20% of the diameter of each beam with the adjacent area

➤ Cross area lighting

Use the focusing sequence as above.

- **Focus the first lantern** of the pair to light the area
- **Focus the second lantern** of the pair to light the area
- **Check the size of the beam** that it overlays and lines up front and back with the beam from the first lantern
- **Compare the area** with the other previously angled areas to see that it is in line, that they cross over and that there is a smooth overlap of light between both areas
- **Check the overlap** with your back to the lighting, using the palm of your hand or the back of the lighting plan to detect any shadows as you pass from one area to the other
- **Look up at the lanterns** as you cross from one area to the next; you should be able to see the beam of light from the next lantern

15 OTHER ANGLES OF LIGHTING

Extras!

➤ **Checking the wash**

When you have finished focusing, check the cover between all the areas across the stage and from front to back:

- **Walk the line of areas** – across the stage and from front to back to check that there are no shadows
- **If you find a shadow** – enlarge the size of the beam or it may be necessary to move the position that the lantern is hanging in

Checking the wash – GMSL

➤ **Focusing side and cross lighting**

This requires a similar process:

- **Stand in the centre of the stage** in line with the lanterns and direct the adjustment of beam size by the shadows cast sideways
- **Walk along the beams of light** to check the cover of the beam across the stage
- **Check the cover** of the beams from the other lighting positions up stage. The cover can be increased by slightly angling the lanterns up stage

➤ **Focusing jargon and actions**

This is covered in Chapter 21 'The lighting process'.

QUICK TIPS

- 'Save your lamps' by turning the lanterns off when they are not in use to keep them cool and to save electricity
- When angling and focusing, run the lamps at 90% to reduce the possibility of damage as the filament of a tungsten lamp burns at white heat when the dimmer control level is at 100%
- Use rigging gloves when adjusting lanterns as they get hot very quickly
- When angling and focusing, use your arms and hands to give directions as well as verbal instructions to the operator when adjusting the size and shape of the beam
- 'Flag' the lanterns by waving a hand in front of the beam from a lantern to check the size of the area of illumination and the spill light from Fresnels and PCs
- When adjusting the 'flat' to 'peak' beam settings on a Profile spot, run it at 30% to save damaging the filament
- Make sure that you have peace and quiet so that you can communicate with your team

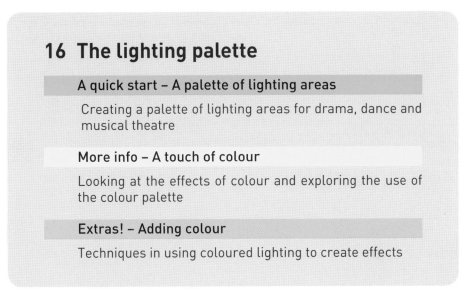

16 The lighting palette

A quick start – A palette of lighting areas

Creating a palette of lighting areas for drama, dance and musical theatre

More info – A touch of colour

Looking at the effects of colour and exploring the use of the colour palette

Extras! – Adding colour

Techniques in using coloured lighting to create effects

A quick start – A palette of lighting areas

The lighting designer aims to create a palette of areas and angles of illumination that can be used to compose scenes of light.

Creating a lighting palette[7]

A grid of areas are planned based on the dramatic requirements of the production to light the main acting areas, solo areas, to provide accent and feature lighting, and broader washes of light.

> **⟫ Fast Forward** on the DVD to **16.1 The lighting palette**

 Lighting for drama

The lighting palette for drama will depend upon whether it is an interior, exterior, realistic or abstract setting. When lighting a drama production, the main emphasis is to illuminate the face and body:

---

[7] Based on *Method of Lighting the Stage*, Stanley McCandless (1897–1967); also developed in *Lighting the Amateur Stage* by Francis Reid

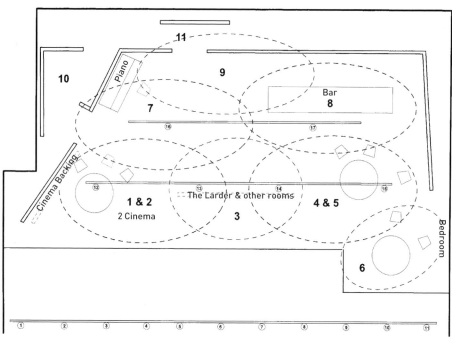

'Allo 'Allo *lighting area plan – Skip Mort*

- **The lighting areas** will be defined by the action. On an interior setting, the focus will be on the position of the furniture and also the entrances. For a small production, this may be based on a nine-area grid: three across and three deep. The areas may not be symmetrical and the size will depend upon the action. Each of the areas will need to overlap and be independently controlled to balance the intensities to produce a seamless wash or to focus the attention to suit the action
- **Specials** reproducing the ambient illumination from practical light fittings on the set
- **Flat frontal or cross area lighting** may be used to illuminate the areas. Direct frontal area lighting tends to be visually flat, and side, cross and back lighting will need to be added to provide highlights, specific natural or dramatic effects
- **Side head lighting** can be used to provide light from natural sources, sun or moonlight through a window, the low glow of a setting sun or from artificial sources through the door from another room, the side light from a candle or table light
- **Cross or back lighting** can provide the effect of high-level sunlight or moonlight; strong colours can be used in the back lighting to create moods without affecting the illumination or the colour of the face

220

Did you know that -

■ Stanley McCandless (1897–1967) was one of the first teachers to offer a college-level course in Stage Lighting. He was a professor at Yale University from 1925 to 1964 and wrote *Method of Lighting the Stage*, where he proposed the technique of dividing the stage into a grid of areas to illuminate the space

➤ Lighting for dance

The emphasis for dance is to illuminate the moving body and less on the face. The addition of side, cross and back lighting is an important element to profile and sculpt the features of the moving body.

Wicked – *Cirencester Creative Dance Academy, Choreographer Katherine Bates, Design and Lighting Design Andy Webb, Photograph © Nik Sheppard*

■ **The lighting areas** for the overhead lighting tend to be based on a regular grid of five areas across by four deep
■ **Flat overhead lighting** with the beams steeply raked at an angle of approximately 80 degrees will provide an overhead wash of precise well-defined downlighting

- **Floor, head and cross side lighting** is positioned either side of the stage in line with the overhead areas across the stage
- **Side lighting** with the lanterns angled straight across the stage, positioned and focused so as to provide a continuous coverage as the dancers move up and down stage. The number of sources of side lighting can be reduced by angling the lanterns up stage and spreading the beams to provide a wider coverage
- **Colour** – warm colours may be used at head height and cool colours at floor level or vice versa. Neutral colours in the overhead wash will tone with the warm and cool colours used in the side lighting. Stronger hot or cold colours tend to be used in the high cross and back lighting

Did you know that –

- Side lighting was introduced to dance in the early 1940s by Jean Rosenthal, a famous American lighting designer who worked for many years with the well-known American contemporary dance choreographer Martha Graham

➤ Musical theatre

Musicals require a mixture of the lighting techniques for both drama and dance. The number of performers at any one time may vary from a full production number to small groups or even solo performers. The lighting requirements can change from a wide wash of the stage to localised areas, also from realistic lighting of a set to lavish fantasy-style colourful lighting.

- **The lighting areas** on a large stage may be based on five across and three or four deep. The up stage areas tend to be less used and therefore reduced to three areas across
- **Flat frontal area lighting** is used to provide a cool and warm wash lighting; the down stage centre and centre stage areas are a major focus and therefore need to be independently controlled, whereas the off-stage areas can be paired across stage if required
- **Specials** are areas of light focused to provide an individual effect which cannot be used as a part of the general palette of lighting, e.g. a small pool of light within a larger area, a close-up on an actor's head and shoulders, gobo down-lighting
- **Follow spots** are used to highlight the faces of the principal actors in a scene or to isolate them as solo performers
- **Side cross lighting** on booms in front of and up stage of the proscenium arch provides additional angles of illumination, profiling the bodies and adding colour

High School Musical – *Tigz Productions, Bacon Theatre, Directed by Adrian Ross Jones, Producer & Lighting Designer Andy Webb, Photograph © Nik Sheppard*

- **Side & high cross area lighting** adds additional angles of illumination and colour, reducing the effects of the shadows created by a large group of performers on-stage
- **Back lighting** to providing colour and effects
- **Moving heads** used to provide special areas, dramatic effects, also for back lighting with either stationary or slow-moving break-up effects
- **Skycloths/cycloramas** illuminated to add realism to the setting or to create a mood
- **'Glitz' effects** – LED strips, mirror balls, chases of lamps, etc. are used to add special effects

> **Quick resources – go to**
>
> **www3.northern.edu/wild/th241/sc12c.htm** – 'An approach to lighting design' Larry Wild, Northern State University, Aberdeen, SD. The article is based on Stanley McCandless's book *Method of Lighting the Stage*, published in the 1930s
>
> Google 'Stage lighting design'/Bill Williams – Part 2 General lighting design

More info – A touch of colour

Designers on colour – *'The use of colour is a key to a lighting designer's craft. I am constantly reminded as I watch the light change from the brilliance of a sunny morning to the early dusk of a winter afternoon, how much colour there is in natural so-called "white light" and how much variety in colour can be made by simply brightening or dimming a light'.*

Jennifer Tipton[8]

> **》** **Fast Forward** on the DVD to **16.2 A touch of colour**

Effects of colour and light

➤ **We respond to colour and intensity of light in our daily life**
- The heat of a midsummers day
- The warmth of the sunshine on a spring afternoon
- The harsh light from a hanging light in a room
- The coolness of early morning
- The chill of a cold and frosty day
- The contrast of a bright to an overcast day

➤ **We associate colour with our feelings**
- Red as warm
- Blue as cold
- On a sunny day, we might feel happy
- On an overcast day, we might feel sad, down or depressed

➤ **Colour association**

The association of colours can be very different depending upon the cultural background and the content of the show.[9]

- White may denote purity or innocence in the West, but is more associated with death in the East
- Red may recall foreboding or violence in the West, and luck or prosperity for a Chinese audience

We can simulate these associated responses by playing with the colour and intensity of light on-stage to create a mood or atmosphere to reflect the feelings and action of drama or dance.

[8] Rosco Guide to Colour Filters – Designers on Colour
[9] Ziggy Jacobs – American Lighting Design student

16 THE LIGHTING PALETTE   **More info**

Using colour

Initially, when selecting and using colour filters or 'gels' for lighting, it can be easier to think of them as five groups.

➤ **Five groups of coloured light and filters**
- **Five basic groups**
- **For drama** we normally use:
- **For dance & musicals** we use:

Hot	Warm	Neutral	Cool	Cold
	Warm	Neutral	Cool	
Hot	Warm	Neutral	Cool	Cold

➤ **Warm, neutral & cool – tints & pastels**

A lighter range of warm, neutral and cool colours are mainly used for drama rather than stronger colours. They are close to 'open white' or 'no color' and provide good natural lighting for the face and enhance the costumes and scenery.

- **Warm colours** – middle rose, amber, golden amber, apricot, salmon, pinks, rose, straw, pale gold, yellow
- **Neutral colours** – lavenders, surprise pink, chocolate, cosmetic tints, frost
- **Cool colours** – ice, mist, pale, steel, dark steel, daylight, summer and glacier blues
- These colours are efficient to use as they have a good transmission factor allowing a high output of light to pass through the filter

➤ **Hot & cold – saturated colours**

A range of rich hot and cold colours of deeper intensity including primary and secondary colours. They are used to create strong moods and more dramatic effects that are suited to dance and musicals and used in naturalistic plays in side and back lighting to create atmosphere and effects.

- **Hot colours** – golden amber, deep orange, pale red, bright red, primary red, magenta, bright rose, bright pink
- **Cold colours** – daylight, bright, medium, deep, dark midnight blues, blue green, pale, leaf, moss and primary greens
- **Deep saturated colours** have a lower light transmission factor, producing less light and therefore need to be used over shorter distances and with more powerful lanterns

GLOBAL JARGON
- **Colour filters** (UK) – Gels (NA)

16 THE LIGHTING PALETTE   **More info**

Extras! – Adding colour

Colour adds another dimension to the lighting palette. It can be used to paint the stage with light to create the feelings and mood suggested by the drama, dance or musical, or set the scene, provide the source of illumination to suggest the time of day or season or just enhance the costumes and setting.

Starting points for using colour

The choice of colour will depend upon the required mood or effect, the direction of the light source and to some extent the position that the colour will be used in the lighting rig.

Frontal lighting – acting areas

Warm, neutral and cool colours – the range of light tints and pastel colours are mainly used for the frontal lighting of acting areas to provide good illumination of the actors. They enhance the face and skin tones and complement the colour of costumes and scenic décor without dramatically affecting their colours.

➤ **Two-tone wash – cross area lighting**
When using cross area lighting, the two lanterns lighting each area can be coloured with two slightly different tints: one from stage left, the other from stage right. The pattern is repeated in lighting the areas across the stage. A two-tone wash helps to model the features of the face and soften the shadows created either side of the nose. This effect is demonstrated on the 'Fast forward on the DVD'.

Starting point: an example of colours for a two-tone wash:

- **Warm** two-tone wash: 152 – Pale Gold with 154 – Pale Rose
- **Bright gold** two-tone wash: 013 – Straw Tint with 763 – Wheat
- **Cool** two-tone wash: 117 – Steel Blue with 118 – Light Blue

There are many other colour combinations that can be experimented with.

Two-tone wash – GMSL

>> **Fast Forward** on the DVD to **16.2 A touch of colour**

(margin) Extras!

(margin) 16 THE LIGHTING PALETTE

➤ Neutral colours

The range of neutral colour filters have a unique characteristic as they mix with both warm and cool colours and are also good for lighting the face. They can be used to provide a general acting area wash with highlighted areas in warm or cool colours.

136 Pale Lavender produces a warm/cool white light that changes when mixed with other complementary colours.

Warm tone wash – GMSL

- 136 – Pale Lavender mixed with 154 – Pale Rose produces a warm lit area
- 136 – Pale Lavender mixed with 118 – Light Blue produces a cool lit area

➤ Natural lighting – front area lighting, cycloramas

A range of medium colours with warm, neutral and cool tones produce atmospheric colours used to simulate natural light creating cool daylight, warm sunlight, a hot day, a cool evening and cold moonlight. More vibrant sky colours being used for cyclorama or skycloth washes to reflect the time of day.

Cool tone wash – GMSL

➤ Key & Fill lighting – cross area lighting

The direction and colour of the main dominant source of illumination lighting the scene is reflected in the pairs of lanterns cross lighting each area. For example, bright sunlight coming through a window which is called accent lighting.

- **Key lighting** lights the acting areas from the same side and direction as the main source of illumination. It is coloured in a lighter tint than the colour of the source of accent lighting. The Key lighting provides a highlight to brighten the face
- **Fill lighting** lights the acting areas from the opposite side to the main source of illumination. It is coloured with a paler shade of the colour than the source lighting as if reflecting the colour of the light falling on to opposite wall. The Fill lighting provides a balance to the Key lighting

Other angles of lighting – side, cross, down & back lighting

Warm & cool, hot & cold colours – more saturated, denser colours can be used from these positions to create atmosphere, mood and effects.

➤ Accent lighting – side, cross, down & back lighting

More saturated warm and cool colours can be used in accent lighting to provide the dominant source of light to show the direction and colour of the natural or artificial source of illumination of the scene. Hot and cold colours can be used to emphasise the mood, create an atmosphere or provide a dramatic effect.

For example:

- **Side lighting** providing shafts of strong sunlight through a window
- **Downlighting** from a hanging light fitting in a room
- **Back lighting** creating the effect of moonlight

➤ **An example of accent, Key and Fill lighting**

- **Accent lighting** – source sunset, low warm red side lighting, catching the side of the actor's head

- **Key lighting** – overhead cross area lighting, providing a warm tint from the same side as the accent lighting at a slightly lower intensity to illuminate the actor's face

Accent lighting – GMSL

Key & Fill lighting – GMSL

- **Fill lighting** – overhead cross area lighting from the opposite side, providing a slightly darker warm tint as the reflected sunlight from the walls of the room

➤ **Special and dramatic effects lighting** – down, side, cross and back lighting

- **Hot and cold** – Stronger, more saturated colours, reds, yellows, greens, blues and mauves can be used to create passionate moods and dramatic effects

An example of accent and Key lighting

Crazy Mary – *Playwrights Horizon production – Set Design John Lee Beatty, Lighting Design Brian Aldous – © Roscolab*

(side margin) **Extras!** **16 THE LIGHTING PALETTE**

Crazy Mary *'Back lighting provides the source of accent light from stage left catching the side of the column echoing the direction of the source of artificial light from the light on the piano. The Key lighting from stage left picks up the source from the standard light. A Kaleidoscope Prismatic gobo projected through the window has been carefully shuttered and focused to heighten the effect, so emphasising the time of day and creating the mood on stage.'*

The effects of colour

Some coloured surfaces respond to and reflect the colour of the filtered light, whereas others tend to lose their colour.

➤ **Selecting colours**
The colours of the costumes and set décor will be affected by the colour that is projected on to them, for example:

- A bright-green backcloth lit with pink will look dull
- A pink dress lit in green will lose its colour

In an extreme case, the following colour change can occur:
- Dark-red light turns green black
- Dark-green light turns red black

Care needs to be taken when selecting saturated colours so that they complement and reflect the colours of the costumes and set décor. However, they can be used to create dramatic effect in side, cross and back lighting.

➤ **Lighting the face**
Strong colours can dramatically change the look of the face. Actors' skin tones can only stand the palest of tints unless you want to create a special effect.

- Select colours that have a pink or red content
- Avoid using filters that have a green or blue content
- Check out the SPD curve for the filter, which gives an indication of the range of colours transmitted; see Chapter 8 'Colour filters – Extras!'

➤ **Using colour**
The above examples are provided merely as starting points and are by no means meant to be prescriptive. Choosing and using colour is a very personal thing and it is very dependent upon experience and knowing the effect the colour will have.

Designers on colour – *'I am aware that my audience, like myself, watch a lot of television so I must light to produce much more natural skin tones than I did thirty years ago. My colour ambience now has to surround the actor, tinting the environment, particularly the airspace that the light passes through and the floor that it hits, while leaving the face and costume as naturally coloured as possible – usually with Supergel 351.'* Francis Reid[10]
(Supergel 351 Lavender Mist; E-Colour/LEE filter match 003 Lavender Tint)

[10] Rosco Guide to Colour Filters – Designers on Colour

16 THE LIGHTING PALETTE Extras!

➤ **LEE 700 Series**

'A unique range of colours created by leading Lighting Designers working in stage, screen, television. The designers are invited to work alongside their Research and Development team to create their own unique colours.'[11] The range has such interesting colours as Electric Lilac, Dirty Ice, Steel Green, Oklahoma Yellow and Magical Magenta, and is included as a part of the LEE Designer swatch book.

Did you know that –

- One in ten males has a colour deficiency and cannot clearly see all colours. So, if you are a male, it is a good idea to get your eyes tested so that you are aware of any colour deficiencies that you may have
- The 'Key' and 'Fill' lighting technique originated in television and it has been adopted and used in the theatre
- Footlights were originally mounted on the front of the stage to light the actors before the development of the modern spotlights used for FOH lighting
- L136 Pale Lavender, formerly known as 'Surprise Pink', is a classic neutral colour widely known and used for its unique colour temperatures; not to be confused with L194 Surprise Pink with the same name

MORE TIPS

- Use a colour swatch to select and check your colours
- Check the colour response on costumes and scenery by looking at them through the selected colour filter
- To check the effect of colour on skin tones, shine a tungsten light source through the filter on to the back of your hand
- If you need a deeper version of the same colour, use two sheets of the colour filter known as 'Double colour'
- Daylight is often portrayed on-stage as pale yellow or gold when it is actually pale blue!

[11] LEE Filters

More resources – go to

www.apollodesign.net

www.gamonline.com – GAM Product inc. colour distribution chart

www.leefilters.com/downloads/assets/4127_LF_Paule_Article.pdf – 'Paule Constable in Colour'

www.maxkeller.org – Max Keller Swiss Lighting designers website, imaginative use of lighting and colour

www.leefilters.com – LEE Filters 'Swatch Ball' – downloadable software to assist colour filter selection; 'The Art of Light' – useful guide to colour listed in colour order with a description of the effect and use

www.rosco.com – Rosco downloadable 'Technotes' resources

Rosco 'Guide to Colour Filters' – useful information, lighting designers' ideas of using colour with examples of productions, colour filters listed by use and application – available online

Roscolab 'e-colour+ range', a handy pocket-sized guide listing the uses of colour effects filters

'A choice of color' by Pete Reader

'How to color stage lighting to enhance the color in scenery, costumes, and makeup'

GLOBAL JARGON

■ **Double colour** (UK) – 'doubling up' (NA)

Points for action

Quickies!

■ Log on to www.leefilters.com – register and download 'Swatchball' – take a closer look at the 700 Series designer colour filters

■ Log on to www.gamonline.com/catalog/gamcolor/index.php – view colour distribution chart

■ Obtain copy of LEE Filters 'The Art of Light'

■ Obtain a copy of Rosco 'Guide to Colour Filters' and Roscolab 'e-colour+ range' pocket-sized guide

Takes longer

- Log on to www.maxkeller.org – view gallery of lighting designs
- Log on to www.leefilters.com/downloads/assets/4127_LF_Paule_Article.pdf – read article on designer's thoughts on using colour and designing and making a new colour filter

A proper job!

- Set up some lanterns and try out some of the colour effects below
- Observe the colour change of 136 – Pale Lavender as it fades from a warm white at full intensity to a rosy glow at a low level
- Split colours; try mixing 136 – Pale Lavender with 154 – Pale Rose; 118 – Pale blue and see the effect
- Key & Fill lighting: try using 193 – Rosy Amber Key light and 152 – Pale Gold Fill light; 170 – Deep Lavender Key light and 009 – Pale Amber Fill light
- Try the effect of some strong saturated colour filters on a coloured panelled golfing umbrella

17 Using the lighting palette

A quick start – The elements of lighting

Using the components of lighting to create different effects

More info – The tools of lighting

Blending the elements of lighting to compose a picture of light

Extras! – Lighting the shows

Looking at the way a lighting designer lit a scene from two shows

A quick start – The elements of lighting

'Stage lighting may be defined as the use of light to create a sense of visibility, naturalism, composition and mood or atmosphere.'[12]

>> **Fast Forward** on the DVD to **17.1 The language of lighting**

The elements of lighting

The key points to consider when using the lighting palette are visibility, motivation, composition and mood.

➤ Visibility

The audience's attention can be focused by selecting a single area of light. The focus can be moved and attention redirected by cross fading one area of light to another; adjacent areas can be combined to produce a larger acting area.

❖ *The light from a candle in darkness focuses our attention but it will need a low-level downlight to illuminate the area*
❖ *A desk light has a similar effect but it creates a larger pool of light, needing a brighter level of downlighting with a touch of side lighting to catch the face*

[12] *A Syllabus of Stage Lighting* – Stanley McCandless, 1933

A quick start

17 USING THE LIGHTING PALETTE

- **The lighting can be selective**, only seeing the head and shoulders of the actor or the lower body or just the legs of a dancer

Berlin – *Silo Theatre, Auckland NZ – Lighting Design & Photograph © Andrew Malmo*

'The warm-coloured side lighting from stage right highlights the face and upper body of the actress as she turns into the light.'

❖ *A highlight can draw attention, for example, an actor in partial silhouette back lit by moonlight*

- **Light, shade and shadows** can be very effective; the areas of the stage or set may not need to be equally illuminated

Decadence – *'Potent Pause' productions, Maidment Studio Theatre, Auckland NZ – Lighting Design & Photograph © Andrew Malmo*

'Caught in the moment of time as a single source of cross lighting catches the actor's head and shoulders, highlighting the face and arm of the actress.'

❖ *Walking through shafts of sunlight through a densely wooded area which can be created by using break-up gobos in overhead profile lanterns downlighting the stage. The shadows created obscure what is seen but can add to the visual interest*

❖ *A subtle variation to the intensity of the quality of a front lighting wash can be created by using large break-up gobos but the number of lanterns will need to be increased to ensure adequate illumination*

❖ *Textured light can add realistic visual effects to the setting, for example, gobo break-ups creating shadows projected by sunlight or shafts of light through a window or blind*

■ **Dramatic lighting** or the effects from moving lights may be very impressive but it is important that the action is still illuminated

❖ *The shape and angle of the beam of light can add a dramatic effect like a vertical shaft of light projecting a Les Mis[13] grille gobo on to the stage*

➤ Motivation – *Where is the light coming from?*

Uncle Vanya – *Birmingham Repertory Theatre production – Lighting Designer Mark Jonathan, Photograph © Robert Day*

'An atmospheric effect as moonlight catches the window frames spilling on to the floor. Low-level side lighting illuminates the actors at either end as if radiating from the lamp in the middle of the table.'

[13] The grille effects as used in the production of *Les Misérables*

17 USING THE LIGHTING PALETTE   A quick start

For a realistic setting, the aim of the designer is to provide natural lighting and a sense of time and place. The motivation or reason for the illumination may be provided by natural or artificial light sources, sun, moon or daylight, lamp, candle or firelight. This dominant light source provides the direction and influences the way in which the rest of the stage is lit, imitating the natural effect.

❖ *Interior settings* may be lit by a natural light source from outside, sun or moonlight, or an artificial source from a light fitting inside
❖ *Exterior settings* are dependent on the effects of natural sources of light, shadows and textures that are created, e.g. sunlight through the trees
❖ *Non-realistic or abstract styles* of productions may require a more stylistic or dramatic form of lighting, e.g. the stark white flat lighting associated with Brechtian epic theatre

➢ **Composition – *What sort of picture do we want the audience to see?***

We Will Rock You – *Tigz Productions, Sundial Theatre – Lighting Design Andy Webb, Photograph © Nik Sheppard*

A picture can be created by using the lighting to:

■ **Complement** the setting with balanced illumination that reveals everything
■ **Contrast** by using highlights and shadows to focus the audience's attention to a part of the setting or a specific part of the action
■ **Reveal** the action and the setting in proportion to their importance as required

> Mood – *What do we want the audience to feel about the scene?*

Creating an atmosphere that reflects the mood of the scene is perhaps the main aim of stage lighting. This is achieved by the careful blending of the other three elements of stage lighting: visibility, motivation and composition.

Our House – *Tigz Productions, Bacon Theatre – Lighting Design Andy Webb,* *Photograph © Nik Sheppard*

237

More info – The tools of lighting

Good lighting should tie together all the visual aspects of the stage with light to paint a picture and create an environment in which the actors can interpret and develop their roles. It should assist them in every way to bring the audience to an understanding of the full meaning and emotion of the unfolding drama.[14]

The tools of lighting

There are four tools that a lighting designer can use to control and blend the elements of stage lighting. The visibility as seen by the eye is affected not only by the reflected brightness but also by the colour, contrast with other illuminated areas, movement of the action and the viewing distance. This all needs to be taken into account.

➤ Intensity

Our House – *Tigz Productions, Bacon Theatre – Lighting Design Andy Webb, Photograph © Nik Sheppard*

The intensity of the light source from the lantern affects the brightness of the reflected light from the object that is being lit. The overall intensity of the lighting can affect the feel of the scene. The intensity and angles of natural light change with the time of day producing different effects.

❖ *Afternoon sunlight through a window changing to low sunset can be created by crossfading from higher- to lower-level side lighting lanterns with different colours*

❖ *The source of light illuminating the room changes from fading sunlight to an artificial light source being switched on. A downlight source of light is switched on with a practical light fitting, with a change in level of Key and Fill lighting*

❖ *Low-level illumination from an overhead hanging artificial light fitting can create an intense feeling of depression with steep angled frontal lighting covering the area illuminated by the practical fitting*

[14] Scene Design and Stage Lighting – Parker & Smith

'The stage lighting designer is more concerned with the brightness of an object than the intensity of its light source. He soon learns that objects of higher brightness generally draw attention on stage. Light attracts! Conversely, darkness conceals.'[15] *But this can grab your attention equally and keep the audience on the edge of their seats.*

➤ Colour

Our House – *Tigz Productions, Bacon Theatre – Lighting Design Andy Webb, Photograph © Nik Sheppard*

Colour is a major component used in composing the lighting picture and in creating the mood. It can also be used to enrich the costumes, emphasise the dimension of the setting and enhance the painted decoration of the set. It can set the scene and create the feeling of the icy coldness of a winter day, the coolness of a wet overcast day, the warmth of a spring morning or the heat of a hot summer day.

The effective use of colour is one of the most challenging aspects of stage lighting. Through practice and experience, one develops feel for the use of colour.

❖ *Light tints can be used to soften the lighting subtly*
❖ *Stronger colours can emphasise the more realistic dominant sources of light*
❖ *Deeper colours can provide a contrast*
❖ *The colour of lighting areas can blend together to create an even wash or they can create a contrast*

---

[15] 'Stage Lighting Design' – Bill Williams

UNIVERS... ...ESTER
LIBRARY

> **Distribution & direction**

War Horse – *National Theatre production – Lighting Design Paule Constable,*
Photograph © Simon Annand

The distribution of the sources of light around the stage, the direction, height and
angle of illumination affect the style of the lighting picture that can be created
and can add to the mood of the lighting.

- ❖ *A single source of light will produce a hard shadow like a follow spot. A row of*
  sources of light produce a soft wash of light with hardly any shadows
- ❖ *A solo spot pinpoints the action*
- ❖ *Changing the distribution of the lighting from one area to another moves the*
  focus of attention
- ❖ *A steeply raked angle of lighting can produce a dramatic effect. A lower level*
  of light will produce a flatter effect. Shadows change depending upon the
  direction and angle of the source of the light

> **Movement**

Comedy of Errors – *Cirencester Youth Theatre, Lighting Design Andy Webb,*
Photograph © Nik Sheppard

'The break-up of the beams in the back lighting can be seen as it is picked up in the
haze. The slow movement of the rotating gobos added to the magical background of the
setting.'

The change in intensity, colour, distribution and direction of the lighting can create
movement in the scene. The movement may be a slow and subtle change that the
audience may hardly notice but feel emotionally or a fast-moving dynamic effect.

❖ *A slow rise in the intensity of light as the level of natural light changes during*
   the day
❖ *The change in the natural colour on a cyc cloth from sunrise to morning light*
❖ *A slow crossfade from one area to another or change in colour*
❖ *The change in the angle and height in the sources of light as the sun from*
   midday to late afternoon
❖ *A change in direction by cutting from one area to another can produce a*
   dynamic effect
❖ *Colour changes in the lighting areas can be made by using duplicate lanterns,*
   colour scrollers or DMX controlled mixing systems on moving heads or LED
   fixtures

241

❖ *Moving heads can provide the unseen flexibility to be repositioned, focused and coloured to light areas during the show or create dynamic moving effects*
❖ *Movement within the beams of light with optical effects, moving projections and rotating gobos*
❖ *Follow spots provide a moving beam of light to follow the main action, focus in on the head and shoulders as used in musical theatre or blend with the general level of lighting to highlight the actor in epic-style drama*

Good facial illumination is important when lighting the show but we have to find ways of combining this with dramatic effects to captivate the audience's imagination and to create that real 'wow' factor of lighting design.

MORE TIPS

■ **Sunlight** – use parallel beams of light from Parcans mounted in the same position to pass through the window in the set to produce a sharp pattern on whatever they strike
■ **Daylight on an overcast day** – a directionless flood of light can be created by a 2.5kW Fresnel with barndoors to produce a soft edged wash
■ **Good lighting** is when the audience doesn't notice it!

More resources – go to

Google 'Stage lighting design'/Bill Williams – Part 1 An introduction to stage lighting – the objectives & qualities of stage lighting

More info

17 USING THE LIGHTING PALETTE

Extras! – Lighting the shows

A lighting designer explains how he has designed the lighting for scenes from two shows.

➤ Lighting for dance – *Swan Lake*

Swan Lake *ballet – Director/Choreographer Mathew Bourne, New Adventures & Backrow Productions – Designer Lez Brotherston, Lighting Design Rick Fisher, Photograph © Mike Rothwell*

'The swans are almost entirely lit with side light which is arranged on lighting booms in each of the bays between the white columns and a boom that is just in front of the proscenium to cover the forestage.

'The booms in this case have 6 lights on each of them. With a "shin" that is focused across the stage but does not hit the floor and lights the full body of the dancer as long as they are about 2m away from the boom. Then there are similar profiles arranged above this lowest unit to cross light the stage with some of the units focusing up stage to help pick out the facial expressions which are such a part of the production of Swan Lake.

'All lights are kept off the floor which is lit solely with either a wash of backlight parcans or large fresnels (5K and 2K if the stage is especially wide) with scrollers to give as close to a single source colour treatment as possible. This helps the stage to look "cleanly lit". The Prince (downstage centre) is lit with a follow spot.

'The footlights visible in the picture (1K open-faced low profile floods) are used to create illumination and shadows; this particular moment is not one of them.'

Rick Fisher

➤ Lighting for musical theatre – *Billy Elliot*

Billy Elliot The Musical – *Director Stephen Daldry, Designer Ian MacNeil, Lighting Design Rick Fisher, Photographer Tristram Kenton*

'This brief moment in the finale of Act 1 of Billy Elliot *(Angry Dance) is a particular favourite of mine. As the police land the riot shields on stage the lighting changes instantly to highlight the shields in deep blue from two overhead VL3500Q spots focused tightly to the line of police.*

'*The rest of the stage uses almost every other available light in deep red including some boom side lights to light Billy and keep in a drastically different space from the riot police. Haze in the air, which is rarely used in this musical, helps the light to appear sculptural and solid.*

'*As the dance progresses, the shapes of the spots change with the choreography and the snaps in colour echo the beats of the music and emotion to create isolation of Billy while he is dancing very close to the police.*'

Rick Fisher

17 USING THE LIGHTING PALETTE

Extras!

Lighting jargon – What's it called?

➤ Rigging

Advance bar	Lighting bar hung in front of the proscenium arch
Boom bar	A vertical bar on the side wall of the auditorium or stage used to mount lanterns on boom arms
Lighting bar	Horizontal aluminium bar on which lanterns are hung
Lighting layout plan	A scale drawing of the stage showing the lighting bars and the positions of the lanterns
Lighting rig	A general term for the lanterns hanging on the lighting bars
Patching	Process of temporarily linking or 'hooking up' lanterns via outlet sockets to dimmers
1:1 soft patch	Control channel fader No.1 controls dimmer No.1
'T' Bar	Bar attached to a spigot, placed in the top of a stand from which to hang lanterns

➤ Lanterns

Field/beam angle	The spread of the cone of light projected by a lantern measured in degrees
Flagging the lantern	Waving your hand in front of a lantern in the beam of light to see the spread and the extent of the spill light
Floats	Original term for footlights, or small lanterns used on the front of the stage to uplight the face
Footlights	A group of floodlight units mounted in a single row used on the front of the stage
Fresnel	Adjustable focus lantern, soft edged diffused beam with more spill light than a PC
Front of House (FOH)	In front of the proscenium arch
PC/Prism/Pebble	Adjustable focus lantern, hard/semi-soft edged intense beam with less spill light than a Fresnel
Profile spotlight	Adjustable focus lantern, precise hard edged beam of light that can be soft focused
Throw	Distance from the lantern to the stage

➤ Stage directions

(SL) Stage left	Actor's left when facing the audience
(SR) Stage right	Actor's right when facing the audience
(PS) Prompt side	Traditionally stage left in the UK
(OP) Opposite prompt	Stage right
House left	Left side of the auditorium viewed from the direction of the audience
House right	Right side of auditorium

Up stage	Away from the audience
Down stage	Nearest to the audience
On-stage	Towards the centre of the stage
Off-stage	Away from the centre of the stage towards the wings

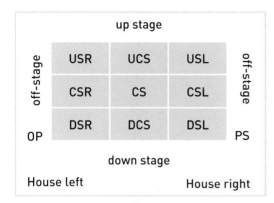

USL – up stage left, **UCS** – up stage centre, **USR** – up stage right
CSL – centre stage left, **CS** – centre stage, **CSR** – centre stage right
DSL – down stage left, **DCS** – down stage centre, **DSR** – down stage right

➢ The lighting palette

Accent light	Dominant lighting which replicates the main natural source of illumination for the scene
Fill light	Lanterns providing a wash of light adding balance to the Key light
Key light	Lantern providing the main dominant source of illumination or highlight
Open white	'No colour', white light, no colour filter being used
Double colour	'Doubling up' (NA), two sheets of the same colour filter mounted in a colour frame to provide a deeper shade of the same colour

Lighting the Show

From page to stage – As a competent technician, the natural progression is to extend your experience by starting to light a show. Lighting the show focuses on the process of lighting design and the contrast between lighting small to large productions. Also, it introduces the use of CAD and the methods of plotting and programming the show.

18 Preparing to light the show

A quick start – Starting points

Introducing the team and starting to prepare the design

More info – Preparing a plan

Making a scaled drawing of a lighting layout plan

Extras! – Working with CAD

Looking at Computer Aided Design software for lighting layout drawings

A quick start – Starting points

There are a number of closely interrelated people involved in the production process, so it is important to know who does what, when and where and how the lighting designer fits into the team.

Who's who & who does what?

➤ **The production team**
    The production team may consist of some or all of the following:

   ■ **Producer** – responsible for all the business arrangements for mounting the stage production and engaging the director. In the commercial theatre, there may be more than one producer or a group who are sharing the financial responsibility

- **Director** – responsible for all the artistic aspects and direction of the production, producing the show on time and within the budget
- **Design team** – artistic team working alongside the director to design and produce the visual look of the production, set, costume, lighting and sound
- **Production Manager** (Technical Director) – used by permanent theatre companies, with similar responsibilities to that of the commercial producers but also responsible for technical preparations and planning

➤ **The Lighting Designer (LD)**

The lighting designer is responsible for the design of the production lighting and effects, and for preparing and producing the drawings and schedules required for the lighting equipment to be installed and connected by the lighting crew. The LD directs the focusing, and supervises the programming/plotting and all artistic elements of the lighting design until the opening of the production.[1]

➤ **Chief Electrician** (Production or Head Electrician)

The chief electrician is responsible in the professional theatre for organising and supervising the rigging of the lighting equipment by the lighting crew and the running of the production. For small college and amateur productions, this role may also be undertaken by the LD.

➤ **Stage management team**

- **Stage Manager (SM)** – head of the stage management team, responsible for coordinating the production team, the welfare of the actors and the oversight of the rehearsals, supervision of all the technical aspects of mounting the production on-stage and running the show. In North America, the Stage Manager would normally call the show from the lighting and sound control room out front
- **Deputy Stage Manager (DSM)** – responsible for coordinating rehearsals and recording the actors' moves as they are blocked and all the artistic, design and technical decisions that develop during rehearsal in the prompt book. In the UK, the DSM is 'normally on the book', calling the cues for the show from the prompt corner, and when necessary 'giving a line', prompting. In North America, there are no DSMs, only assistant stage managers (ASMs)

Did you know that –

- Traditionally in the UK, the stage has been managed and the show 'run' from the prompt corner which is on the stage left
- In some theatres, the prompt corner and stage manager desk may be on the stage right because of the layout of the building and the position of the dressing rooms related to the stage, and it is referred to as a 'bastard prompt' but this is no reflection on the DSM running the corner!

[1] *Stage Lighting Design*, Bill Williams

- However, the term Prompt Side is always stage left and Opposite Prompt stage right, no matter the position of the prompt corner
- It is important to retain this convention, as the scenery on touring productions is traditionally marked as PS and OP to show the side of stage that it is to be used or positioned
- The stage manager's desk traditionally has a set of cue lights to all lighting, sound, orchestra, flies, follow spots, etc. that are used to cue the show: red (stand by) and green (go)
- Headsets or 'cans' are now used by the DSM to call the cues, although lights can still be used for a visual reinforcement. The DSM may well be positioned along with lighting and sound in an FOH control position

Preparation before you start to design the lighting

'The designer must know what he is lighting and how he wants the production to look. The designer must be very familiar with the script and all lighting requirements of the production. He must use the qualities of light and objectives of stage lighting to allow him to fully visualize, verbalize and define his design concept and intentions.'[2]

➤ **Read the script**
Prior to meeting with the director, read the script at least twice and record your thoughts.

- First time, try to get the overall feel of the production
- Second time, look for clues that could affect the lighting of each scene, time of day, season, general mood or emotional flash points
- For musical theatre and dance, listen to and become familiar with the music

➤ **Meet with production team**
This may not always be possible and you may have to just attend the rehearsals, watch, gather your own information and make some creative decisions. However, if you do have the opportunity to meet, talk, listen and discuss with the director and the designers, try to find out:

- How the production is going to be staged and the basic lighting requirements
- The lighting requirements of the set design
- What colours will be used in the set and costumes
- The style of lighting required, natural, realistic, abstract, lighting for dance
- The feel of the production reflecting the emotional qualities developed by the playwright or the director's and designer's interpretation of the script
- The changes in mood or atmosphere, season or time of day that need to be created
- How the lighting will be used to select areas and to create special effects

[2] *Stage Lighting Design*, Bill Williams

- The positions of the main acting areas, 'specials', solo areas and any special effects
- Budget available for the hire of additional equipment and purchase of colour filters, gobos, etc.
- Production timetable, time available for rigging, focusing, plotting, tech run and dress rehearsals

➤ Research

- **Set design** – study the model of the set, identify any obvious source of illuminating windows or light fittings, photograph the model and scene changes, obtain a copy of the plan and elevation
- **Costume designs** – study the sketches for the designs, photograph the designs and endeavour to obtain samples of the main coloured materials to be used
- **Visit the theatre space** – walk the stage, view all the rigging positions, estimate the lengths of throw and the angle of illumination of the lanterns, check out the local electrics staff available for the production. Obtain a copy of the stage plan and elevation showing the layout of the lighting bars and the permanently installed circuit outlet socket numbers or make a survey drawing to produce your own plans
- **Check the equipment available:**
  Lanterns – the numbers of each type, make and model
  Dimmer packs/racks – the total number of dimmers mains electrical power available
  Control desk – make and model, specification control circuits, memory facilities, moving fixtures
- **Attend rehearsals** – note the positions of the main acting areas, entrances and movement of the actors, as this can suggest the direction of the lighting; check the blocking with the DSM
- **Play around with your ideas** – try to visualise the lighting of the action and the set, the angles of the lighting, the colours that might be used and the changes in the states of lighting
- **Record your ideas** – sketch out visual ideas and plans, experiment, talk and share ideas with the director and designers

'Creative lighting is the technique of reproducing the characteristics of natural lighting in order to stimulate specific subconscious feelings.'

> **》** **Fast Forward** on the DVD to **18.1 Designing the show**

GLOBAL JARGON

- **Chief Electrician** (UK) – Production/Head/Master Electrician (NA)

More info – Preparing a plan

It is important to have a lighting layout plan of the venue that you are working in to fully understand the layout of the lighting system and to use it efficiently. The plan is like a 'Road Map' that will guide you to success and without it you may get lost.

Lighting layout plan

A layout plan of the stage and auditorium should show the positions of lighting bars and the layout of all the outlet sockets and circuit numbers. The plan is used to record the position of the lanterns and the dimmer circuit numbers that control them.

➤ **Making a survey and plan of the lighting system**

If a plan is not available when working in a new venue, the first thing to do is to make a survey plan, even if it is only a quick sketch. The basic measurements of the space will also be required.

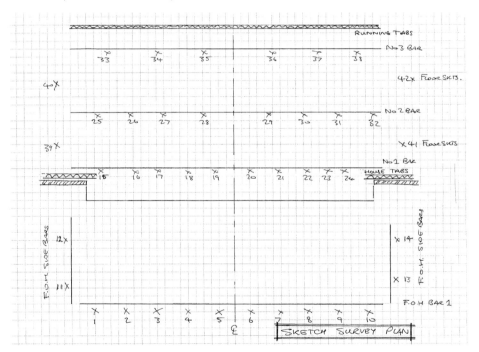

Sketch survey plan – GMSL

■ Draw up a sketch survey plan with the positions of all the lighting bars. If possible, use squared paper – it will help you keep the drawing in proportion. Find out where all the circuit outlet sockets are and mark their positions using a cross and record the socket numbers

253

- If the sockets are not numbered, work out a sequence starting from stage right to left on each lighting bar, and from front of house to the up stage bars
- Number all the sockets, so that they can be clearly seen from the stage, as this will help with rigging and the identification of the lanterns
- Draw up a scaled plan using a CAD program or
- Make an accurate scaled drawing of the lighting layout plan on a sheet of A3 or A4 squared paper, depending upon the size required, using the information from the sketch survey drawing. Use a centre line as marked on the example plan to help keep the layout and the positions of the bars and sockets symmetrical
- Use a stencil to draw small circles to mark the positions of the outlet sockets and place the circuit number inside the circle
- Keep the original copy safe and use it as the master for photocopying. A3-size plans are used for designing the layout of lanterns. Reducing the size on a photocopier to A4 will provide a useful size to carry round with you to quickly identify the circuit outlet socket numbers

➤ **Scaled plans**

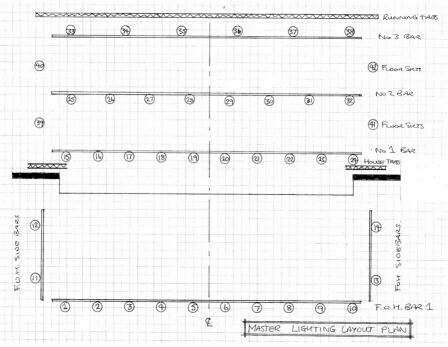

Lighting layout plan scaled drawing – GMSL

Using a scaled drawing of the plan gives a better idea of the usage of space and the positioning of the lanterns and it is essential to use when working on a medium- to large-size stage

- A measured survey will be needed to draw up an accurate scaled plan
- The lantern stencils are produced to fit either a 1:25 or 1:50 metric scale
- The most common scale used in the theatre is 1:25 or ½" to 1ft in the American system or what is sometimes called the 'English units'. Theatre designers also use this scale for their drawings and models in order to provide sufficient detail
- 1:50m or ¼":1ft scales are used for very large venues where it would be impossible to fit the drawing on to a large enough sheet
- 1:25 is a standard metric scale used for theatre drawings that is:

1mm Drawing size		Represents 25mm Actual (full) size	
1mm	=	25mm	(.025m)
4mm	=	100mm	(.100m)
10mm	=	250mm	(.250m)
20mm	=	500mm	(.500m)
40mm	=	1000mm	(1.000m)
80mm	=	2000mm	(2.000m)
160mm	=	4000mm	(4.000m)
500mm	=	5000mm	(5.000m)

- On a 1:25 metric scale drawing, 1mm represents 25mm full-size measurement. The use of a scaled rule removes the need to calculate the scaled measurement as the graduations are marked with the full-size measurement
- Start with a centre line and construct the position of the proscenium arch, front of stage, side and rear walls. Draw in the positions of the lighting bars
- When working on a scale drawing, it is possible to plan the accurate positions and the spacing of the lanterns on the bars, which can then be replicated by Lx crew when rigging on-stage

18 PREPARING TO LIGHT THE SHOW   **More info**

GLOBAL JARGON

- UK – A4 & A3 is a standard metric size of paper and you can see from the A3 measurements that it is the equivalent of putting two sheets of A4 side by side: A4 = 210mm x 297mm; A3 = 297mm x 420mm
- NA – A4 = 8¼" x 11¾"; A3 = 11¾" x 16½"
- American units of measurement

American system scale 'English units' ½" : 1ft	
Measurements on the drawing =	**Full-size measurement**
½" =	1 ft
1" =	2 ft
2" =	4 ft
2½" =	5 ft

MORE TIPS

- Metric and Imperial (ft and inches) scale rules can be purchased from drawing equipment suppliers
- Laminate a copy of the lighting layout plan and use a non-permanent OHP pen to record the position of lanterns; the plan can then be wiped clean and reused
- Large self-adhesive numbers for numbering outlet sockets are available from most stage lighting suppliers
- A4 size plans are easier to carry around when identifying lanterns and circuit outlet socket numbers. They can be easily made by reducing an A3 plan on a photocopier to A4

GLOBAL JARGON

- **Lx crew** (UK) – shortened term used for the electric crew

Points for action

Quickies!
■ Check out if there is a plan of the stage that you are going to use

Takes longer
■ If there is no plan available, make a sketch survey plan of the lighting rig

A proper job!
■ Draw up a lighting layout plan

18 PREPARING TO LIGHT THE SHOW

More info

Extras! – Working with CAD (computer aided design)

Lighting layout plans and elevations can be constructed by using a computer drawing program, 2D plan drawing software or a dedicated stage lighting Computer Aided Design (CAD) program.

Computer software

➤ Draw/ 2D CAD programs

Drawings can be produced by using the CIE basic lantern symbols which can be easily constructed.

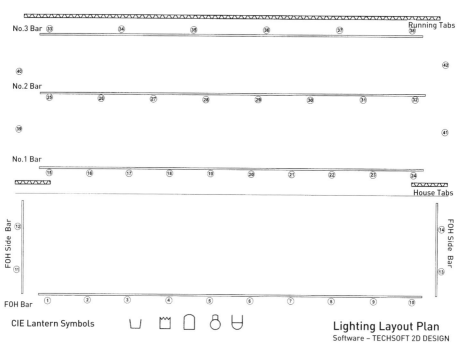

CAD plan – GMSL

- Draw programs can be found on most standard computer software and they can be used to produce a schematic lighting plan. A4-size printouts can be enlarged to A3 on a photocopier to provide a larger working plan. The major drawback is that these drawings will not be to scale which makes it little more than a sketch but it can be used for a small production
- 2D CAD programs can be used to construct the basic CIE lighting symbols and lighting layout plans plans or 'plots' to scale

Extras!

18 PREPARING TO LIGHT THE SHOW

Stage lighting CAD programs

CAD lantern symbols are available from the lantern manufacturers but they can only be used with a dedicated stage lighting CAD program. The programs available provide a range of levels of outcome:

- 2D plans of the stage and lantern layout to scale
- Sectional elevation drawings
- 3D views
- Generate paperwork direct from the plan to produce equipment lists of lanterns, accessories, control channels and patching, colour call and power calculations
- Rendered photo realistic 3D visuals of the lighting designs
- Pre-visualisation allowing the design of cue structure and the pre-programming of the show

Stage lighting software

The following software is commercially available and has been custom designed to produce scaled lighting drawings for the entertainment industry:

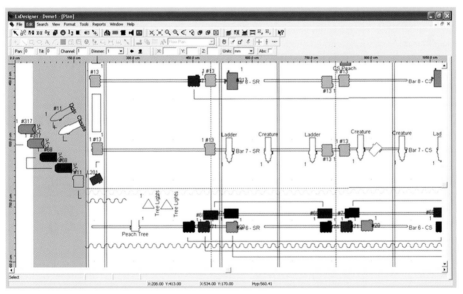

LxDesigner plan – Michael Mackie-Clark

LxDesigner – suitable for FE college use and possibly small venues

LxDesigner is an easy-to-use design environment for stage lighting, suitable for use in schools, colleges and small venues. 'Included are a number of libraries which contain symbols for the various set, rigging and fixtures used in the design process. The plan is built up by simply dragging and dropping the required symbols on to the drawing area or by using one of the built-in tools such as the

259

truss builder. The package has a number of built-in reports which can be used to generate the paperwork associated with the design such as gel, rigging and equipment calls.' There are additional add-on features available, providing side, front and perspective views. The website provides a comprehensive set of demo movies providing online training tutorials that click automatically through the stages of its use.[3]

➤ **CAST wysiwyg** – industry standard
wysiwyg, named after the abbreviation of What You See Is What You Get, is an industry standard dedicated stage lighting design software. With wysiwyg it is possible to pre-visualise (virtually) the set and stage lighting designs before installing the rig or even occupying the venue. Its powerful pre-cueing and pre-visualisation can be used offsite on a PC linked to a lighting control desk to plot cues for an entire show in virtual realtime for generic lanterns, moving lights and other DMX fixtures. It can also replicate the streaming of media content to coordinate with the lighting. The pre-cueing and pre-visualisation facilities can make significant savings in energy and the time used in the venue.

There are three versions of wysiwyg:

- **Report** – 2D CAD plans and elevations generation of paperwork
- **Design** – Photo realistic 3D renderings of the proposed designs
- **Perform** – Pre-visualisation of the lighting plot, design of cue structure and programming online from the lighting desk

➤ **Vectorworks Spotlight** – industry standard
Spotlight is part of a sophisticated suite of CAD design software for the entertainment industry. 'It marries precision 2D drafting and flexible 3D modelling with advanced lighting-design, visualization, and production tools. It can easily draft light plots, create stunning set designs, automate paperwork and visualize design concepts in 3D.'[4]

➤ **Industry standards**
wysiwyg & **Vectorworks** are regarded as an industry standard, and they are used in Higher Education, so it is worthwhile trying to gain some experience in using either of these programs. The ability to use AutoCAD is steadily growing in demand as a skill required of an assistant lighting designer, so the more experience you can get the better.

[3] www.lxdesign.co.uk; www.kave.co.uk – Kave Theatre Services information on LxDesigner
[4] www.nemetschek.net/spotlight

GLOBAL JARGON

- **Lighting plan** or I prefer lighting layout plan (UK) – Lighting plots (NA)
- **Colour call** (UK) – Color schedule (NA)

Extra resources – go to

www.onstagelighting.co.uk – stage lighting blog 'useful resource to help those new to stage lighting'

www.modelboxplans.com – free CAD lantern symbols available for use on AutoCAD

www.lxdesign.co.uk – online training tutorials

www.kave.co.uk – Kave Theatre Services information on LxDesigner

www.nemetschek.net/spotlight – Vectorworks Spotlight demo copies available

www.cast-soft.com – CAST software Ltd, wysiwyg demo copies available

www.autodesk.com – request a free student copy of AutoCAD

Points for action

Takes longer

- View LxDesign online demo/training tutorials

A proper job

- Download and evaluate demo copy of LxDesign
- Download and evaluate demo copy of wysiwyg

18 PREPARING TO LIGHT THE SHOW

Extras!

19 Planning the design

A quick start – Lantern layout plan

'Planning on paper gives me the space to play around creatively and form my ideas. I like to start by working on a large 1:25 scale A1 size plan of the stage and set on a drawing board as it helps me to visualise the space and the position of the sources of light. As I draw in the positions of the lanterns with a stencil I plan the spacing on the lighting bar as it is in "real time". When the creative thinking is complete then I transfer my plan to the computer to do all the detailed planning and paper work.' Andy Webb, Lighting designer

Constructing a lantern layout plan

Some designers find it easier to start to visualise their ideas and plan their design on paper, while others will start using a CAD program.

When working on a scaled plan drawing, it is essential to use lantern stencils to plan the positions of the lanterns. The CIE international symbol stencils are fairly satisfactory for small-size rigs. For larger rigs, the 1:25 scaled manufacturer's symbol stencils should be used in order to make sure that there is enough space to fit all the lanterns on to the lighting bars.

➤ **Guidelines when drawing a plan**
- Draw the lantern in the position and angled in the direction that it is going to be used

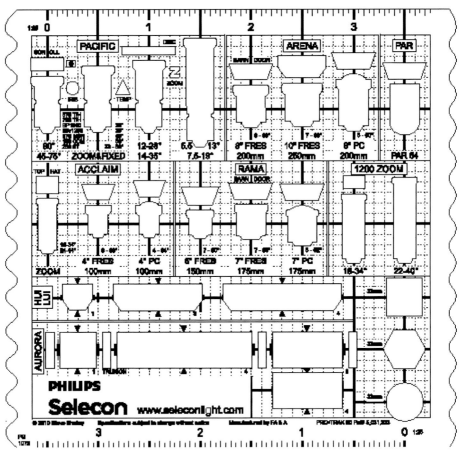

Selecon lantern stencil – Field template Steve L Shelly

- Allow enough space where lanterns are crossing in front of each other, i.e. lighting the opposite side of the stage especially if one lantern is smaller in length than the other, e.g. Acclaim Fresnel next to Source Four Profile
- Allow space where barndoors or moving effects are going to be used on lanterns
- Record the control channel number that will operate the lantern or fixture at the rear of the lantern symbol
- Record the colour filter number in front of the lantern symbol
- If there are circuit outlet sockets marked on the plan indicate with a line to which socket the lanterns will be connected

---

Quick resources – go to

www.stage-electrics.co.uk – Selecon Lighting stencils
www.whitelight.ltd.uk – generic-style lighting stencils

More info – Which lantern to use & where

Profiles, PCs, Fresnels, Parcans, Floods – each lantern produces a different type of beam and quality of light, so it is important to consider their individual characteristics and match them to their use.

> **»** **Fast Forward** on the DVD to **19.1 Which lantern to use where**

Selecting lanterns

There are a number of things that you should consider when deciding which lantern to use and where.

➤ **Points to consider:**
- **The effect** that you want to create
- **The position** of the light source, FOH or on-stage, side, cross, back lighting or special effects
- **Length of throw** that is required
- **The size** of the beam required
- **The quality** of the beam of light required, hard, semi-hard, semi-soft, soft, accurately shaped or profiled
- **Types and numbers** of the lanterns available
- **Intensity/wattage** of the lanterns available

➤ **Position and length of throw:**
- **Short throw** lanterns are generally used overhead on small stages and for medium throw on larger stages
- **Medium/long throw** lanterns are used FOH in medium-sized auditoriums and long throw in larger spaces

The potential range of a lantern

This can be identified by the name of the model and wattage, and for Profiles their field/beam angle. For full details, see Part 3: 'Lighting Resources – Technical info. – Lantern reference guide'.

   For example, the following are lanterns from the Philips Selecon range:

- **Name and wattage** of Fresnels, PCs and Profiles
  Acclaim 500W/650 watt – short throw distance
  Rama 1000W/1200 watt – medium throw distance
  Arena 2000W/2500 watt – long throw distance
  Pacific 1000W – medium/long throw

19 PLANNING THE DESIGN

More info

- **Field/beam angle**, e.g. 24/44° are frequently used to identify the type of Profile spot
  Acclaim 24/44° zoomspot – short throw distance
  Acclaim 18/34° zoomspot – medium throw distance
  Acclaim Axial 18/34° zoomspot – long throw distance
  Pacific 12/28° – long throw distance

- **North America** lanterns are identified by the lens diameter and the focal length
  Altman Ellipsoidal 360Q 6 x 12 – 6 inch dia. lens x 12 inch focal length but this doesn't give any information on the beam angle or spread

NB: each manufacturer produces their own range of lanterns with their own model names

Field/beam angle

The size of the cone of light projected by a lantern increases with the distance and length of throw.

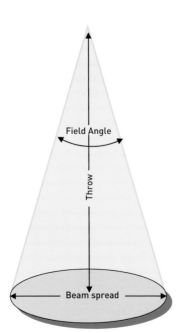

Field Angle

Throw

Beam spread

Field/beam angle of light

> **The field/beam angle** quoted in degrees by a manufacturer indicates the size of the beam, e.g. 18° a narrow beam, 34° a wide beam. The minimum/maximum angles quoted by the manufacturers for each model indicate the characteristics and performance of the lantern and how and where they can be used. The diameter of the cone of light projected by a lantern can be calculated by making a scaled drawing of the length of throw from the lantern and the field/beam angle.

> **The length of throw from a lantern**
> It is necessary to calculate the true length of throw by constructing a right-angle triangle using the vertical height of the lantern to the stage and the horizontal distance to the centre of the lighting area. This can be measured on-stage or found from the lantern layout plan and side elevation drawing of the lighting rig. The triangle can be constructed as a scaled drawing on 5mm square grid paper using a 1:50 scale where 4 squares represent 1m as below. The third side represents the true length of throw that can be measured with a scale rule or calculated from the grid by rotating the length of the side with a compass into the vertical position.

(sidebar) **More info**

19 PLANNING THE DESIGN

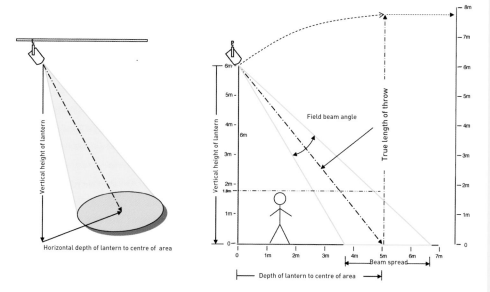

Constructing the true length of throw of a beam of light

➤ **The true length of throw from a lantern can be found on the following chart:**

True length of throw (metres) – lantern to centre of the area							
10m	10.40	10.70	11.20	11.60	12.20	12.80	13.40
9m	9.50	9.80	10.30	10.80	11.40	12.00	12.70
8m	8.50	8.90	9.40	10.00	10.60	11.30	12.00
7m	7.60	8.10	8.60	9.20	9.90	10.60	11.40
6m	6.70	7.20	7.80	8.50	9.20	10.00	
5m	5.80	6.40	7.10	7.80	8.60		
4m	5.00	5.65	6.40	7.20			
	3m	**4m**	**5m**	**6m**	**7m**	**8m**	**9m**

*(Left axis: **Vertical height of lantern**)*

Horizontal depth from lanterns to centre of the area

➤ **The spread of a beam of light**

The spread or the diameter of a beam of light can be found on the following chart by relating the true length of throw from the lantern to the centre of the area and the field/beam angle.

Beam spread diameter (metres)[5]

Field angle										
5°	0.3	0.3	0.4	0.5	0.6	0.7	0.8	0.9	1.0	1.1
10°	0.5	0.7	0.9	1.0	1.2	1.4	1.6	1.7	1.9	2.1
19°	1.0	1.3	1.7	2.0	2.3	2.7	3.0	3.3	3.7	4.0
26°	1.4	1.8	2.3	2.8	3.2	3.7	4.2	4.6	5.1	5.5
36°	1.9	2.6	3.2	3.9	4.5	5.2	5.8	6.5	7.1	7.8
50°	2.8	3.7	4.7	5.6	6.5	7.5	8.4	9.3	10.3	11.2
	3m	4m	5m	6m	7m	8m	9m	10m	11m	12m

True length of throw/distance of lantern to centre of the area

> **The intensity of light**

The intensity of the light output is measured in Lux. This will vary depending upon the size of the beam and the length of throw. The light output from a lantern decreases as the beam is enlarged and the length of throw increased, as can be seen in the diagrams in 'Extras!'. Therefore, it is important to consider the position and the length of throw when selecting the type of lantern.

■ **Fresnels & PCs** – a narrow beam of light from a spot focus produces the maximum output: as the beam is widened to a Flood focus, it decreases in intensity. Fresnels and PCs can be used with a fairly wide focus over a short throw and a spot focus over a medium throw without losing too much intensity

■ **Zoomspot Profiles** – on a short throw, a 24/44 wide-angled zoomspot set with a spot focus will produce slightly more light than a 18/34 narrow-angled zoomspot set with a wider Flood focus, as can be seen on the table in 'Extras!'

> **Which lantern to use where and why**

■ **Fresnels** – 6/60 degree beam angle provides a wide range of beam sizes; they are fast-to-set the focus and ideal for over stage use where precision may not be as important as the flexibility of the size of beam

■ **PCs** – 4/64 degree beam angle provides an even greater flexibility from a narrow near parallel beam to wider washes. Ideal for use over stage for tight semi-hard edged acting areas or in FOH positions, e.g. in Europe

■ **24/44 Zoomspot Profile** has a wide beam angle with a short throw, making it ideal for use over stage for special areas and projecting gobos

■ **18/34 Zoomspot Profile** has a narrower beam angle with a medium throw making it ideal for use in FOH positions in front of the stage

With experience, you will soon get to know how each type of lantern performs; its length of throw, size of beam and the best position to use it.

[5] Stage Electrics – Hire & Sales Catalogue 1998

MORE TIPS

■ Profile spots – the narrower the angle, the longer the throw

■ The light output on Profile spots can be slightly increased by adjusting the beam distribution from 'flat' to 'peak' field

■ Axial Profile spots can be fitted with either a GKV or a GLB Long Life lamp. The light output from the GLB Long Life lamp is reduced to less than 75% of the light from the GKV lamp

■ Use the performance information supplied by the lantern manu-facturers to compare the size of the beams and the optimum throw of lanterns. A summary of all the major manufacturers' specifications can be found in Part 3: 'Lighting Resources – Technical info. – Lantern reference guide 2'

Points for action

Quickies!

■ Identify the wattages and names of lanterns produced by different manufacturers

May take a bit longer

■ Make a scaled drawing to calculate the true length of the beam spread for lantern:

Measure the vertical height and the horizontal distance of the lantern to the centre of the lighting area. Construct a 1:50 scaled drawing on 5mm grid paper of the base and upright of a right-angled triangle, 4 squares = 1m. The long side of the triangle represents the true length of the throw of the beam of light. This length can be calculated by rotating it into a vertical position by using a compass from the base point and counting the number of squares

Extras! – Beam spread/field angles

When planning your lighting, it is useful to know the basic characteristics of each lantern, its potential throw, the size of the beam spread over a set distance and how bright the pool of light will be.

Understanding the data

Manufacturers' catalogues provide the specifications for their range of generic lanterns specifying the size of lens, beam spread and light output. This may be different for a similar lantern from another manufacturer. Following are some examples from one manufacturer:

➤ **Selecon – Fresnel & PC lantern data:**

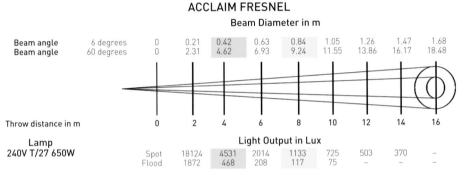

ACCLAIM FRESNEL

Beam Diameter in m

Beam angle	6 degrees	0	0.21	0.42	0.63	0.84	1.05	1.26	1.47	1.68
Beam angle	60 degrees	0	2.31	4.62	6.93	9.24	11.55	13.86	16.17	18.48

Throw distance in m: 0, 2, 4, 6, 8, 10, 12, 14, 16

Lamp 240V T/27 650W	Light Output in Lux							
Spot	18124	4531	2014	1133	725	503	370	–
Flood	1872	468	208	117	75	–	–	–

Fresnel beam angle – Philips Selecon

- **Beam diameter** measured in metres
- **Length of throw** measured in metres
- **Light output** measured in Lux
- **The optimum length of throw** should have a light output of around 2000 Lux

ACCLAIM PC

Beam Diameter in m

Beam angle	6 degrees	0	0.14	0.28	0.42	0.56	0.70	0.84	0.98	1.12
Beam angle	64 degrees	0	2.50	5.00	7.50	10.00	12.50	15.00	17.50	20.00

Throw distance in m: 0, 2, 4, 6, 8, 10, 12, 14, 16

Lamp 240V T/27 650W	Light Output in Lux							
Spot	18748	4687	2083	1172	750	521	383	–
Flood	1436	359	160	90	57	–	–	–

PC beam angle – Philips Selecon

Extras!

19 PLANNING THE DESIGN

The beam diameter and light output vary depending upon the:

- **Length of throw** of the beam
- **Size of the beam** spot to Flood focus
- **Optimum length of throw – 6m**

➤ **Comparing Fresnel & PC lantern data**

	Field/beam angle	Throw	Beam dia	Light output
Fresnel	Spot focus – 6 degrees	6m	0.63m	2014 Lux
PC	Spot focus – 4 degrees	6m	0.42m	2083 Lux
Fresnel	Flood focus – 60 degrees	4m	4.62m	458 Lux
PC	Flood focus – 64 degrees	4m	5.00m	359 Lux

Spot focus at a 6m throw

- **Fresnel** has a slightly wider beam but a lower light output
- **PC** has a narrower beam and a slight increase in the light output

Flood focus at a 6m throw

- Compare the beam sizes and light outputs for the Flood focus

➤ **Selecon – Axial zoomspot lantern data:**

ACCLAIM AXIAL ZOOMSPOTS 18°–34° & 24°–44°

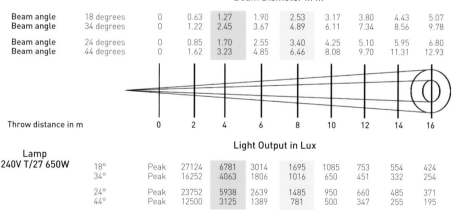

Acclaim Axial beam angle – Philips Selecon

The beam diameter and light output vary depending upon the:

- **Lantern beam angle** – 18/34 or 24/44
- **Length of throw** of the beam
- **Diameter of the beam** – spot or Flood focus

- **Lamp tray position** – the position of the lamp providing a peak or flat beam affects the light output
- **The optimum length of throw** – 6/8m

	Field/beam angle	Throw	Beam dia.	Light output Peak	Light output Flat
18/34 Axial	Spot focus – 18 degrees	8m	2.53m	1695 Lux	1028 Lux
18/34 Axial	Flood focus – 34 degrees	8m	4.59m	1016 Lux	570 Lux
18/34 Axial	Flood focus – 34 degrees	6m	3.44m	1806 Lux	1014 Lux
24/44 Axial	Spot focus – 24 degrees	6m	2.55m	2639 Lux	972 Lux
24/44 Axial	Flood focus – 44 degrees	6m	4.85m	1399 Lux	695 Lux

Comparing 18/34 and 24/44 Axial
- Compare the light output between the spot and the Flood focus for each lantern – the wider the beam, the less the light output
- Compare the peak light output for the 18/34 and 24/44 Axial with a 2.5m diameter beam – 8m throw 1695 Lux and 6m throw 2639 Lux
- Note that the peak setting has a brighter light output than the flat setting

➢ **Cyc Flood Selecon lantern data:**

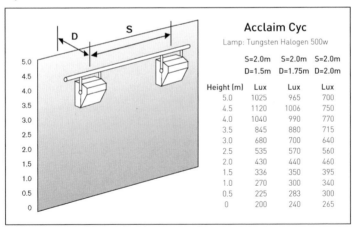

Position of Cyc Floods – Philips Selecon

The light output from Cyc Floods vary upon the:

- **Distance** from the vertical surface
- **Height** above the vertical surface
- **Cyc Floods** are hung at 2.0m centres
- **What is the optimum distance from the surface to be illuminated?** Check the light output for 1.5m, 1.75m, 2.0m distance from the vertical surface

EXTRA TIPS

■ A wide-angle 24/44 zoom Profile spot on a short throw over stage will produce a brighter light for the same area than a 18/34 Profile

Extra resources – go to

www.mts.net/~william5/sld.htm – Stage Lighting Design 101 – Part 6 Lighting Mechanics/6.04 Beam Spread Concept

More info resources – go to

www.seleconlight.com – Click on Resources – the lighting calculator can be used to calculate the beam diameter and the light output of Selecon lanterns by selecting the lantern, lamp and inputting the length of throw

20 The design process

A quick start – Lighting a small show

Introducing *'Allo 'Allo* – an example of the planning and design for a small show

More info – Planning & preparing the lighting design

Looking at the stages of planning a lighting design and preproduction preparation

Extras! – Designing a larger show

Our House – an example of a technical specification and lighting design for a larger show

A quick start – Lighting a small show

Lighting a small show can be a good learning experience for the trainee technician. As the person lighting the show, you may well be performing all the roles of designer, chief electrician and desk operator. Resources may be limited but the process for the lighting will be almost the same as that for lighting a larger show. Once you have completed the preparation of the design, you are ready to start planning the lighting for the show.

Planning a small show

When you are working in a small space with a limited range of equipment, the planning can be worked out practically while assembling the rig on-stage using the following method:

- **Plan the areas** – draw the acting areas and specials on a layout plan, and number them in a logical sequence as viewed from the FOH position of the control desk
- **Plan the lantern positions** – walk the space, sight the best position to hang the lanterns to light each area and record it on the plan with an 'x'
- **Check the lanterns** – check the number of lanterns available and sort them into types – which type will you use and where?
- **Lantern positions** – draw the positions on the lighting layout plan using CIE lantern symbols which can easily be drawn by hand if a stencil is not available

- **Lantern distribution** – if there are not enough lanterns, consider whether you can reduce the number of areas, use single lanterns to light an area or borrow or hire additional units
- **Plan the circuit connections** – assign the lighting desk control channels to the lanterns and number them on the plan at the rear of the lantern symbol. Where possible, hard patch the outlet circuits to the dimmers so that the control channel matches the lighting area numbers

You will find that, after you have gained some practical experience, it will be easier to visualise and plan the lighting layout directly on to the plan.

A small show profile

Show info.
Production: 'Allo 'Allo comedy/farce based on BBC TV series
Company: Chedworth Players, small amateur dramatic society producing two plays a year
Venue: Chedworth village hall, small stage with limited technical facilities, no wing space
Equipment: 16 lanterns, 12-way 2 preset desk, 2 x 6-way dimmer packs, incoming main supply 32 amps

Planning the design

➤ **Lighting requirements**
- **Setting** – permanent interior set of a rural French café having two entrances, outside door, interior door, both having backing scenery. Window non-practical due to lack of wing space. Bedroom area set down stage left
- **Scene changes** – small inset scenes played within the permanent set, cinema, larder and other rooms
- **Requirements** – basic warm wash of areas, lighting for exterior and interior backings, candle lighting for bedroom area, special areas – cinema and room insert scenes

➤ **Planning the areas**
Because of the limited number of lanterns, the plan was based on three down stage areas, two mid stage and one up stage area

- **Acting areas** – focused around the positions of the furniture in the main café scene, the two entrances and the bedroom DSL
- **Entrances** – CSR included in mid stage area also including the piano, USR cover in rear stage areas to cover the actors when making their entrances
- **Specials** – special areas, cinema DSR, larder and other rooms in DSC. The lanterns to be selected from the cross area lighting rig
- **Side and back lighting** – lighting the actors on their entrances, provided by lanterns illuminating the backing pieces

- **Area numbers** house left to right – DS areas, 1 & 2, 3, 4 & 5, 6 – CS areas 7 & 8 – US areas 9 – backings 10, 11
- **Colours** – acting areas two-tone warm wash, CS specials neutral, DSR special candle light

Lantern layout plan

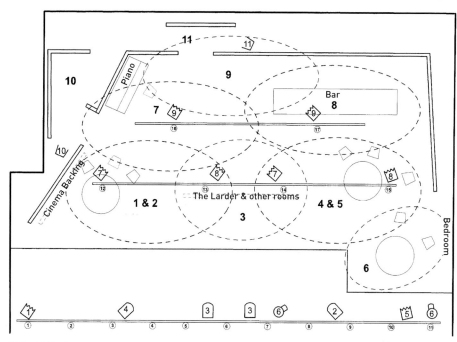

'Allo 'Allo *lantern layout plan – Skip Mort*

➤ Positions & types of lanterns

Lanterns marked on the plan using the CIE lighting symbols, the control channel number to the rear and the colour filter number in the centre of the lantern symbol:

2 x Fresnels lighting areas 1 DSR & 5 DSL, separate circuits for use as specials
2 x PCs lighting areas 2 DSR & 4 DSL, separate circuits for use as specials
2 x PCs lighting area 3 CS, flat frontal lighting to reduce overshoot when used as special
2 x Profiles lighting area 6, special area for bedroom scene
6 x Fresnels lighting areas: 7, 8 & 9
2 x Floods on stands lighting areas 10 & 11 backings for entrances

➤ Colour

Key lighting stage right L152 Pale Gold, Fill lighting stage lighting L154 Pale Rose, Specials 136 Pale Lavender.

277

> **Preproduction preparation**
  - **Equipment list/instrument schedule**
    Showing the position and type of lantern, colour filter, circuit outlet socket number, dimmer and channel control number

Hanging position	Lantern no. plan L–R	Lantern	Colour filter no.	Circuit socket no.	Dimmer no.	Desk control channel no.
				Hard patching/Hook up		
Lx 1.	1	Fresnel	L152	1	1	C1
Lx 1.	2	PC	L152	3	4	C4
Lx 1.	3	PC	L136	5	3	C3
Lx 1.	4	PC	L136	6	3	C3
Lx 1.	5	Profile	L152	7	6	C6
Lx 1.	6	PC	L154	9	2	C2
Lx 1.	7	Fresnel	L154	10	5	C5
Lx 1.	8	Profile	L154	11	6	C6
Lx 2.	9	Fresnel	L152	12	7	C7
Lx 2.	10	Fresnel	L152	13	8	C8

  - **Patching/hook-up** – the lanterns are connected via the outlet circuits that are hard patched to the dimmer packs so that the lighting desk control channel numbers match the lighting areas
  - **Basic hard patch plan** – showing the layout of the numbered dimmer units and sockets on the dimmer pack, e.g. the plug top of the outlet circuit No.1 is patched to dimmer No.1, control by channel No.1

Dimmer pack No.1

Dimmer No Channel No	Dimmer 1/C1	Dimmer 2/C2	Dimmer 3/C3	Dimmer 4/C4	Dimmer 5/C5	Dimmer 6/C6
Socket	1	9	5	3	10	7
Socket			6			

Dimmer pack No.2

Dimmer 1/C7	Dimmer 2/C8	Dimmer 3/C9	Dimmer 4/C10	Dimmer 5/C11	Dimmer 6/C12
12	13	16	Flood	Flood	
14	15	17			

QUICK TIPS

■ **Planning a lighting rig** – lay out the lanterns on the stage under the bars in the position they will be hung to light the areas; stand back and check your layout and make any adjustments; record on to a plan

■ Lighting small shows provides practical experience and helps to develop a greater understanding of the effects produced by individual lanterns, the size and quality of the beam of light and the length of throw

■ The experience gained will assist you to be able to visualise effects of the lighting when planning on paper and creating a lighting design

More info – Planning & preparing the lighting design

The planning and preparation of the design is crucial for the success of the lighting for the production. For a larger show, the design needs to be carefully thought through, visualised and prepared on paper. The demands of each production are very different but the following outline provides a process to follow.

Planning the design

➤ **Decide on the look of the lighting**
- **Style** – soft and diffuse, stark white downlighting, low-level frontal lighting, steep shafts of light, dominant accent lighting
- **Areas** – selective acting areas, specials, broad washes
- **Colours** – OW 'open white', natural light, warm, neutral, cool, tints or pastels, hot and cold, romantic hues, contrasting saturated colours
- **Special effects** – projected effects, moving beams of light, follow spots
- **Decide on the setting** – time and place and changes during the course of the action

➤ **Plan the areas & colour**
Copy the ground plan of the set on to the stage lighting layout plan (the lighting plot).

- **The lighting layout plan** is drawn and laid out to be viewed from the direction of the audience, which is the same view that the lighting designer has of the stage when setting and plotting the lighting. It is therefore viewed from house left to house right (stage right to stage left)
- **Acting areas** – sketch out the approximate areas of the stage to be illuminated; musicals may tend to have a more symmetrical pattern, whereas drama may be far more random and variable in size. The lighting areas on the plan represent the area to be lit at the actors' head height and not the position of the beam of light on-stage
- **Specials** – draw in the position of the individual special areas
- **Accent lighting** – decide the source and direction of the accent lighting and add to the plan
- **Side, cross & back lighting** – draw in the areas that will be covered from these sources
- **Number the areas** – use a logical sequence from house left to right on the plan (stage right to left)
- **Colours** – indicate the colour of each area in general terms as decided above – do some areas need to double up as warm and cool, can some be in neutral colours?

> ## Designing the lantern layout plan
Use a copy of the lighting plan with the set and acting areas marked on it.

- **Lantern positions** – decide on the best position for each lantern to light each area – one lantern or two? Mark the positions with a small cross on the plan
- **Select the lanterns** to be used to light each area – consider the length of throw, quality and size of beam required; add the lantern symbols to the plan
- **Wash lighting** – will the acting areas provide a full wash or do you need to add additional lanterns?
- **Do any of the areas need to be lit in two colours** requiring additional lanterns, dimmer ways and power requirements?
- **Numbers of lanterns** – have you a sufficient number of lanterns available or the budget to hire additional equipment, colour scrollers or moving heads? Do you need to rationalise the number of areas and lanterns being used?
- **Lighting bars** – check that the total weight of the lanterns is within the safe working load for each bar – do you need to reduce the number of lanterns?
- **Moving head fixtures** – could you reduce the number of lanterns on a bar by using moving head fixtures to cover multiple areas?
- **Special effects** – mark in the positions of any gobos, moving effects, LED fixtures, smoke or pyrotechnics
- **Are you within the budget?** – check your hire/rental costs – what can you leave out of the plan?

> ## Adding colour
- **Select the colour filters** from a colour swatch to light each area
- **Check the effect** of the colours selected on the colours of the set and costumes
- **Mark the filter** numbers on the plan either in the lantern symbol or in front of it using a **#** followed by **L** for LEE, **R** for Rosco followed by the filter no – **# L105**

Preproduction preparation

> ## Additional planning & paperwork
This additional paperwork is produced on separate sheets not on the lantern layout plan.

- **Patching/hook-up schedule** – record the position & type of lantern, circuit connection, dimmer, DMX address, desk channel number
- **Equipment list/instrument schedule** – record the position & types of lanterns, wattage, colour and frame size
- **Lighting bar list** – record the lantern and patching information listed bar by bar
- **Colour call** – list of the colour filters and sizes to be cut, positions where they are to be used
- **Cable call** – cable requirements listed bar by bar

- **Hire/shop list** – list of equipment and accessories to be hired in
- **Risk assessment** – produce a risk assessment for all aspects of the lighting installation
- **Magic sheet**[6] – make a lighting area crib sheet/plan, a simplified diagrammatic plan showing the direction, colour and control channel numbers of the lanterns lighting each of the main areas on an A4 sheet of paper

➤ Preproduction paperwork

There are various lists that can be generated from CAD lighting software direct from the lighting plan. Also there is other stand-alone software that will create all the paperwork from an initial input of data, see 'More resources – Lightwrite 5'.

➤ Check your designs

- **Talk** to the director and designer about your designs
- **Check** the colours selected on the colours of the set and costumes
- **Attend** rehearsals to check there are no major changes to the blocking of the actors' moves that may affect the lighting areas
- **Confirm** with the director the sequence of lighting changes and the intended feel to each state of the lighting
- **Produce** a cue outline sheet, a numbered list of all the changes in the states of lighting, discuss or circulate to the director and DSM; expect some feedback and modifications
- **Attend** the final run-through rehearsals; check the cue synopsis and familiarise the actors' positions and moves related to the intended lighting of the acting areas

➤ Communicate your designs

- **Confirm hire list** and expenditure with the producer/production manager and place order
- **Confirm cue list** with DSM who will be running the show
- **Provide copies** of the lantern layout plans, equipment, patching, lighting bar lists, colour and cable call to the chief electrician and Lx crew
- **Meet** with the chief electrician and/or crew to talk about your intentions for the lighting design and to discuss any problems over the rig

[6] 'Magic list' name credited to Tom Skelton circa 1970 – Bill Williams; a similar process is also described by Francis Reid in *Lighting the Amateur Stage*

20 THE DESIGN PROCESS   More info

GLOBAL JARGON

- **Open white (OW)** (UK) – 'no color' (NA) NC or N/C standard abbreviation used when marking up a plan
- **Equipment list** (UK) – Instrument schedule (NA)
- **Rigging to hang the lanterns** (UK) – The Hang (NA)
- **Lantern layout plan** (UK) – The lighting plot (NA)
- **Hard patching of lanterns to dimmers** (UK) – Hook-up (NA)
- **Hire list** (UK) – Shop order (NA)
- **Hire** (UK) – Rental (NA)

MORE TIPS

- An hour spent planning and preparing is worth two wasted on-stage!
- Use a mini Mag-lite torch with a colour swatch to try out the effects of the colour filters on the set model, samples of costume materials and the back of your hand for flesh tones

More resources – go to

www.mckernon.com – Lightwrite 5 is a unique cross between a spreadsheet and a database, designed specifically to manage professional lighting design paperwork.

'Lightwrite understands what designers and electricians do with their paperwork. It knows that dimmers and circuits shouldn't be overloaded, that striplights have more than one color, it organizes your worknotes, and provides tools to design color scrolls and specify moving light wheels. It can find mistakes, reconcile two sets of paperwork, figure circuit and dimmer needs, renumber or rearrange channels and dimmers, and assign dimmers automatically.'[7]

Points for action

Quickies!

- Log on to www.mckernon.com: click on to a short video tour

[7] www.mckernon.com – product information

Extras! – Designing a larger show

'Any lighting design begins with the designer having a complete understanding of just what it is that he is lighting. Not only must the lighting designer be able to accurately visualize his proposed design, he must see it in the context of the actual venue or performance space. This only comes from a thorough understanding of the script, the scenic design and the venue. All of this is very important!'[8]

Planning a larger show

A larger show requires far more planning and preparation than a small show requiring the design work to be carried out on paper prior to arriving at the venue.

Large show profile

Show info.

Production:	*Our House The Musical* by Tim Firth, with music by Madness
Company:	Music Theatre Youth Company, Tigz Productions
Venue:	Bacon Theatre, Cheltenham, 550-seat college venue with 10m x 10m stage with half height flying facilities
Equipment:	To be hired as tech spec

Planning the design

➤ **Lighting requirements**
- **Setting** – a street scene in Camden Town, North London. Two houses centre stage left and right with raised upper levels in front down stage and two front walls with rotating doors. In between the two raised house fronts is a main entrance for the main scenes just to the left of centre
- **Scene changes** – additional scenes played within the permanent setting of the street scene. Other locations of a Car Yard, Prison, Pub, Vegas, Law Office and Primrose Hill created with props and lighting
- **Concept** – to create a dark realistic, location-based lighting design, using strong amounts of side lighting, and follow spots to highlight the main characters/action. The overall stage level of light to remain dark and moody creating elements of the 'film noir' style. The key effect within the design is the rear cyclorama to achieve a realistic backdrop to the set, and allow images and scenes to be projected
- **Requirements**
  General lighting – basic warm/cool wash of areas, lighting for daylight and late-evening exteriors, a wash of gobo break-ups to provide back lighting

[8] *Stage Lighting Design* – Bill Williams

Sidebar: **Extras!** | **20 THE DESIGN PROCESS**

Special areas – rear raised platforms need to be isolated, intense centre stage downlight for prison scene, bright colourful cheesy Vegas showgirl number

Special effects – cloud gobos and video images, snow, rain, time-travel effect to be projected on to the cyc cloth, low-level uplighting front of stage to create shadow effects in prison scene

➤ **Planning the areas**
- **Acting areas** – down stage is divided into three main areas, 2 areas on the raised platforms either side mid stage with an additional area in between
- **Entrances** – 11 entrances
Down stage: 2 entrances either side of the stage in front and behind the wall scenic pieces, 2 entrances either side through the rotating doors
Up stage: 2 entrances to the raised areas, 2 entrances centre left and right from behind the raised platforms, 1 entrance down the stairs from the stage right raised area
- **Special areas** – centre stage prison scene, up stage centre stage the car yard
- **Side and back lighting** – 1 boom either side up stage of the pros arch
- **Area numbers** house left to right as plan – DS areas Nos.1, 2, 3, CS areas Nos.4 & 6 raised platforms, CS area No.5 between the raised areas

➤ **Planning colours & gobos**
- **Frontal wash lighting** – warm wash L103 Straw, cool wash L117 Steel Blue, floor ground row L058 Lavender
- **Back lighting** – warm wash L103 Straw, cold wash L132 Medium Blue
- **Cyc lighting** – L106 Red, L132 Medium Blue, L089 Moss Green, L022 Dark Amber
- **Gobos** – break-up DHA 805, perpendicular window DHA146, Cloud 16 DHA 99501

➤ **Moving fixtures**
Mainly to be used for back lighting the stage with colour washes with slow gobo rotation, also rain animation movement on to the stage and set

- 3 x Profile lights moving head fixture
- 5 x wash lights moving head fixtures

Analysis of lantern layout plan & the design

➤ **Lx 1 Bar**
- 4 x 1000W Fresnels, # L103 lighting area 4, CSR raised area
- 2 x 1.2kW Fresnels, # L103 lighting area 6, CSL raised area
- 2 x 600W Pacific 23–50° lighting area 5, CS
- 1 x 600W Pacific 90° specials, area 4 steps
- 2 x 650W Acclaim Axial 24–44° specials, downlighting rotating doors DSL, DSR

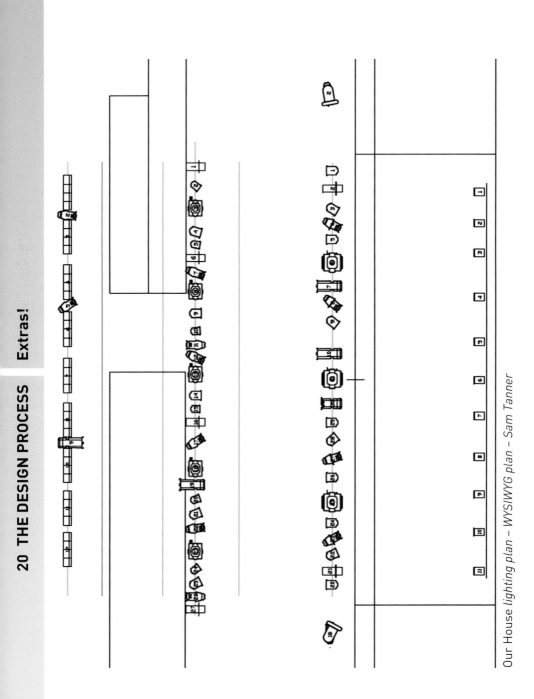

Our House lighting plan – WYSIWYG plan – Sam Tanner

- 4 x 1000W Fresnels, # L132 back lighting forestage centre
- 4 x 575W Source Four 50°, break-up gobos back lighting forestage centre
- 3 x Robe Colorspot special effects back lighting forestage area

➤ **Down stage Booms**
On either side of stage cross side lighting areas 1, 2 & 3

- 2 x Source Four Juniors + colour scrollers
- 1 x PAR 64 + colour scrollers effects back lighting down stage area

➤ **Lx 2 Bar**
- 4 x 650W Acclaim Axial 24–44° specials, cloud gobos on to cyc cloth
- 2 x 650W Source Four 50° specials, stained glass window gobos on to cyc cloth
- 6 x 1000W Fresnels, # L132 back lighting areas 1, 2 & 3
- 6 x 1000W Fresnels, # L103 back lighting areas 1, 2, & 3
- 4 x 575W Source Four 50°, break-up gobos back lighting areas 1, 2 & 3
- 5 x Robe Colorwash special effects back lighting areas 1, 2 & 3

➤ **Lx 3 Bar**
- 9 x 4 cell Coda Cyc Batten, 4-way cyc colour wash
- 2 x 650W Source Four 50°, break-up gobos back lighting area 6, CSL raised area
- 1 x 600W Pacific 23–50° back lighting area 4, CSR raised area

 # as marked on the plan denotes colour filter number

Tech spec equipment

➤ **Fixtures spec.**
- **Fixed generic lanterns**
  12 x Source Four 50°
  4 x Source Four Junior 25–50° with Apollo colour scroller
  6 x Selecon Acclaim 24–44°
  4 x Selecon Pacific 23–50°
  1 x Selecon Pacific 90°
  15 x CCT Starlette Fresnel
  9 x Selecon Acclaim Fresnel
  6 x Strand Cantata Fresnel
  6 x Par 64 (CP62)
  9 x 4 cell Coda Cyc Batten

- **Moving fixtures**
  3 x Robe Colorspot 700at
  5 x Robe Colorwash 250at

- **LED fixtures**
  8 x Anolis Arcline LED 1200mm Batten
  1 x Anolis Arcline LED 400mm Batten

20 THE DESIGN PROCESS

Extras!

- ■ **Effects**
  2 x Apollo colour scrollers (Source Four Junior)
  4 x Apollo colour scrollers (Par 64)
  1 x Unique Hazer
  1 x Antari Low Smoke Machine
- ■ **Projection** 1 x DT7000 Robe projector
- ■ **Control** – Jands Vista

Detail of the lighting plan

The numbering sequences on the plan relate in the following way:

- ■ **Unit/fixture number** – middle of the lantern symbol
- ■ **Control channel No.** (red) – above the lantern
- ■ **Colour filter No.** – below the lantern
- ■ **Outlet circuit Nos.** – not shown on this plan

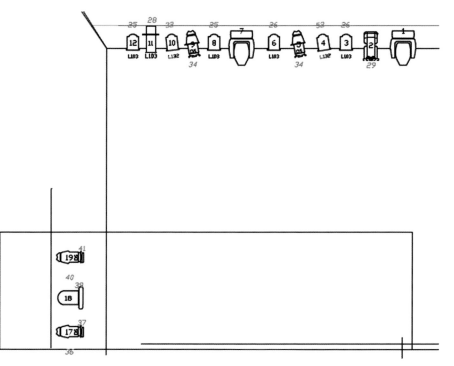

Detail of the lighting plan showing stage right section of Lx1 lighting bar and the down stage right boom. WYSIWYG drawing – Sam Turner

Abbreviations used:

BD – Barndoor; **L103** – LEE Filters No.103, **OW** – Open white, **NA** – not applicable, **RB1** – right boom circuit outlet socket No.1, **Lx1/1** – electrics bar No.1 circuit outlet socket No.1, **D30** – dimmer No.30, **CB1** – circuit breaker No.1, **Fix.1** – fixture/attribute (moving head)

Combined equipment list & patching/hook-up schedule

Hanging position	Unit/ Fixture – No.	Fixture – type	Accessories	Wattage	Colour	Outlet Circuit No.	Dimmer No. Circuit Breaker No.	No DMX channels req.	DMX 512 (start) address	Control Channel No.
						Hard patching			Soft patching	
Boom DSR	1	Source Four Junior	Scroller	575W		RB1	D30	1	030	36
Boom DSR	1A	Scroller for Source Four Junior			scroller			1	101	37
Boom DSR	2	Par 64 (CP62)	Scroller	1000W		RB2	D31	1	031	38
Boom DSR	2A	Scroller for Par 64			scroller			1	102	39
Boom DSR	3	Source Four Junior	Scroller	575W		RB3	D31	1	032	40
Boom DSR	3A	Scroller for Source Four Junior			scroller			1	103	41
Lx 1.	20	CCT Starlette Fresnel		1000W	L103	Lx1/1	D40	1	040	25
Lx 1.	21	Selecon Axial 24/44		600W	L103	Lx1/2	D41	1	041	28
Lx 1.	22	CCT Starlette Fresnel	BD	1000W	L132	Lx1/3	D42	1	042	32
Lx 1.	23	Source Four 50	Gobo	575W	OW	Lx1/4	D43	1	043	34
Lx 1.	24	CCT Starlette Fresnel		1000W	L103	Lx1/5	D44	1	044	25
Lx 1.		Robe Colorspot		700W	NA	Lx1/6	CB1	36	110	Fx.1
Lx 1.	25	CCT Starlette Fresnel		1000W	OW	Lx1/7	D45	1	045	26
Lx 1.	26	Source Four 50	Gobo	575W	OW	Lx1/8	D46	1	046	34
Lx 1.	27	CCT Starlette Fresnel	BD	1000W	L132	Lx1/9	D47	1	047	52
Lx 1.	28	CCT Starlette Fresnel		1000W	L103	Lx1/10	D48	1	048	26
Lx 1.	29	Selecon Pacific 90		600W	L103	Lx1/11	D49	1	049	29
Lx 1.		Robe Colorspot		770W	NA	Lx1/12	CB2	36	146	Fix.2
Lx 1.	34									

> ### Reading the equipment list & patching schedule
With reference to the detail of the lighting plan:
- **Hanging position** – Boom DSR, lighting boom down stage right
- **Unit/fixture No.** – Unit No.1
- **Fixture type** – Source Four Junior lantern type
- **Accessory** – colour scroller
- **Hard patching, circuit & dimmer Nos.** – Unit No.1 is connected via RB1, right boom circuit No.1 patched to D30, being powered by dimmer No.30
- **Soft patching** – Control channel No.36 on the lighting desk assigned to DMX address 030
- **Control channel fader No.36** controls Unit No.1, a Source Four Junior hanging on the stage right lighting boom

Notes:
- **No. of DMX channels req.** – 1 DMX channel is required to control a dimmer unit and a lantern
- **DMX 512 start addresses** – dimmer units controlling generic lanterns DMX 001, Scroller units DMX 100, moving fixtures DMX 110
- **Unit 25** – Robe Colorspot is patched to CB1, being powered by a non-dim circuit that is controlled by circuit breaker No.1 on the distribution board

20 THE DESIGN PROCESS Extras!

> **Equipment list**
>   ■ **Full list can include:** lamp type, weight of fixture, frame size, gobo & size to provide additional information for the preparation of the show
>   ■ **Equipment lists** can be created on a spreadsheet by manually entering in the data as above. Lightwrite 5 software has a database that automatically provides all the additional information related to the lighting fixtures wattage, colour, frame size, weight, etc. Equipment lists and other paperwork can automatically be generated from a CAD lighting design on dedicated software, e.g. Cast WYSIWYG, LxDesigner

CAD drawings

A number of different drawings and views can be generated from the CAD plans, three-dimensional views and elevation drawings showing the cover of the beam spread from the lanterns.

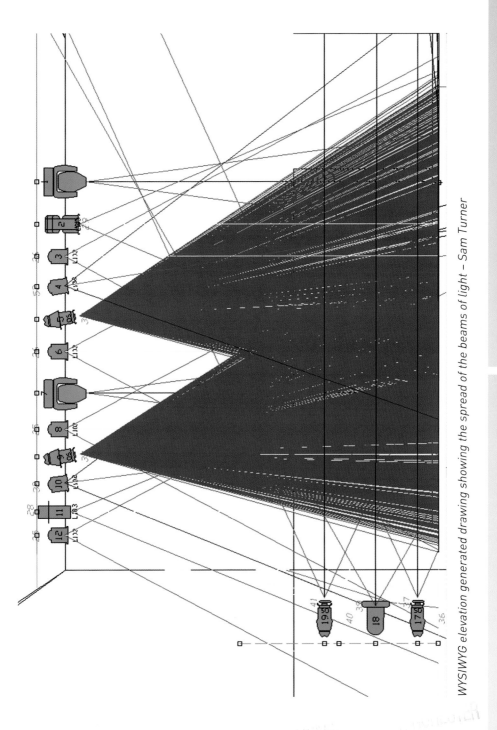

WYSIWYG elevation generated drawing showing the spread of the beams of light – Sam Turner

21 The lighting process

A quick start – Rigging & focusing a small show

'Allo 'Allo – a way of rigging & focusing a small show

More info – The lighting process

Looking at the stages of the lighting process

Extras! – Rigging & focusing a larger show

Our House – the method of rigging & focusing a larger show

A quick start – Rigging & focusing a small show

The lighting system in a drama studio or on a small stage should be fairly straightforward to understand and use. The main difference from a larger stage is that the lighting bars are usually on fixed suspensions with the circuit outlet sockets mounted either on or above the bar, removing the need for the use of extensive cabling. In some installations, the outlet circuits are connected to the dimmer packs via a hard patch panel allowing the lanterns to be controlled by the lighting desk in a logical layout.

Rigging

In small amateur venues, the lanterns are often left hanging from the previous production so it may be necessary to de-rig all the equipment and accessories before starting to rig the show.

➤ **Preparation**
- **Prep equipment** – all available lanterns and cables
- **Cut & prepare** colour filters and lantern accessories
- **Hard patching/hooking up** – pre-patch the circuit outlet sockets to the dimmer units as previously prepared on the lantern layout plan
- **Pre-patching** saves a lot of time when rigging, as the circuit can immediately be flashed through to check that it is working and the lantern can be immediately focused

- **Strike lanterns** that are already hanging in the grid, leaving any that are in the right place
- **De-rig** – accessories, colour frames and clear filters

➤ Rigging

The lighting bars/pipes in drama studios and on small stages are often suspended in a fixed position. The rigging therefore has to be done from an access system.

- **Lay out the lanterns** on the stage under the bars in the positions that they will be hung
- **Colour frames & accessories** – fit them to the lanterns before hanging
- **Hang the lanterns** for the first area and connect them to the outlet circuit socket on the lighting bar as indicated on the plan; open up the shutters and barndoors
- **Hard patching/hook up** – connect the outlet circuit to the dimmer unit as allocated on the plan if this has not already been done
- **Flash out the lantern** – raise the channel fader; check that the lantern is connected and working
- **Focus the lantern** to roughly light the intended area
- **Hang, patch and focus the lanterns** for the next area in a similar way
- **Flash out** – check all the lanterns to see that the connection to the control channels and dimmers is as the plan

The focus

On a small lighting rig, it is possible for the LD to focus the lighting with the assistance of another person to walk the stage, providing the lighting control desk is positioned on the stage for easy access. If the lanterns have been roughly focused, they will need to be checked and the beams trimmed. Ideally, the fine focusing of the lanterns needs to be carried out once the set is completed and the masking is in place. The stage and auditorium need to be in darkness in order to see precisely the effect of each beam of light. It is best to arrange a time when others are not working.

➤ Checking the focusing

- **Check the focusing** – check each area is adequately illuminated. Walk in the beam of light and observe how it covers your shadow
- **Check the wash effect** – do the beams overlap with the next area, are there any shadows? Walk through the areas and check for any drop in intensity using the palms of your hands or the white surface of the lighting plan
- **Fine focus the lanterns** – adjust the size of the beams. Profiles adjust the focus hard or soft. Soft edged spots adjust barndoors to remove unwanted spill light
- **Check the colours** – check that the filters are producing the colour that you expected
- **Patch/hook-up plan** – record the circuit outlet socket numbers connected to each dimmer unit and control channel

➤ **An alternative method**

The above method is suitable when working on a small lighting rig when time is limited and you may possibly be working on your own. On a larger show, it is common to first rig all the lanterns and then to focus them altogether in a separate session. Working along the lighting bar, focusing each lantern in order, is a more logical approach and saves the possibility of knocking previously focused lanterns.

QUICK TIPS

■ Position the lighting desk on the front of the stage to save time when rigging and focusing
■ A mini Mag-lite torch on your belt can be very useful on a darkened stage when rigging, focusing and setting the lighting

21 THE LIGHTING PROCESS

A quick start

More info – The lighting process

The rigging for a larger show will involve a greater number of technicians, and a more organised approach is required in order to complete a lot of work in a relatively short space of time. The following outline provides a plan for carrying out the necessary work. Note the references to earlier chapters which cover the correct ways of handling the equipment and carrying out the procedures.

The fit-up

The fit-up is a relatively short period of time of intense work on-stage during which the set is assembled and the lighting equipment is rigged. In some cases, it might be possible to rig all the lighting before the set arrives but in reality this is rarely the situation. The requirements of a great variety of work requires a degree of planning and careful cooperation to prevent the stage and electrics crew getting in each other's way causing delays and wasting time.

➤ **Preparation**
- **Prep the lanterns and cables** – check that the equipment is working, see Chapter 3 'Working with lanterns – A quick start'
- **Cut colour filters** – cut and number the colour filters as listed on the colour call, sort into groups by lighting bars/pipes or position, fit into the colour frames, box and clearly mark
- **Lantern accessories** – fit gobos into holders, check out other accessories and sort into groups by lighting bars/pipes or positions, box and clearly mark
- **Sort out the flying** – position the lighting bars/pipes while the stage is clear – this can save a lot of time during the fit-up

➤ **The 'get-in'**
- **The set and equipment** is unloaded from the trucks brought into the theatre and stored in the scene dock or on the side of the stage prior to the commencement of the fit-up
- **Lighting equipment** – sort out equipment according to where it is to be positioned and store off-stage in the wings and auditorium clear of the scenery ready for rigging

➤ **Rigging**
Hanging the lanterns/fixtures on the bars/pipes and connecting them to the circuits and back to the dimmers; see Chapter 3 'Working with lanterns – A quick start'. This is usually done in the following order to fit in with the stage crew working on the set:
- **Over stage lighting bars/pipes** – if possible, rig these bars during the get-in, while the stage is clear

(left margin) More info   21 THE LIGHTING PROCESS

- **FOH positions** – rigged while the stage is occupied and the set is being constructed
- **On stage** – additional lighting booms and stands rigged off-stage while the set is completed
- **Hard patching** – connecting the outlet circuits to the dimmers
- **DMX** – setting addresses of the dimmer units and fixtures
- **Soft patching** – allocating the lighting desk control channels to the DMX addresses of the dimmers and fixtures. (Setting the DMX addresses and soft patching can be preset prior to rigging)
- **Flash out** – check all lanterns/fixtures that the connections with the control channels and dimmers as on the plan

The focus

'Lighting design is a two part process. First the designer must create the lighting in his mind. Next he must create it in the real world.'[9]

➤ **Focusing**

The focusing of the lanterns can start when the construction of the set is completed and the masking is in place. It is best carried out when the stage crew have left the stage and there is peace and quiet for the LD to direct the focusing. However, this can often mean working late and through the night. Focusing can take a long time, depending upon the number of lanterns. This is the start of realising the lighting design so it is important to have sufficient time to accurately position and adjust the beam of light projected from each lantern.

- **Check the heights of the lighting bars/pipes** that they are hung at the correct height before starting to focus the lanterns
- **Focusing** was covered in Chapter 3 'Working with lanterns – A quick start' and Chapter 15 'Other angles of lighting – Extras!'

GLOBAL JARGON
- **'Get-in' or 'Fit-up' (UK)** – 'Bump in' (NZ)

EXTRA TIPS
- It is quicker to fit colour frames, barndoors, gobos and irises to the lanterns when they are at stage level rather than at the top of an access system in semi-darkness
- Flash out the lanterns to check that they working and correctly connected before flying the lighting bars

[9] *Stage Lighting Design* – Bill Williams

21 THE LIGHTING PROCESS

More info

Extras! – Rigging & focusing a larger show

The requirements for lighting a larger show are very different for those needed for a small show, although the basic process is the same. The larger installation is more complicated to understand and to use, requiring more detailed planning. There is far less flexibility to make alterations on a large rig, so the lighting designer needs to be totally committed to ensuring that the lighting layout plan works.

Rigging a large show

Larger installations are more complicated and difficult to understand with a greater use of temporary cabling, localised hard patching panels, DMX distribution and the soft patching control circuits requiring detailed planning.

➤ **Preparation**
The weight of each lighting/Lx bar and the dimmer load can be calculated on the Lx bar equipment list and it should be checked against the specification of the venue.

- The max weight distributed along the lighting bar must not exceed the sum of the safe working load of each of the points of suspension
- Where the total weight of the bar exceeds the safe working suspension load, it will be necessary to reduce the number of lanterns
- A triangular aluminium truss is used to distribute the weight of the lanterns on a heavy rig where the suspension points are widely spaced, which could cause the lighting bar to bend. The truss also provides additional space for fixing temporary cables clear of the hanging tube
- Calculate the total load of the power requirements of the rig and check that it matches the dimmer capacity and the incoming mains power supply. Caution: if you are exceeding the mains supply, calculate the diversity factor

➤ **Rigging**
On larger stages, the lighting/Lx bars or pipes are suspended from an overhead grid allowing them to be repositioned according to the lighting demands of the production. The bars can be suspended from fixed-position winches or by hemp or counter-weight flying systems or motorised hoists. These systems should be handled with care and should only be operated by a specialist technician.
The Lx bars should be hung to match the positions as marked on the lighting layout plan prior to the start of the fit-up. The first priority while the stage is clear is to rig the over stage Lx bars/pipes at stage level. Once the set is erected, it will be difficult to access the over stage Lx bars at stage level.

Lanterns – order for rigging[10]

- ✓ **Fly the bar** in to a reasonable working height from the stage
- ✓ **Work from the down stage side** of the bar
- ✓ **Hang the lanterns** with the side of the hanging clamp with the set screw facing down stage so that it is easily accessible to adjust the position if necessary when focusing
- ✓ **Check the spacing** with the plan using scale rule and measure out the positions from the centre of the bar
- ✓ **Tighten the hanging clamp** and secure safety bond
- ✓ **Point the lanterns** in the direction that they will be used to check for spacing problems
- ✓ **Fit accessories:** colour frame, iris, barndoor, gobo
- ✓ **Spot focus lantern**, open shutters and barndoors to prepare for focusing and flashing out
- ■ **See Rigging checklist:** Chapter 3 'Working with lanterns – A quick start'

Cabling the bar

Where there are no circuit outlet sockets on or above the lighting bar, temporary cabling will need to be used to connect the lanterns. Single TRS extension cables can be used or Socaplex multicore cables with 6-way plugging boxes or spiders. Short 'jumper' cables are used to distribute the power from the boxes or spiders along the bar to the fixtures.

- ✓ **Cabling the bar**, start with the longest run of cable first so that it can be attached along with the shorter cables as they are added along the bar. Attach the outlet socket close to each fixture, ensuring that there is enough cable to allow sufficient movement for focusing
- ✓ **Tape the cables** on to the underside of the bar, leaving the hanging clamps free; do not coil the cable around the bar
- ✓ **Check the lamps and cables** are OK by using a live socket and that any pairing of lanterns is correct
- ✓ **Don't tape the lantern cable to the bar** so that it can be removed if a fault occurs and make sure that there is enough length for the lantern to be angled
- ✓ **DMX fixtures** require a direct mains supply 'non-dim' circuit, as damage may occur if they are connected to a dimmer controlled circuit. It is good practice to run a separate multicore to power the DMX fixtures
- ✓ **Moving heads** with tungsten lamps will require a dimmer control circuit
- ✓ **Connect DMX fixtures** – 5 pin XLR DMX cable daisy chained from 'DMX Out' to 'DMX In' on each fixture
- ✓ **Set DMX addresses** – set each fixture as planned on the equipment list
- ✓ **Record the cable connections** to the lanterns on the lighting bar equipment list, e.g. Lx1BM/1=Lx1 bar, Blue multicore circuit No.1. This is essential to check out the connections to the lanterns when hard patching or for checking out faults

[10] 'Intro to Stage Lighting' – Steve Marshall, www.seleconlight.com

✓ **Fly out the bar** – with a sash cord measuring twice the required height over the bar to set the Trim/Dead height of the bar as the side elevation drawing

✓ **Fly out the loom** of singles or multicore cables

➤ **Hard patching** – power distribution
The distribution of the power via dimmer circuits to lanterns and via circuit breakers to DMX fixtures.

■ **Hard patch up the loom** to the localised house patching panels or 'Waylines' as planned on the Lx bar equipment list

➤ **Soft patching** – use the control desk software to:
■ **Assign the control channels** on the lighting desk to the DMX 512 addresses of the dimmers, fixtures and effects as planned on the patching/hooking-up schedule

The focus – a large show

When focusing on-stage lighting, designers use a combination of hand actions and phrases to direct the operators.

The method of focusing was covered in detail in Chapter 3 'Working with lanterns – A quick start' and Chapter 15 'Other angles of lighting – Extras!'.

Each LD may use their own variations so you should be ready to adapt to their style. The following will give you some starting points:

➤ **Actions when focusing**
■ **Standing on-stage with back facing the focuser** – spot focus the beam and centre it on to the back of the head and shoulders – lock off the adjustments
■ **Arms raised moving hands outwards** – enlarge the beam until the hands stop moving
■ **Arms raised moving hands inwards** – reduce the beam size
■ **Arms raised hands stop** – lock off the zoom focus on the lantern
■ **Single arm raised hand moving in** – Profile/Axial: cut the beam in using the shutter on the opposite side of the lantern; Fresnel/PC: cut the barndoor in on the same side of the lantern

➤ **Focusing jargon**
■ **'Can I see number 6'** – raise channel 6 to 90%
■ **'Hit my shoulders'** – spot focus the beam and centre it on the back of the shoulders
■ **'Beam at my heels'** – focus the beam to start from the heels, used by dance LDs to direct side lighting
■ **'Open it up', 'Close it down'** – enlarge and reduce the size of the beam
■ **'Flag that'** or **'Flaggit'** – wave your hand in the beam of light to indicate the cover

- **'Move it on-stage'** or **'Move it off-stage'** – move the beam towards the centre stage and away from the centre
- **'Lock it off'** or **'Lock that'** – tighten the adjusting nut or wing nut on the lantern suspension and tilt so that it doesn't move
- **'Shutter in the top'** – Profile/Ellipsoidal: move the bottom shutter in
- **'Shutter in the bottom'** – Profile/Ellipsoidal: move the top shutter in
- **'Sharpen it'** or **'Soften it'** – harden and soften the focus
- **'Top door in'** – Fresnel/PC: move the top barndoor down
- **'Hold it'** – stop moving the shutter or barndoor
- **'Ghost it'** – take the level of light down to 25%
- **'Next'** – moving on to focus the next lantern on the bar

Focusing moving fixtures

Moving fixtures are focused in a similar way to generic lanterns: tilt and pan followed by adjustments to the beam size, colour and pattern. The main difference is that the change is produced on the lighting desk by moving the control wheels assigned to the fixture personality. The new position, beam size, colour and pattern will be programmed as a 'follow on' cue in preparation for the next cue.

- Moving fixtures can take a long time to focus so it is a good idea to pre-program a number of preset focused positions that can be stored in the memory as named palette or focus group
- It is important to store them with meaningful names that can easily be identified with the limited number of characters that can be used on the small lighting desk screen if a monitor is not being used
- If it is necessary during the rehearsals to readjust the position or any other attributes of a preset focused position, the other cues where the palette has been used will automatically be updated

GLOBAL JARGON

- **Waylines** (SH) – hardwired circuit outlet sockets from the dimmer racks
- **Loom** (SH) – **Snake** (NA) – Socapex/Lectriflex, a group of multicore cables taped together (UK)

21 THE LIGHTING PROCESS   Extras!

MORE TIPS

■ 'Allow 15 minutes per lantern to rig, colour, patch and focus eg 100 lanterns x 15 mins = 25 tech-hours. A 100 lantern rig will take 4 technicians 8 hours to set up (excluding rigging hanging positions and flying the rig)'[11]

■ When focusing moving fixtures, move the 'tilt' first followed by the 'pan' to prevent the head from 'flipping' over to get from one position to another

Extras!

21 THE LIGHTING PROCESS

[11] 'Intro to Stage Lighting' – Steve Marshall, www.seleconlight.com

22 Lighting the show

A quick start – Plotting a small show

Setting the lighting and creating a manual plot for a small show – *'Allo 'Allo*

More info – Lighting the show

Examining the stages of lighting the show

Extras! – Programming a larger show

Programming a lighting memory desk – *Our House*

A quick start – Plotting a small show

Lighting the show is the process of creating pictures or scenes of light in the form of a series of states of light. Each state of light is created by setting the individual level of light from each lantern saved as a cue related to a point in the script. The cue may be saved either manually as a written plot or as a stack in the memory of the lighting control desk.

Setting the lighting

A provisional cue list of the states of lighting and changes should be previously prepared with the director and the DSM prior to setting the levels of the lighting.

➢ **Preparation**
   ■ Produce a simplified A4-sized lighting layout plan with the lantern channel control numbers marked in the lighting areas
   ■ Set up a table with the lighting control desk and a working light in a central position in the auditorium. You will need the director, designer and the DSM who will plot the position of all the lighting cues in the master copy of the script which is called 'the book'
   ■ You will need a member of the stage management team or an actor to walk the stage in order to see the effect of the state of lighting as it is set for each cue. Also a lighting desk operator will be needed or a programmer for a large show using an advanced memory desk. On a small show, the lighting desk may be operated by the LD

- If it is not possible to move the position of the control desk, a communication system will be required between the LD in the auditorium and the desk operator

➤ **'Setting' the levels or 'cue setting'**

Lighting a scene is like painting a picture. The three components of accent, Key and Fill lighting[12] are used to compose each state of lighting by slowly raising the level of light of each lantern until the desired effect is achieved.

The cue sequence starts with the first state of light to be set up by the desk operator which is usually a preset state set up before 'the half' – before the audience comes into the auditorium.

- **Preset lighting** – the light that the audience will see before the show, 'tab warmers' lights on the house curtain, or for an open stage some lighting of the set
- **Fade house lights and preset lighting** – taking house lights down just in advance of the preset lighting can help focus the audience's attention
- **Lx Cue 1 – Opening light**[13]
  For a realistic setting, it is logical to start with the natural source of illumination or the 'motivating light'

1 **Raise the accent light** to suggest the direction and source illumination for the scene and set the level to suggest the mood, time of day, etc.
2 **Start with the down stage lighting** areas lit from the Lx 1 or the advance lighting bar
3 **Position your 'walker'** in the main lighting area to see the effect of the lighting
4 **Add the Key light** to that area to provide directional lighting from the main source of illumination, setting the level to match the accent light
5 **Set a similar level of Key lighting** to each of the other on-stage areas unless some light and shade is required
6 **Add the Fill light** from the other side to the main lighting acting area to provide the effect of the reflection of the direct lighting, setting the level at a slightly lower level to discreetly complement the Key light and maintain the main direction of the lighting
7 **Set a similar level of Fill lighting** to the rest of the on-stage areas
8 Where the lanterns lighting each area are paired together on a single dimmer circuit, the contrast between the directional and Fill light has to be created by the choice of colour in a two-tone wash
9 **Add the FOH lighting** in a similar way
10 **Walk the area** – ask the 'walker' to walk though all the actors' positions, keeping their face to the front so as to check the cover and to see how it looks
11 **Check** that the director is happy with the state of lighting

---

[12] Check out Chapter 16 'The lighting palette – Extras!'
[13] *Lighting the Amateur Stage*, Francis Reid

A quick start

22 LIGHTING THE SHOW

12 Plot/program the state of lighting

13 Confirm the time of the raise for the cue

- **Lx Cue 2 – Next lighting state**
  Crossfade Preset Masters and build next state of lighting on the other set of preset faders

  1–10 Repeat the previous actions and set up the next cue

  11 Crossfade between Cue 2 to Cue 1 to compare the change in lighting

  12 Check that the director is happy with the state of lighting

  13 Plot the state of lighting

  14 Confirm the type and time for the cue

  15 Confirm the point of action for the cue with the director and DSM

➤ **A change of lighting in a scene**

Changes in the realistic source of illumination in the scene will create a lighting cue as the direction, intensity and colour of the accent lighting, Key and Fill lighting changes, e.g.:

- The bright sunlight coming in through a window turns to sunset
- A practical light fitting is switched on to provide some artificial light
- The practical light is switched off leaving the stage in darkness and moonlight coming in through the window

Plotting

When using a manual control desk, the levels of each channel fader are recorded on a written plot sheet on which all the actions required to execute the lighting cue are recorded.

➤ **Types of cues**

■ **Snap**	Jump from one lighting state to another
■ **Build**	Raising the level of the state or scene of lighting
■ **Add**	Levels of light being added to an existing state or scene of lighting
■ **Fade**	Lowering the level of the state or scene of lighting
■ **'X' Crossfade**	Changing from one state of lighting to another state
■ **Fade to DBO**	Fade to Dead Black Out, everything off!
■ **Snap to DBO**	Instant Dead Black Out, all circuits directly switched off

22 LIGHTING THE SHOW   **A quick start**

➢ **Plot sheets**

The following information is recorded on the plot sheet for *'Allo 'Allo*:

- **Cue No.**   Q 1 – note that the lighting cues have their own dedicated sequence numbering as separate from sound and other cue sequences
- **Time & type**   Time in secs. Build, Fade, X Fade
- **Action**   Levels and movements of presets A & B
- **Levels**   Channel number followed by level
                     3 – 12/6 = channels 3 to 12 level 6 or 60%; *4 + 5/7* = channels 4 & 5 at level 7 or 70%
- **After cue**   Preparation for the next cue normally carried out after the last cue
- **Notes**   Inserted in between cues – Act & Scene numbers, setting, action, cue line

Lighting Plot Sheet   Show: *'Allo Allo' Chedworth Players*   Sheet No: **1 / 6**

Act / Scene	Action: Line:				
CUE	TIME	ACTION	LEVELS 1 - 6	LEVELS 7 -12	AFTER CUE
	AUDIENCE PRESET				
	PRESET	B / 10	3 -12 / 6		
	SLOW FADE WITH HOUSE LIGHTS				
	5 SEC FADE	B / 0	3 – 12 / 6		
	FLICK ON STAGE – AN ANOUNCEMENT -				
Q 1	2 SEC RAISE	A / 10	4 + 5 / 7	SET UP PRESET B: 1 / 6 2 – 12 / 10	SET UP PRESET B
	FLICK ON STAGE – AN ANOUNCEMENT -				
Q 2	2 SEC FADE	A / 0	4 + 5 / 7		
Act 1 Scene 1	RENE'S CAFÉ: SLOW RAISE				
Q 3	5 SEC RAISE	B / 10 ADD A / 10	1 / 6, 2 – 12 / 10 2 / 10		ADD PRESET A
Act 1 Scene 1	RENE MOVES DOWN STAGE - CAFÉ LIGHTS FADE LEAVING CENTRE SPOT Rene: ' Y'vette hurry with the tables. I must go to the larder to see if the brie is young and firm'				
Q 4	3 SEC FADE	B / 0 A / 10	1 / 6, 2 – 12 / 10 2 / 10		
Act 1 Scene 1	Rene: 'This is of course a lie. I am not interested in brie. I am going to feel if Mimi is young and firm'				
Q 5	1 SEC FADE TO BO	A / 0	2 / 10		

The plot sheet for 'Allo 'Allo – *Skip Mort*

Rehearsals

It is difficult to set the lighting without having the full cast on-stage in costume, and inevitably fine adjustments may need to be made to the levels and plot during the technical and dress rehearsals.

>> **Fast Forward** on the DVD to **22.1 Lighting a scene**

GLOBAL JARGON

■ **Lighting rehearsal/programming/plotting** (UK) – Level/Cue setting (NA)

QUICK TIPS

■ When setting and plotting the lighting, always light a face rather than the floor in order to see the true effect
■ Start by setting lighting levels at 80%–90% to keep some extra light in hand
■ The golden rule of stage lighting is *'When in doubt, up half a point'*[14]

Points for action!

Quickies!

■ Look through the *'Allo 'Allo* plot sheet

Takes longer

■ Try setting up the *'Allo 'Allo* lighting plot on a two preset lighting desk and run through the cues to understand how the plot has to be made

---

[14] *Lighting the Amateur Stage*, Francis Reid

'Allo 'Allo – *A rural French café, midday with the bright sunlight coming in through the stage right door – Skip Mort*

'Allo 'Allo – *evening, the main focus of the lighting is on the action in the centre – Skip Mort*

'Allo 'Allo – *The pantry inset scene; the acting area was larger than the scenery backing* – Skip Mort

'Allo 'Allo – *The scenery backings to the doors need to be lit* – Skip Mort

More info – Lighting the show

There is a common sequence of events in the process of lighting a show through to the first night.

Lighting the show

There are two common terms used:

- Plotting, level or cue setting – terms formerly used for a written recording of the lighting states when using a manual control desk
- Programming – term now used in the age of advanced memory desks and moving fixtures

➤ **Lighting session**
Traditionally, lighting has been set and plotted in a separate isolated lighting session as described in 'A quick start – Plotting a small show'. This was necessary due to the time taken to record a manual plot. A separate lighting session provides more time to compose the states of lighting but lacks having the cast and action to light as part of the picture. This method is suited to small drama productions but it has been superseded by the use of memory desks, where cues can be programmed instantaneously during a lighting rehearsal as used for larger shows.

➤ **Technical rehearsal**
The main aim of the 'tech run' is for the actors to become used to the set and scenery changes and for the sound and lighting technicians to run their cues. The rehearsal is shortened by cutting the action to jump to the next cue in order to save time, and cues may be repeated in order to get them right. The tech run is the first time that the lighting will have been seen with the actors and it may be necessary to rebalance some of the lighting levels and adjust the lighting of some of the areas to match the action. Notes should be made and adjustments done before the dress rehearsal.

➤ **Lighting rehearsal**
For larger-scale musical theatre and dance, the lighting designers tend to prefer to program during an extended lighting rehearsal. This has the advantage of being able to light the action as it happens with the cast in costume and the scene changes. The lighting rehearsals can be very long for the cast but it does allow them to become used to the set, entrances and their costumes, and maximises the use of the stage during a limited preproduction period. It also replaces the need for a further 'tech run'. However, the lighting designer still needs to take time to try out their rig and prepare a palette of states of lighting and positions for moving lights prior to the lighting rehearsal to maximise the use of time.

➤ **Dress rehearsals**

The first dress rehearsal provides the opportunity to practise the cues and become familiar with all of the action and the running of the show. Adjustments may still need to be made to the levels of the lighting and the plot, but they can be done live, providing there is adequate time in between the cues.

The final dress rehearsal is run as a performance and may well be held during the day prior to the opening night. Only minor alterations should be made to the lighting, providing that they are not apparent to the actors.

➤ **Running the show**

The cues for lighting, sound and stage are called by the DSM or SM so that they can be coordinated with the action of the show. On small shows, the lighting operator may take his own cues, but it is difficult to prepare for a cue on a manual desk and keep track of the script and the progress of the scene. The cues for lighting, sound, flying and automation are frequently dependent on each other and must follow a sequence that can only be coordinated centrally.

The cues may be given by cue light – Red warning/stand by and Green for go – or they may be called verbally by using headsets or 'cans', e.g.:

- 'Stand by Elx cue 3' – usually given half a page of script before the cue
- 'Elx cue 3 Go!' – cue number always comes first to remind the operator; the 'Go' comes last to action the cue

>> **Fast Forward** on the DVD to **22.1 Lighting the show**

22 LIGHTING THE SHOW   More info

Did you know that –

- The first electronic lighting control designed by Strand Electric was called the Light Console which used a Crompton organ console keyboard to control the lighting channels and thyratron valve dimmers. The first one to be installed was at the London Palladium in 1949 with 152 channels

311

Extras! – Programming a larger show

With the increased demands of large shows and the development of the technology used in advanced lighting control desks, the programmer has become a key member of the lighting production team. The programmer will have the detailed knowledge and experience of the specific memory desk being used, allowing the lighting designer to concentrate on composing the scenes of light and leave the means of achieving it to the specialist.

➤ Preparation

It is good to prepare some states of lighting, especially if the programming is going to be carried out during a lighting rehearsal as described in the 'More info' section.

- **Moving fixtures** – palettes can be composed of set positions, moving sequences and effects can be created and saved so that they can be added to the final plot
- **Sub-masters** – preset settings of groups of lanterns to produce area lighting or specific effects that may be used a number of times in the lighting plot, e.g. blue back lighting, coloured stage and side lighting washes, cyclorama colours. The levels of lighting on

Programming the show – Skip Mort

a sub-master can be instantly added to and saved as part of a state of lighting. Any adjustments made to the sub-master states will be immediately updated in all the cues in which they have previously been used
- **Visualisation software** – preprogramming can be done on CAD programs used to create the lighting plans, WYSIWYG or LD Capture. This is commonly used for shows and concerts using large numbers of moving fixtures. It does have some limitations in visualising the effect of illuminating the moving body, but it provides an initial canvas that can be touched up and tweaked during the running of the lighting rehearsal

➤ Programming fixtures

- **'Move while Dark'** feature can be found on most current lighting desks – it provides an automatic follow-on cue facility, allowing the moving fixtures to be programmed to change colour, position, gobo, etc. ready for the next cue. Where this facility is not available, additional sub cues are inserted in between the generic cues in order to program the fixtures
- **Colour scrollers** – programming colour changes

Cue Nos.	Type of Cue	Generic Lanterns	Colour Scroller
Q 1		Fade to BO	
Q 1.1	Follow-on		Change colour
Q 2		Raise	

Creating a cue list

The cue list is a sequence of preprogrammed states of lighting, which are saved in the memory stack of the lighting desk and which are played back by pushing the 'Go' button.

➤ **Two methods of recording cues on memory desks**
  - **Cue only** – recording the output of every control channel used in the cue
  - **Tracking cues** – recording only the changes in the output from control channels from the previous cue. This has the advantage of being able to make an edit to a cue that will run through the following cues, e.g. we need to add a light for the conductor; add the lantern setting to the first cue and it will run through the following cues until it is changed, saving the need to edit each individual cue

➤ **Types of cues**
  - **Cue** – preprogrammed state of lighting having an allotted time change called the 'cue time'
  - **Dynamic cue** – lighting changes within the cue/state, chases, movement of moving fixtures or attributes, e.g. gobos or colour
  - **Live cue** – a slow fade or raise that may continue over an extended cue time running in the background of the lighting plot. We refer to this as the 'cue is still running'[15]
  - **Multilayered cues** – having several independent cues running at the same time without affecting each other, which simplifies the use of moving fixtures

➤ **Additional changes or transitions of cues** available on advanced memory desks
  - **Split time crossfade** – change from one state of lighting to another, each at different speeds
  - **Delayed time** – the change in one state of lighting starting after the other
  - **Follow-on (FO)** – following on from the previous cue either manually by the operator or programmed automatically
  - **Step cue** – a running sequence of individual lanterns, fixtures or states of lighting run as a chase

The procedure for programming the show will depend upon the protocol of the lighting control desk that you are using, so it is important that you know how it functions before you start to even think about programming the show.

[15] *Performance Lighting Design* – Nick Moran

22 LIGHTING THE SHOW   Extras!

Did you know that –

- Tracking cue method was originally used by manual dimmer operators who were only concerned with changes in dimmer levels

EXTRA TIPS

- When focusing moving fixtures, move the 'tilt' first followed by the 'pan' to prevent the head from 'flipping' over to get from one position to another
- Know your lighting desk and how it works before you start to program the show

Points for action

Takes longer

- If you have access to a colour scroller, try setting it up and programming some colour changes

A proper job!

- Explore your lighting desk to find out the programming protocol
- If you have access to a moving head fixture, try setting it up and programming a simple set of positions for the beam

Lighting from the show – *Our House*

Our House – *Tigz Productions, Bacon Theatre – Lighting Design Andy Webb,*
Photographer Nik Sheppard

'*The umbrella dance sequence, note the gobo patterned back lighting*' – © Nik Sheppard

'*The rain effect projected from the front with the strong blue back lighting from the moving heads and light blue side lighting.*' – © Nik Sheppard

'The prison visiting scene: strong down lighting with precise follow spots lighting the faces of the two down stage actors, cutting in at an acute angle from either side.'
– © Nik Sheppard

'The car sequences with moving projected background and the three actors in the front illuminated by steeply raked cross lighting to avoid spill light falling onto the screen.'
– © Nik Sheppard

'The dance sequence: note the lead actor's face being lit by two tightly focused follow spots cutting in at an acute angle from either side FOH and not from the standard rear of the auditorium positions.' – © Nik Sheppard

22 LIGHTING THE SHOW

Extras!

UNIVERSITY OF WINCHESTER
LIBRARY

Lighting jargon – What's it called?

➤ Abbreviations & stage terms

ALD	Association of Lighting Designers
ASM	Assistant stage manager
Blocking	Recording the actors' moves and entrances related to the text
Cyclorama/Cyc	White rear wall or backcloth used to mix coloured light and create sky effects
DSM	Deputy stage manager (UK), attends all rehearsals, keeps the 'book' and runs the show
LD	Lighting designer
SM	Stage manager
Stage director (NA)	Performs the same role as the DSM in the UK
The 'book'	The master copy of the script which contains blocking, lists of furniture and props, cues for the show
'Walker'	An ASM who walks the stage when setting and plotting to check the level of illumination

➤ The lighting control desk

Chase	Continuous repeated sequence of flashing lights produced by the effects function on a lighting control desk as used on neon signs
Dipless crossfade	Channel levels set at the same level on both presets remain at the same intensity
Flashing through	Raising each control channel in succession to check that the lantern or fixture is working after rigging and before each performance
Light board	Alternative term for lighting control desk
Master fader	Having the overriding control of a group of channel faders
'On the board'	Lighting operator referring back to when the lighting was controlled by a switchboard and resistance dimmers
Preset lighting	Lighting an open set prior to the audience entering the auditorium
Scene preset	Group of individual channel faders on a lighting control desk that control the dimmers
Soft patching	Electronic patching a DMX address to a control channel on the lighting desk
'Tab warmers'	Lanterns focused to light the front curtain 'tabs', often with a warm colour

Side tabs: What's it called? / LIGHTING JARGON

➤ Lanterns

Cyc – asymmetrical	Fixed focus Flood, soft edged even wash directed downwards by an asymmetrical reflector
Generic lanterns	Non-automated lanterns, often referred to as Generics
PC/Prism/Pebble	Adjustable focus lantern, hard/semi-soft edged intense beam with less spill light than a Fresnel
Profile spotlight	Adjustable focus lantern, precise hard edged beam of light that can be soft focused
Flood – symmetrical	Fixed focus lantern, soft edged even wash having a symmetrical reflector
Fresnel	Adjustable focus lantern, soft edged diffused beam with more spill light than a PC
Parcan	Fixed focus lantern, intense near parallel oval beam of light that can be rotated

➤ Rigging on-stage

Dips	Floor circuits/sockets mounted under the stage floor to connect practical fittings or side lighting
Dip traps	Metal flaps mounted in the stage floor providing access to floor sockets
Hard patching	Process of temporarily linking or 'hooking up' lanterns via outlet sockets to the dimmers
IWB	Internally Wired Barrel, having outlet sockets mounted on the bar internally wired to an end box
Jumper	A short extension cable – not a woolly jumper!
Ladders	Suspended framework in the wings to hang lanterns from for side lighting
Lighting rig	General term for the lanterns hanging on the lighting bars
Loom	A group of cables tied together as from a lighting bar
Patch panel	Hardwired circuits terminated with flexible cables and numbered plug tops passing through a holed comb panel mounted below the dimmer units
Practical	A light fitting, e.g. a desk light, which may be switched on by the actor
Rigging	Term used for hanging lanterns and equipment
TRS	Extension cables are made up from tough rubber shield cable, which is used as an abbreviated name

LIGHTING JARGON

What's it called?

Part three: Lighting resources

- » Fast forward DVD video clips

- Technical info.

- Websites

- Key notes!

Credits

Bibliography

» Fast forward – watch on the DVD

Part 1 – Lighting Technician

Lanterns, Dimmers & Control

1.1   Understanding the lighting system

2.1   Five types of lanterns

3.1   Adjusting lanterns

4.1   Dimmers

4.2   Dimmers, patch panels & power supplies

5.1   Manual control desks

5.2   Memory control desks

7.1   Safety when working at heights

Colour, Gobos & Effects

9.1   Using gobos

10.1   Moving effects and fixtures

11.1   Gobo slide projection

12.1   Special effects

Part 2 – Lighting Designer

Lighting the Performance Space

14.1   Angles of illumination

14.2   Three angles of lighting

14.3   Flat and Cross area lighting

15.1   Focusing lanterns

15.2   Side, cross and back lighting

16.1   The lighting palette

16.2   A touch of colour

17.1   The language of lighting

Lighting the Show

18.1   Designing the show

21.1   Which lantern to use & where

22.1   Lighting a scene

22.2   Lighting the show

Technical info. – Lanterns, Dimmers & Control

> **Makes & models of lanterns – a quick guide**

Fresnels, PCs, Profiles, Parcans

Makes – manufacturers	Country of origin	Models – lantern names
Altman Stage Lighting	North America	**Fresnels, Ellipsodial, PAR 38/46/56/64, Border lights, Ground & Sky Cyclorama; Comet & Luminaire follow spots**
ADB Lighting Technologies	Belgium	**Europe range & Warp**
CCT Lighting Mainly used in UK educational market	United Kingdom	**Minuette, Freedom Eco, Starlette, Silhouette ranges; Freedom follow spot**
ETC	North America	**Source Four Axial, PAR and Parnel**
Philips Selecon	New Zealand	**Acclaim, SPX, Pacific, Rama, Arena, Hui & Lui, Aurora ranges; Pacific and Performer follow spots**
Robert Juliat	France	**'LUTIN', Le CIN'K, SX ranges; Foxie, Ivanhoe and Manon follow spots**
Strand Lighting No longer manufacturing lanterns	United Kingdom	**Quartet, Prelude, Nocturn, Coda, SL, Brio, Harmony and Cantata ranges**
Teatro Teclumen	Italy	**Forma, Curva, Atto ranges; Arena follow spots**
Thomas Engineering	UK, North America	**PAR 36, PAR 56, PAR 64**

Ellipsodial lanterns

Makes – manufacturers	Country of origin	Models – lantern names
Altman Stage Lighting	North America	Ellipsoidal Fixed Focus
CCT	United Kingdom	Freedom 2000 Zoomspot
ETC	North America	Source Four Zoom, Junior, Fixed Focus
Philips Selecon	New Zealand	Acclaim Axial Zoomspot, Pacific Zoomspot, Pacific Fixed Focus & Long Throw
Strand Lighting	United Kingdom	SL Zoomspot, Brio Zoomspot (no longer manufactured)

> **Most commonly used lamps**

T18	T26	T11	T29	GKV600	HPL575	HPL750
500 watt	650 watt	1000 watt	1200 watt	600 watt	575 watt	750 watt
Focus lanterns CCT, Philips Selecon & Strand				**Axial lanterns** Acclaim, SPX, Pacific, SL	**Axial lanterns** Source Four	

TECHNICAL INFO.

Lanterns, Dimmers & Control

TECHNICAL INFO.   Lanterns, Dimmers & Controls

> Lantern reference guide

Make	Lantern Model	Wattage	Voltage	Lamp Type	Frame Size	Gobo Holder	Gobo Size
Altman							
Altman	6" Quarz Fresnel	750W	120V	T6 120V	7½" x 7½"		
Altman	8" Quarz Fresnel	1000W	120V	T7 120V	7½" x 7½"		
Altman	3.5" Ellipsoidal MT	500W	120V	EHC	4⅛" x 4⅛"	3.5Q	
Altman	Shakespeare S6	600W	120V	HX754	7½" x 7½"	1KL6	
Altman	4.5" Ellipsoidal	750W	120V	HX754	6¼" x 6¼"	360Q	
Altman	6" Ellipsoidal	550/575W	120V	EHD/GKE 120V	7½" x 7½"		
Altman	PAR	500/1000W	120V	PAR 120V			
Altman	Comet follow spot	410W	82V	MR-16 82V			
Altman	Luminator fs	410W	82V	MR-16 82V			
ADB							
ADB	Eurospot	500/650W	240V	GY9.5	125x125mm	SP/GO	DS/DW
ADB	'A' Range	500/650W	240V	GY9.5	155x155mm	A6	A56C
ADB	Warp	600/800W	240V	G9.5	185x185mm		'B'
ADB	Europe	1000/1200W	240V	GX9.5	185x185mm		
ADB	Europe	2000W	240V	GY16	245x245mm		
CCT							
CCT	Minuette	500/650W	240V	T18/T26	125x125mm	GH15	'M'

326

	Model	Wattage	Voltage	Lamp	Size	Code	Notch
CCT	Freedom Eco	600/800W	240V	HX600/800	190x185mm		'A' 'B'
CCT	Freedom 2000	600/800W	240V	HX600/800	190x185mm	Z0120	'A'
CCT	Silhouette Turbo	1000/1200W	240V	T19/T29	190x185mm	GH01	'A'
CCT	Silhouette	2000/2500	240V	CP92/CP91	190x185mm	GH01	'A' 'B'
CCT	Starlette	1000/1200W	240V	T19/T29	190x185mm		
CCT	Starlette	2000/2500W	240V	T11/T29	190x185mm		
CCT	Starlette Flood	1000/1250W	240V	K4	375x265mm		
ETC							
ETC	Source Four Junior	375/575W	240V	HPL375/575	159x159mm	GH63	'M'
ETC	Source Four Zoom	575/750W	240V	HPL575/750	159x159mm	GH59	'B'
ETC	Source Four fixed angle	575/750W	240V	HPL575/750	159x159mm	GH59	'B'
ETC	Source Four Par	575/750W	240V	HPL575/750	190x190mm		
ETC	Source Four Parnel	575/750W	240V	HPL575/750	190x190mm		
Robert Juliat							
Robert Juliat	Lutin 306	1000W	240V	CP70/T19	180x180mm		
Robert Juliat	310H Range	1000/1200W	240V	CP70/CP90	215x215mm		
Robert Juliat	329H Range	2000/2500W	240V	CP91/CP92	245x245mm		
Robert Juliat	600SX	1000/1200W	240V	T19,CP70/T29,CP90	190x190mm		
Robert Juliat	700SX2	2000/2500W	240V	CP92/CP91	215x215mm		
Rober Juliat	Aledin 630SX	LED 85W	240V	LED lamp unit	190x190mm		

TECHNICAL INFO. — Lanterns, Dimmers & Controls

Make	Lantern Model	Wattage	Voltage	Lamp Type	Frame Size	Gobo Holder	Gobo Size
Philips Selecon							
Selecon	**Acclaim**	500/650W	220/240V	T18/T25	125x125mm	GH60	'M'
Selecon	**Acclaim Axial**	600W	220/240V	GKV600LL	125x125mm	GH60	'M'
Selecon	**Leko Lite**	575/750W 800W	115V 230V	Philips High-Brite			
Selecon	**SPX**	600/800W	220/240V	GKV600/800LL	185x185mm	GHB	'B'
Selecon	**Pacific**	600/1000W	220/240V	GKV600LL	185x185mm	GHPB	'B'
Selecon	**High Performance**	1000/1200W	220/240V	T11/T29	185x185mm		
Selecon	**Compact**	1000/1200W	220/240V	T11/T29	185x185mm		
Selecon	**Rama**	1000/1200W	220/240V	T11/T29	185x185mm		
Selecon	**Arena**	2000/2500W	220/240V	CP92/CP91	245x245mm		
Selecon	**Acclaim Cyc/Flood**	500W	220/240V	K1 Frosted	230x204mm		
Selecon	**HUI**	500/800W	220/240V	K1/P211	265x203mm		
Selecon	**LUI**	1000W	220/240V	K4 Frosted	265x203mm		
Selecon	**Aurora**	625/1000/1250W	220/240V	P2/10/7/12	305x315mm		
Strand							
Strand	**Patt. 23**	500W	240V	T28	100x100mm	GH08	'B'
Strand	**Patt. 123**	500W	240V	T25	165x165mm		
Strand	**Prelude**	500/650W	240V	T18/T26	150x150mm	GH73	'B'
Strand	**Quartet**	500/650W	240V	T18/T26	150x150mm	GH33	'M'
Strand	**Cantata**	1000/1200W	240V	T11/T29	185x185mm	GH06	'B'
Strand	**Alto**	2500W	240V	CP91	245x245mm		

Make	Model	Wattage	Voltage	Lamp	Size		
Strand	**Patt. 60 Flood**	500W	240V	GLS Clear	300x300mm		
Strand	**Brio**	600W	240V	HX600	150x150mm	GH06	'B'
Strand	**SL**	600W	240V	GKV600LL	158x158mm	GH73	'B'
Strand	**Coda/Nocturne**	500/1000W	240V	K1/K4 Frosted	215x245mm		
Strand	**Leko**	1000W	240V	CP77			
Strand Century							
Strand	**Leko**	500W	120V	EHD			
Strand	**Leko**	750W	120V	EHG			
Strand	**Leko**	1000W	120V	CP77			
Teatro							
Teatro	**Forma**	500/650W	240V	T18/T26			
Teatro	**Curva**	650/1000/1200W	240V	T21/T19/T29			
Teatro	**Atto**	2000W	240V	CP55/CP75			
Teatro	**Ribalta**	300/500W	240V	K9/K1			
Teatro	**Linea**	625/1000/1250W	240V	P2/10/7/12			
Zero 88							
Zero 88	**Focus 650**	550/650W	240V	T18/T26	125x125mm		
Thomas							
Thomas	**Par 64**	1000W	240V	CP60 Narrow / CP61 Medium / CP62 Wide / CP95 Ex Wide	254x254mm		

➤ Cable connectors

Country	Amps	Volts	Connector name	Pins
United Kingdom	15 amp	230 volts	Cable plugs & sockets	3 pin round
United Kingdom	16 amp	230 volts	CEE P17	3 pin round
Europe	10 amp	230 volts	IEC	3 pin flat
Europe	16 amp	230 volts	CEE P17	3 pin round
Europe, Germany	16 amp	230 volts	Schuko	2 pin round & earth
Australia & New Zealand	10 amp 20 amp	230 volts	3 pin Piggy circuit plug 3 pin Piggy circuit plug	3 pin flat blade
North America	20 amp	120 volts	Edison SPC Stage Pin Connectors	flat 3 in line parallel round pin '3-pin stage cable'
North America	20 amp	120 volts	Edison stage pin	twist lock

- **Amps** are the measurement of the rate of flow of the electrical current in a circuit
- **Volts** are the measurement of the constant electrical pressure or force of the mains supply of the country of origin: UK, Europe, Australia & New Zealand 230 volts, North America 120 volts
- **The size of the connectors** and diameter of the pins depends upon the maximum power handling of the cable being used that is measured in amps
- **16 amp CEE P17** are used in the UK for moving heads with discharge lamp sources to prevent them being connected to a dimmer circuit.[1] They are also used for outdoor installations as the circular body of the male and female connector is fully enclosed when joined together providing a waterproof connection

➤ Dimmer ratings

Country	Voltage	Rating	Dimmer ratings
UK	230 volts	Amps	10A, 16A, 25A
Europe	230 volts	Watts	2.5kW, 3kW, 5kW, 12kW
Australia/New Zealand	230 volts	Amps Watts	10A, 13A, 15A, 25A 2.5kW, 3kW, 5kW, 12kW
North America	120 volts	Watts	600W, 1.2kW, 2.4kW

[1] Moving heads/discharge lamps, see Chapter 6 'DMX fixtures – A quick start – Animated fixtures'

> ## Safe working loads – Power-handling capacity 230 volt supply

Safe 'rule of thumb': 10 amps = 2kW – 15 amps = 3kW – 16 amps = 3.5kW

Mains supply – 230 volts	Dimmer rating amps	Max power watts	Approx load kilowatts	Safe working load no. of lanterns
Dimmer units	10 amps	2300 watts	2kW	3 x 650W lanterns 2 x 1000W lanterns
Dimmer units & sockets	13 amps	2990 watts	3kW	4 x 650W lanterns 2 x 1200W lanterns
Dimmer units, sockets & extension cables	15 amps	3450 watts	3kW	5 x 650W lanterns 3 x 1000W lanterns
Dimmer units, sockets & extension cables	16 amps	3600 watts	3.5kW	5 x 650W lanterns 2 x 1200W lanterns
Dimmer units	25 amps	5750 watts	5.5kW	4 x 1200W lanterns 2 x 2000W lanterns
Mains electrical supply	32 amps	7360 watts	7kW	10 x 650W lanterns 6 x1200W lanterns
Mains electrical supply	63 amps	14490 watts	14kW	20 x 650W lanterns 12 x1200W lanterns
Mains electrical supply	100 amps	23000 watts	20kW	35 x 650W lanterns 19 x 1200W lanterns

> ## Safe working loads – Power-handling capacity 120 volt supply

Safe 'rule of thumb': 10 amps = 1kW – 20 amps = 2kW

Mains supply – 120 volts	Dimmer rating amps	Max power watts	Approx load kilowatts	Safe working load no of lanterns
Dimmer units & extension cables	10 amps	1200 watts	1kW	2 x 575W lanterns
Dimmer units & extension cables	20 amps	2400 watts	2kW	4 x 575W lanterns 3 x 750W lanterns
Mains electrical supply	30 amps	3600 watts	3.5kW	6 x 575W lanterns 4 x 750W lanterns
Mains electrical supply	60 amps	7200 watts	7kW	12 x 575W lanterns 9 x 750W lanterns
Mains electrical supply	120 amps	14400 watts	14kW	24 x 575W lanterns 19 x 750W lanterns

TECHNICAL INFO.

Lanterns, Dimmers & Controls

331

Lanterns, Dimmers & Controls

TECHNICAL INFO.

➤ Three phase supply – colour coding

Country	EU/IEC 2004 harmonised colours	UK pre-2004	USA	Canada	Australia New Zealand
Phase L1	Brown	Red	Black	Red	Red
Phase L2	Black	Yellow	White	Black	White – (previously Yellow)
Phase L3	Grey	Blue	Green	Blue	Dark Blue

IEC – International Electrotechnical Commission

➤ Lighting control desks – makes and models

Manufacturer	Country of Origin	Manual Control	Basic Memory Control	Advanced Memory Control
ADB Lighting Technologies	Belgium	**SWING** 6 & 12 cf*	**MIKADO** 12/24 cf **DOMINO** 24/48 cf	**DOMINO/XT** 48/96 cf **HATHOR** cc infinite
ETC	North America	**Smartfade** 12/24 or 24/48 cf	**Smartfade ML** 48 cf 1024 DMX outputs **Element 60** 250/500 cc*	**Congo JR** **Congo** 3072 cc 6144 DMX outputs **Congo Kid** **Ion** 1000/1500/ 2000 cc **Eos** 5000cc
Jands Pty Ltd	Australia	**Stage 24** 24/48 cf **ESP II** 24 & 48 cf **Event 24 & Plus 48**	**Event 408** 24/48 cf **Event 416** 36/72 cf	**Jands HOG 500** **Jands HOG 1000** **Jands Vista**
LSC Lighting Systems	Australia	**MINIM** 12/24 cf		**maXim** 24 – 120 cf
Philips Strand	United Kingdom	**100 series** 12/24 cf	**200 series** 12/24 or 24/48 cf	**preset Palette** 32/64 or 48/96 cf **classic Palette** 150, 250 or 500 cc **Light Palette classic** 800 cc **300 Series** 125 cc **500 Series** 500 cc

* cf channel faders/cc control channels

332

Zero 88	United Kingdom	**Juggler** 12/24 cf	**Jester & ML** 24/48 cf **Jester TL** 200 cc	**Leap Frog 48 or 96** cf 248 or 296 devices **ORB** 2048 cc
MA Lighting	Germany		**Lightcommander 2** 24/6 48/6 cf	

Live & moving lights control desks

Avolites	United Kingdom		**Diamond 4 Elite** **Diamond 4 Vision**	**Sapphire** **Pearl** Live control desks
ChamSys **'Cam' 'Sis'**	United Kingdom			**MagicQ:** **Expert, Pro,** **Pro Execuite**
High End Systems	North America			**Whole Hog 3** **Road Hog** Specialist moving lights desks
MA Lighting	Germany			**grand MA2**

➤ Moving heads – makes & models

Company	Country of origin	Fixtures: MH – Moving Heads, LEDs
ADB Lighting Technology	Belgium	WARP/M motorised Axial zoom Profile EUROPE motorised Plano/Prism- convex, Fresnel
Clay Paky	Italy	MH – Alpha moving body projectors, beam & washlight
ETC	North America	Source Four, Autoyoke, Revolution integrated colour scroller
High End Systems	North America	Wash & Spot effects lantern
Martin	Denmark	MAC Beam, Profile effects & Wash lanterns MAC Tungsten Wash
Philips Vari-Lite	North America	VL – Spot, Wash luminaires VL ERS Ellipsoidal Reflector Spotlight luminaire
Robe	Czech Republic	Colour & Robin – Wash, Spot, Beam
Qmaxz Lighting	Netherlands	QM Spot, Wash

TECHNICAL INFO.

Lanterns, Dimmers & Controls

➤ LED fixtures – makes & models

Company	Country of origin	LED Fixtures
ADB Lighting Technologies	Belgium	**ALC4 asymmetrical Cyc Flood**
Chroma-Q	United Kingdom	Colour Block, Colour Split, Colour Punch
ETC	North America	**Selador – Lustr, Palletta, VIVID-R, Fire & Ice, Desire**
Gekko Technology Ltd	North America	Gekko kedo LED focusable luminaire
GLP German Light Products	Germany	LED – Volslicht
High End Systems	North America	SHOWPIX moving head
Martin	Denmark	**MAC 301/ 401 Zoom Wash moving head** **MAC Entour Profile moving head** MH – Stagebar, **EvenLED light wall**
Philips Vari-Lite	North America	**VLX Wash luminaire**
Pulsar	United Kingdom	Chroma Flood, Batten, Bank, Flood, Strip
Robe	Czech Republic	Robin – Wash, Plasma Spot
Robert Juliat	France	**Aledin 630SX LED profile**
Thomas	United Kingdom	Pixel Range

➤ Health & Safety – Risk assessment

HEALTH & SAFETY – Risk Assessment		Venue:			
Activity					
Description of operation					
Who is affected by this operation	Staff	Students		Public	Others

Description of hazards/risk – Before	Probability Accident 1–5	Severity Injury 1–5	Risk Factor P x S
1 2 3 4			

5			
6			
7			
8			
9			
10			

Probability	1 Very unlikely	2 Unlikely	3 Could occur	4 Likely	5 Will occur
Severity/injury	1 Very minor	2 Minor	3 Serious	4 Major	5 Fatal
Risk Factors	Multiply Probability x Severity to obtain Risk Factor				

Risk factor **Low 0–6**	Risk factor Medium **7–14**	Risk factor **High 15–25**
Above 5 – improve if possible	**Above 10 – further action required**	**15+ immediate action required**

Recommended precautions

1
2
3
4
5
6
7
8
9
10

Description of hazards/risk – After	Probability Accident 1–5	Severity Injury 1–5	Risk After 1–5
1			
2			
3			
4			
5			
6			
7			
8			
9			
10			
Further action to be taken *			

TECHNICAL INFO.

Lanterns, Dimmers & Controls

Technical info. – Colour, Gobos & Effects

➢ Ranges of colour filters

LEE & Rosco E-Colour+

LEE Filters
- **234** – Colour effects filters, diffusion, correction and reflection materials
- **Use** – first made in the late 1960s to meet the demands of the film production industry
- **Material** – surface-coated polyester film
- **Properties** – high melting point, good resistance to dye fade in hot lights and impervious to water
- **Sheet sizes:** 53cm x 61cm and 53cm x 1.22m, **Rolls:** 1.22m x 7.62m

Rosco E-Colour+
- **331** – Colour effects filters, diffusion, correction and reflection materials
- **Use** – a comprehensive range of European colours and correction filters, based on the earlier Cinemoid filter numbering system originally produced by Strand Electric
- **Material** – surface-coated polyester film
- **Properties** – high melting point, good resistance to dye fade in hot lights and impervious to water
- **Sheet sizes:** 53cm x 61cm and 53cm x 1.22m, **Rolls:** 122cm x 7.62m

Rosco – Supergel & Roscolux

Supergel
This range is more of a hybrid but there are many similarities with the E-Colour+ range of filter colours:

- Many exact, close matches or similar colours in both ranges
- No relationship between the colour reference numbers
- Supergel has one or two additional colours not found in E-Colour+
- E-Colour+ has a wider range of colours
- **144** – Colour effects filters and diffusion materials
- **Use** – premium filter range introduced to Europe in 1976, popular with lighting designers, having evolved through dialogue worldwide offering fresh alternatives to the older Cinemoid colour range
- **Material** – a body-colour polycarbonate, 3 rolls of plastic film tri-extruded simultaneously on a polycarbonate base
- **Properties** – very good colour durability and heat resistance, providing a long life under intense heat of theatre and TV lighting. The polycarbonate construction

Colour, Gobos & Effects

TECHNICAL INFO.

eliminates 'stress', preventing the material from buckling and shrinking, this makes it highly suitable for building colour strings for scrollers[2]

- **Sheet sizes:** 50cm x 61cm, **Rolls:** 61cm x 7.62m

Roscolux
More of a stand alone colour range originating in North America.

- Many different additional colours in its range
- Very few colours match Supergel but some can be found in the E-Colour+ range
- **135** – Colour effects filters
- **Use** – now available throughout Europe, first choice of North American lighting designers and widely specified throughout the world
- **Material** – deep-dyed polyester
- **Properties** – slightly more resistant to fading than surface-coated filters
- **Sheet sizes:** 53cm x 61cm and 53cm x 1.22m, **Rolls:** 1.2m x 7.62m

GAM – GamColour
Manufactured in North America.

- **138** – Colour effects filters
- **Use** – North America, available from distributors worldwide
- **Material** – deep-dyed polyester colour
- **Properties** – clear polyester base is highly resistant to tears, punctures, cracking and deterioration from heat
- **Sheet sizes:** 20" x 24", **Rolls:** 24" x 198" junior roll, 24" x 50', 48" x 25'

Apollo – Apollo Gel
Manufactured in North America.

- **150** – Colour effects filters, diffusion and colour correction
- **Use** – mainly used in North America
- **Material** – double coated and double dyed on 3mm polyester
- **Properties** – colour consistency from batch to batch
- **Sheet sizes:** 20" x 24", 22" x 24", **Rolls:** 2' x 12', 2' x 25'

➢ Dichroic glass filters

Rosco Permacolour
- **23** – Colour effects filters, 12 Architectural series colours
- **Use** – suited for high-temperature lanterns, metal halide discharge sources and high-wattage tungsten lamps. Ideal for permanent installations, long productions to save recolouring lanterns and especially inaccessible lanterns
- **Material** – Dichroic glass containing multiple micro-layers of metal oxide films
- **Properties** – accurate, high-quality filters that selectively pass the light of a small range of colours, reflecting rather than absorbing the others and so reducing

---

[2] Rosco 'Guide to Colour Filters'

the premature fading and creating of heat experienced with standard saturated colour filters

■ **Size** – available in any shape or size

LEE Dichroic Glass Colours

■ **36** – Colour effects filters and Architectural colours

Apollo Dichroic filters

Few saturated colours, mainly pale and some tints

■ **41** – Colour effects filters and Architectural colours

➤ **Makes of gobo rotators**

Type/ motor	Single Gobo	Dual Gobo	Double Gobo	Double Gobo	Indexing
Apollo	Smart Move Jr (M)	Smart Move		Smart Move DMX	
Chroma-Q	Junior FX (B)		Twin FX	Twin FX DMX	
GAM		Twin Spin Jr (M) Twin Spin		Dual Motor Twin Spin	
Rosco	Single Rotator	Vortex	Double Rotator	Double Rotator	Indexing Rotator
Control	**Stand alone**	**Stand alone**	**Remote controller**	**DMX**	**DMX**

Technical info. – Lighting the Show

➤ Scales – metric and 'English units'

1:25 metric scale

1mm Drawing size		Represents 25mm Actual (full) size	
1mm	=	25mm	(.025m)
4mm	=	100mm	(.100m)
10mm	=	250mm	(.250m)
20mm	=	500mm	(.500m)
40mm	=	1000mm	(1.000m)
80mm	=	2000mm	(2.000m)
60mm	=	4000mm	(4.000m)
500mm	=	5000mm	(5.000m)

American system scale 'English units' ½" : 1ft

Measurements on the drawing =	Full-size measurement
½" =	1ft
1" =	2ft
2" =	4ft
2½" =	5ft

➤ True length of throw and beam spread from a lantern

True length of throw (metres) – lantern to centre of the area

Vertical height of lantern	3m	4m	5m	6m	7m	8m	9m
10m	10.40	10.70	11.20	11.60	12.20	12.80	13.40
9m	9.50	9.80	10.30	10.80	11.40	12.00	12.70
8m	8.50	8.90	9.40	10.00	10.60	11.30	12.00
7m	7.60	8.10	8.60	9.20	9.90	10.60	11.40
6m	6.70	7.20	7.80	8.50	9.20	10.00	
5m	5.80	6.40	7.10	7.80	8.60		
4m	5.00	5.65	6.40	7.20			

Horizontal depth from lanterns to centre of the area

	Beam spread diameter (metres)[3]									
5°	0.3	0.3	0.4	0.5	0.6	0.7	0.8	0.9	1.0	1.1
10°	0.5	0.7	0.9	1.0	1.2	1.4	1.6	1.7	1.9	2.1
19°	1.0	1.3	1.7	2.0	2.3	2.7	3.0	3.3	3.7	4.0
26°	1.4	1.8	2.3	2.8	3.2	3.7	4.2	4.6	5.1	5.5
36°	1.9	2.6	3.2	3.9	4.5	5.2	5.8	6.5	7.1	7.8
50°	2.8	3.7	4.7	5.6	6.5	7.5	8.4	9.3	10.3	11.2
	3m	**4m**	**5m**	**6m**	**7m**	**8m**	**9m**	**10m**	**11m**	**12m**

(left axis label: Field angle)

True length of throw/distance of lantern to centre of the area

> **Lantern reference guide – Wattage, beam/field angles, optimum throw**

Fresnels

Make	Lantern Type	Wattage	Beam Angle	Optimum Throw
Altman				
Altman	**6" Fresnel**	**500/750W**	**4.2ft dia**	@ 21ft – Short
Altman	**8" Fresnel**	**1000W**	**6.3ft dia**	@ 30ft – Medium
ADB				
ADB	**Eurospot**	500/650W	**9°–65°**	Short
ADB	**'A' Range**	500/650W	**9°–66°**	Short
ADB	**Europe** Prism-convex	1000/1200W	**7°–61°**	Medium
	Plano-convex	1000/1200W	**10°–65°**	Medium
	Prism-convex	2000W	**8°–58°**	Long
	Plano-convex	2000W	**5°–65°**	Long
CCT				
CCT	**Minuette** F	650W	**10°–59°**	Short
CCT	**Starlette** F	1200W	**7°–38°**	Medium
CCT	**Starlette** F	2000W	**5°–50°**	Medium/Long

[3] Stage Electrics – Hire & Sales Catalogue 1998

(left margin vertical text: Lighting the Show / TECHNICAL INFO.)

Make	Lantern Type		Wattage	Beam Angle	Optimum Throw
Robert Juliat					
Robert Juliat	**Lutin**	6"	1000W		Short
	Lutin 310H	8"	1000W		Medium
	Lutin 329H	8"	2000/2500W		Long
Interchangeable Fresnel, Pebble & PC lenses available					
Selecon					
Selecon	**Acclaim** F		500/650W	**4°–64°**	Short
Selecon	**Rama** F		1000/1200W	**5°–60°**	4M–18M Medium
Selecon	**Rama 175 HP**		1000/1200W	**4.5°–62°**	4M–20M Medium
Selecon	**Arena** F		2000/2500W	**4.5°–60°**	6M–25M Long
Strand					
Strand	**Patt 123**		500W	**15°–45°**	5M Short
Strand	**Quartet** F		500/650W	**7.5°–55°**	6M Short
Strand	**Prelude** F		500/650	**7.5°–55°**	8M Short
Strand	**Cantata** F		1200W	**4°–49°**	15M Medium
Strand	**Alto** F		2000/2500W	**7°–62°**	20M Medium/Long
Teatro					
Teatro	**Forma F eco**		500/650W	**7°–60°**	2–16M Short
	Forma F 650		500/650	**7°–60°**	2–16M Short
	Curva F eco		1200W	**10°–56°**	2–18M Medium
	Curva F 1200			**10°–56°**	2–18M Medium
	Atto F 2000		2000W	**10°–70°**	3–25M Long
Zero 88					
	Pebble Con		500W	**10°–59°**	Short

PCs				
Make	**Lantern Type**	**Wattage**	**Beam Angle**	**Optimum Throw**
Altman – PCs not included in this manufacturer's range of lanterns				
ADB				
ADB	**Eurospot** PC	500/650W	**9°–65°**	Short
ADB	**'A' Range** PC	500/650W	**9°–66°**	Short

341

Lighting the Show

TECHNICAL INFO.

Make	Lantern Type	Wattage	Beam Angle	Optimum Throw
ADB	**Europe**			
	Prism-convex	1000/1200W	**7°–61°**	Medium
	Plano-convex	1000/1200W	**10°–65°**	Long
	Prism-convex	2000W	**8°–58°**	Long
	Plano-convex	2000W	**5°–65°**	Long
CCT				
CCT	**Minuette** PC	650W	**10°–59°**	Short/Medium
CCT	**Starlette** PC	1200W	**7°–38°**	Medium/Long
CCT	**Starlette** PC	2000W	**5°–50°**	Medium/Long
Robert Juliat				
Robert Juliat	**Lutin** 6"	1000W		Short
	Lutin 310H 8"	1000W		Medium
	Lutin 329H 8"	2000/2500W		Long
Interchangeable Pebble, PC & Fresnel lenses available				
Selecon				
Selecon	**Acclaim** PC	500/650W	**4°–64°**	Short
Selecon	**Rama** PC	1000/1200W	**5°–60°**	4m–18m – Medium
Selecon	**Rama 175 HP**	1000/1200W	**4.5°–62°**	4m–20m – Medium
Selecon	**Arena** PC	2000/2500W	**4.5°–60°**	6m–30m – Long
Strand				
Strand	**Quartet** PC	500/650W	**7.5°–55°**	6m Short
Strand	**Prelude** PC	500/650	**7.5°–55°**	8m Short/ Medium
Strand	**Cantata** PC	1200W	**4°–49°**	15m Medium
Strand	**Alto** PC	2000/2500W	**4°–58°**	20m Medium/ Long
Teatro				
Teatro	**Forma PC eco**	500/650W	**7°–60°**	2m–16m Short/ Med
	Forma PC 650	500/650	**7°–58°**	2m–16m Short/ Med
Teatro	**Curva PC eco**	1200W	**8°–60°**	2m–20m Medium
	Curva PC 1200	1200W	**8°–60°**	2m–20m Medium
Teatro	**Atto PC 2000**	2000W	**9°–70°**	3m–27m Long
Zero 88				
Zero 88	**Pebble Con**	500W	**10°–59°**	Short

342

Profile Spots

Make	Lantern Type		Wattage	Beam Angle	Optimum Throw
Altman					
Altman	**Ellipsoidal** 3.5"–MT		500W	**18° 23° 28°**	Short/Medium
			500W	**38° 48°**	Short
Altman	**Shakespeare**		600W	**5° 10° 20°**	Short/Medium
	Ellipsoidal S6		600W	**30° 40° 50°**	Short
		S6-1535Z	600W	**15°–35°**	Short/ Medium
		S6-3055Z	600W	**30°–55°**	Short
Altman	**Ellipsoidal** 4.5"–MT		750W	**15°–30°**	Medium
			750W	**25°–30°**	Short/Medium
			750W	**30°–60°**	Short
Altman	**Ellipsoidal** 6" Series		750W	**6"x 9", 12", 16", 22"**	Medium/Long
ADB					
ADB	**Eurospot**	D54	500/650W	**18°–30°**	Medium
		D54		**30°–47°**	Short
ADB	**'A' Range**	A59Z	500/650	**16°–35°**	Short/Medium
ADB	**Warp**		660/800W	**12°–30°**	Medium
				22°–50°	Short
ADB	**Europe**	DW105	1000/1200W	**15°–38°**	Medium/Long
		DS105	1000/1200W	**15°–31°**	Medium/Long
		DSN105	1000/1200W	**11°–23°**	Long
		DN105	1000/1200W	**9°–20°**	Long
		DVW105	1000/1200W	**38°–57°**	Medium/Long
		DS205	2000W	**13°–36°**	Long
		DN205	2000W	**10°–22°**	Long
		DVW205	2000W	**30°–54°**	Medium/Long
CCT					
CCT	**Minuette**				
	Fixed lens		650W	**26°**	Short
	Reflector zoom		650W	**21°–36°**	Short
	Condenser zoom		650W	**17°–36°**	Medium
	Condenser zoom		650W	**30°–48°**	Short
	Condenser zoom		650W	**6°–14°**	Long
CCT	**Freedom**		600/800W	**7°–17°**	Long
			600/800W	**16°–30°**	Medium/Long
			600/800W	**25°–58°**	Short/Medium

TECHNICAL INFO.

Lighting the Show

343

Lighting the Show

TECHNICAL INFO.

Profile Spots

Make	Lantern Type		Wattage	Beam Angle	Optimum Throw
CCT	**Silhouette Turbo**		1000/1200W	**11°–26°**	Long
			1000/1200W	**15°–32°**	Long
			1000/1200W	**28°–52°**	Long
CCT	**Silhouette**		2000/2500W	**11°–26°**	Long
			2000/2500W	**15°–32°**	Long
			2000/2400W	**28°–52°**	Medium/Long
ETC					
ETC	**Source Four**	fixed	575W	**26° 36° 50°**	Short
	Junior	zoom	575W	**25°- 50°**	Short
ETC	**Source Four**		750W	**5° 10° 14°**	Long
	fixed lens		750W	**19° 26° 36,**	Medium
			750W	**50° 70° 90°**	Short
ETC	**Source Four**		750W	**15°–30°**	Long
			750W	**25°–30°**	Medium/Short
Robert Juliat					
Robert	**600 SX Series**	611	1000/1200W	**11°–26°**	Medium
Juliat		613	1000/1200W	**28°–54°**	Short/Medium
		614	1000/1200W	**16°–35°**	Medium
Robert	**700 SX2 Series**	710	2000/2500W	**10°–25°**	Long
Juliat		711	2000/2500W	**8°–16°**	Long
		713	2000/26500W	**29°–50°**	Long
		714	2000.2500W	**15°–40°**	Long
Robert	**Aledin 630SX**	631	LED 85W	**11°–26°**	
Juliat		633	LED 85W	**16°–35°**	
		634	LED 85W	**28°–54°**	
Selecon					
Selecon	**Acclaim**		500/650W	**18°–34°**	Short/Medium
			500/650W	**24°–44°**	Short
Selecon	**Axial**		600W	**18°–34°**	Medium
			600W	**24°–44°**	Short
Selecon	**Pacific**		600/1000W	**12°–28°**	Medium/Long
			600/1000W	**23°–50°**	Short/Medium
			600/1000W	**90° Wide**	Short/Medium
Strand					
Strand	**Patt. 23**		500W	**26°**	6m	Short
Strand	**Quartet**		500/650W	**18°–34°**	8m	Medium
			500/650W	**24°–44°**	6m	Short

Profile Spots

Make	Lantern Type	Wattage	Beam Angle	Optimum Throw
Strand	**Prelude**	500/650W 500/650W	**16°–30°** **28°–40°**	8m Medium 6m Short
Strand	**Cantata**	1200W 1200W 1200W	**11°–26°** **18°–32°** **26°–44°**	18m Medium 15m Medium 12m Short/Med
Strand	**Alto**	2000/2500W 2000/2500W 2000/2500W	**8°–16°** **14°–32°** **20°–38°**	25m Long 20m Medium/Lng 15m Medium
Strand	**Brio**	600W 600W	**18°–30°** **28°–40°**	10m Medium 8m Short
Strand	**SL Zoom**	600W 600W	**15°–32°** **23°–50°**	12m Medium 10m Short/Med
Strand	**SL 5°/10°/19°** **SL 36°/ 50°**	600W 600W	**5° 10° 19°** **36°/50°**	Long Short Medium
Strand	**Leko 11** 8"x13" **Leko 18** 6"x16" **Leko 26** 6"x12" **Leko 40** 6"x9"	1000W 1000W 1000W 1000W	**14°** **21°** **30°** **45°**	Long Long Short/Medium Short

Strand Century

Make	Lantern Type	Wattage	Beam Angle	Optimum Throw
Strand	**Leko 6"x12"**(=L26) **Leko 6"x13"**(=L11)	500/750/1000W 500/750/1000W	30° 14°	Short/Medium Medium/Long

Teatro

Make	Lantern Type	Wattage	Beam Angle	Optimum Throw
Teatro	**Forma**	650W 650W	**10°–28°** **20°–40°**	2m–14m Short 2m–12m Short
Teatro	**Curva**	1200W 1200W	**8°–22°** **18°–36°**	5m–25m Med/L 5m–25m Long
Teatro	**Atto**	2000W 2000W	**8°–22°** **18°–36°**	6m–30m Long 6m–25m Long

Zero 88

Make	Lantern Type	Wattage	Beam Angle	Optimum Throw
Zero 88	**Focus**	500/650W	**21°–36°** **30°–45°**	Short/Medium Short

TECHNICAL INFO.

Lighting the Show

Websites

➤ Lantern manufacturers

www.altmanltg.com	Altman Stage Lighting: NA
www.adblighting.com	ADB Lighting Technologies: Belgium
www.cctlighting.com	CCT Lighting: UK
www.etcconnect.com	ETC: NA
www.seleconlight.com	Philips Selecon: New Zealand
www.robertjuliat.fr	Robert Juliat: France
www.strandarchive.co.uk	Strand Lighting archive
www.jthomaseng.com	James Thomas Engineering: UK
www.teclumen.it	Teatro Teclumen: Italy

➤ Dimmers & control desks

www.adblighting.com	ADB Lighting Technologies
www.avolites.org.uk	Avolites
www.etcconnect.com	ETC
www.highend.com	High End Systems
www.jands.co	Jands Pty Ltd
www.lsclighting.com	LSC Lighting Systems
www.strandlighting.com	Philips Strand Lighting
www.zero88.com	Zero88

➤ Moving heads

www.adblighting.com	ADB Lighting Technologies
www.etcconnect.com	ETC
www.highend.com	High End Systems
www.claypaky.it	Clay Paky
www.martin.com	Martin Professional
www.vari-lite.com	Philips Vari-Lite
www.qmaxz.com	Qmaxz Lighting
www.robelighting.com	Robe Lighting

➤ LED fixtures

www.adblighting.com	ADB Lighting Technologies
www.chroma-q.com	Chroma-Q
www.etcconnect.com	ETC
www.gekkotechnology.com	Gekko Technology Ltd
www.glp.de	GLP German Light Products
www.highend.com	High End Systems
www.martin.com	Martin Professional

Websites

LIGHTING RESOURCES

www.pixelrange.com	Thomas Engineering
www.pulsarlight.com	Pulsar
www.robelighting.com	Robe Lighting
www.robertjuliat.fr	Robert Juliat
www.vari-lite.com	Philips Vari-Lite

➤ Health and Safety

www.hse.gov.uk/publications	HSE – Health and Safety Executive
http://ladderassociation.org.uk	The Ladder Association
www.pasma.co.uk	PASMA – Prefabricated Access Suppliers' & Manufacturers' Association
www.scottint.com	Scott Health & Safety Bump Hats

➤ Access systems

www.zargesuk.co.uk	Zarges Skymaster ladder
www.escauk.co.uk	ESCA UK
www.airborne-ind-acc.co.uk	Instant UpRight Span towers
www.tallescope.co.uk	Tallescope – Aluminium Access Products Ltd

➤ CAD – Computer aided design

www.autodesk.com	AutoCAD
www.cast-soft.com	CAST Software Ltd, wysiwyg
www.lxdesign.co.uk	LxDesigner
www.modelboxplans.com	CAD lantern symbols for use on AutoCAD
www.nemetschek.net/spotlight	Vectorworks Spotlight

➤ Colour filters

www.leefilters.com	LEE Filters
www.rosco.com	Roscolab
www.gamonline.com	GAM Products
www.apollodesign.net	Apolo Design & Technology

➤ Associations

www.abtt.org.uk	ABTT – Association of British Theatre Technicians
www.ald.org.uk	ALD – Association of Lighting Designers
www.theatrestrust.org.uk	The Theatres Trust
www.womeninlighting.com	WISE – Women in Stage Entertainment

➤ Stage lighting equipment & hire UK

www.aclighting.com	A.C. Lighting Ltd – High Wycombe Bucks
www.ajs.co.uk	AJS Theatre Lighting & Stage Supplies – Ringwood, Hampshire
www.black-light.com	Black Light Ltd – Edinburgh
www.centraltheatresupplies.co.uk	Central Theatre Supplies – Birmingham
www.hawthorns.uk.com	Hawthorn – Leicester
wwww.kave.co.uk	Kave Theatre Services – West Sussex, Derbyshire
www.lancelyn.co.uk	Lancelyn Theatre Supplies – Oxford, Merseyside
www.northernlight.co.uk	Northern Light – Edinburgh
www.productionireland.com	Production Services Ireland – Belfast
www.nstage.co.uk	Northern Stage Services Ltd – Oldham
www.stage-electrics.co.uk	Stage Electrics – Bristol, London, Tyneside
wwww.whitelight.ltd.uk	White Light (Electrics) Ltd – London

➤ Stage lighting equipment & hire global

www.northamerica@aclighting.com	A.C. Lighting Ltd – Toronto Canada
www.gamonline.com	GAM Products – Los Angeles USA
www.apollodesign.net	Apollo Design & Technology – Fort Wayne IN, USA

➤ Equipment & accessories UK

www.flints.co.uk	Theatrical Chandlers (Quad spanners and Caritools)

➤ Additional training resources

www.stagelightingtraining.co.uk	'Give Me Some Light!!!' DVDs and student resources
skipmort@stagelightingtraining.co.uk	Skip Mort Stage Lighting Training – educational resources

➤ 'Give Me Some Light!!!'

Three interactive lighting workshops on DVD for students providing self-directed study, support for examination coursework options GCSE, A2 & BTEC, fast-track training, health & safety and teachers' Continued Professional Development.

Key notes!

➤ Make a note of what you have done

You will be asked to provide curriculum vitae when you make an application for a job or a place on a college course. CVs are a brief account of your education and experience, in other words what you have done. It can be quite useful to start making a list of the types of equipment that you have used, any specialist courses that you have taken, the shows that you have worked on and the roles that you have been responsible for.

Lanterns used

Make	Model	Type	Make	Model	Type

Lighting control desks

Make	Model	Familiar with	Can use	Plotted & run show

Live & moving lights desks: e.g. Sapphire, Pearl, Hog, grand MA

Make	Model	Familiar with	Can use	Plotted & run show

Specialist courses	Organising body – certification	Date
Working at heights		
Using access equipment		
Risk assessment		
Electrical testing		

Shows

Date	Show	Role/responsibility

Industry contacts – people you have met or worked for

Name	Position	Theatre/company

> Make a note of the contacts that you have made

Trade contacts

Company	Contact	Phone number	Website

> Notes

Credits

'Fast Forward' video clips

Extracts from '**Give Me Some Light!!!**'
Three interactive stage lighting workshops on DVD for students. 'Need a Technician', 'Taking the Drama out of Lighting!' & 'So You're Lighting the Production?'

Written & directed by Skip Mort
Assistant director & presenter Andy Webb
Filmed & edited by Mike Hill – an Attic Studios production
© SKIP MORT LIGHTING SERVICES 2005

The making of the original DVDs were sponsored by Philips Selecon, Roscolab, Zero 88, ESCA, Stage Electrics, and supported by Strand Lighting, LEE Filters, CCT Lighting UK, Skyhigh FX, Scott Health & Safety.

Other contributions

Article on 'War Horse' video design by Julie Harper for Lighting & Sound International (www.lsionline.co.uk)
Designers on Colour – Guide to Colour Filters Roscolab
Introduction to DMX by David Whitehead – Stage Electrics
Electricity – how does it work? by David Whitehead – Stage Electrics
Swan Lake – lighting the transformation scene – Rick Fisher
Lighting the shows – *Swan Lake* & *Billy Elliot* – Rick Fisher
Designing a larger show – *Our House* – Andy Webb

Production photographs

Photographs of Tigz Productions – Nik Sheppard www.sheppardphotography.com
Uncle Vanya, Birmingham Repertory Theatre – Robert Day
Billy Elliot – Tristram Kenton
War Horse – Simon Annand
Hamlet, *Berlin 2006*, *Decadence* – Andrew Malmo
Crazy Mary – Brain Aldous
'Give Me Some Light!!!' – Skip Mort

Product photographs

Reproduced by courtesy of:
ABTT Sightline – Bob Morgan
ALD-TTV Technologies
Apollo Design Technology, Inc. – Apollo Gelbook
Clay Paky
Colin and Lindsey Ockwell – St Augustine Theatre

ESCA
ETC
GAM Products Inc
Instant UpRight
Le Maitre – Pyrotechnics & Special Effects
LEE Filters – Art of Light
Martin Professional
Philips Selecon – Performance Lighting
Philips Strand
Philips Vari-Lite
Robert Juliat
Roscolab Ltd – Product Guide, Guide to Colour Filters, Guide to Motion Effects
Stage Electrics
Strand Electric – Education in Stage Lighting
Thomas Engineering
Jands Pty Ltd
White Light
Zarges UK
Zero 88 Cooper Controls – Product Guide

Drawings

Michael Mackie-Clark, Kave Theatre Services – LxDesigner plans
Steve Shelly – Selecon lantern stencil drawing
Sam Tanner – wsyiwyg plans

Bibliography

Alpha 300/700 Product Guides – Clay Paky

Apollo Design Technology inc. website – www.apollodesign.net

Basics – A Beginners Guide to Stage Lighting – Peter Coleman

'Calculating power' – Virgina Tech. www.the12volt.com/ohm/ohmslaw.asp

Chromarange catalogue – Pulsar Light of Cambridge Lighting, Hire & Sales

'Code of Practice for In-Service Inspection and Testing of Electrical Equipment' – The Institution of Electrical Engineers

Current trends in video design for theatre – Sightline ABTT, Dick Straker

Educational Guide to Stage Lighting – Strand Lighting

'Electrical Maintenance including Portable Appliance Testing' – The Institution of Electrical Engineers

Five steps to risk assessment – HSE UK

GAM Products inc. website – www.gamonline.com

Health & Safety, Risk Assessment – Central School of Speech and Drama

Hire & Sales Catalogue 1998 – Stage Electrics

Intro to Stage Lighting – Steve Marshall, www.seleconlight.com

Introducing projected computer images – Teaching Drama, Paul King

Jands Vista Control desks – Neil Vann Jands Europe

Lantern information – Philips Selecon

MAC TWI Product Guide – Martin

Making of War Horse – More 4

Martin Professional website – www.martin.com

Moving Effects Catalogue – DHA Lighting

Performance Lighting Design – Nick Moran

Pixel Range – LED Lighting – www.pixelrange.com, Thomas Engineering

Rosco Guide to motion effects – Roscolab

Rosco Product Catalogue – Roscolab

Scene Design & Stage Lighting – W. Oren Parker & Harvey K. Smith

Selecon beam angles data – Philips Selecon

Stage Lighting Design – Bill Williams

Step into the Limelight – Strand Lighting Drama Resource Pack

Strand Electric, Rank Strand, Strand lighting Luminaires – Brian Legge, ABTT Archaeology Committee

The Art of Light – LEE Filters

The Art of Stage Lighting – Frederick Bentham

The Hire Store Catalogue – Stage Electrics

The Strand Archive – www.strandarchive.co.uk

Theatre Craft – www.theatrecrafts.com

Theatre Projects – resources – Theatre Projects website

War Horse – Lighting & Sound International – Julie Harper

White Light Catalogue reference section – White Light Entertainment

Wikipedia the Free Encyclopaedia – www.wikipedia.org

Zero 88 Product Guide – Cooper Controls

Index

INDEX

UNIVERSITY OF WINCHESTER LIBRARY